THE TRANSATLANTIC RELATIONSHIP

Also by Jarrod Wiener

MAKING RULES IN THE URUGUAY ROUND OF THE GATT
A Study of International Leadership

* THE UNITED NATIONS IN THE NEW WORLD ORDER: The
World Organization at Fifty (*co-editor with Dimitris Bourantonis*)

* *From the same publishers*

The Transatlantic Relationship

Edited by

Jarrod Wiener
Lecturer in International Relations
University of Kent at Canterbury

First published in Great Britain 1996 by
MACMILLAN PRESS LTD
Houndmills, Basingstoke, Hampshire RG21 6XS
and London
Companies and representatives
throughout the world

A catalogue record for this book is available
from the British Library.

ISBN 0–333–64818–8 hardcover
ISBN 0–333–66986–X paperback

First published in the United States of America 1996 by
ST. MARTIN'S PRESS, INC.,
Scholarly and Reference Division,
175 Fifth Avenue,
New York, N.Y. 10010

ISBN 0–312–16203–0

Library of Congress Cataloging-in-Publication Data
The transatlantic relationship / edited by Jarrod Wiener.
p.   cm.
Includes bibliographical references and index.
ISBN 0–312–16203–0 (cloth)
1. Europe—Foreign relations—United States.   2. United States–
–Foreign relations—Europe.   3. Europe—Foreign relations—1989–
I. Wiener, Jarrod.
D1065.U5T715   1996
327.7304—dc20   96–10526
                                                                                    CIP

10   9   8   7   6   5   4   3   2   1
05   04   03   02   01   00   99   98   97   96

Printed and bound in Great Britain by
Antony Rowe Ltd, Chippenham, Wiltshire

Contents

Preface: A Transatlantic Community – Myth or Emerging Reality?
  Nicholas Sherwen   vii

Acknowledgements   xiv

Notes on the Contributors   xv

1   The Transatlantic Partnership in the 1990s
    Jarrod Wiener and Dan Hiester   1

2   NATO After the Cold War
    Lawrence S. Kaplan   26

3   American Strategies Towards the Enlargement of European
    Security Institutions: Partnership or Cold Peace?
    Sean Kay   44

4   The EU: From Civilian Power to Speaking with a
    Common Voice – The Transition to a CFSP
    Juliet Lodge   67

5   Manifest Destiny and the Pacific Century: Europe as No.3?
    Robert O'Brien   95

6   Transatlantic Trade: Economic Security, Agriculture,
    and the Politics of Technology
    Jarrod Wiener   128

7   EU-US Commercial Relations and the Debate on a
    Transatlantic Free Trade Area
    Stephen Woolcock   164

Index   185

Preface:
A Transatlantic
Community – Myth or
Emerging Reality?

Nicholas Sherwen[*]

Observers of international affairs are currently reeling from the shock of witnessing yet another damaging rift in the transatlantic relationship. This time it has taken the form of an object lesson on how not to go about building consensus on the selection of a new Secretary General for NATO. Some have interpreted this episode as evidence of a far-reaching change in the nature of transatlantic relations. More of a superficial crack in the link than a deep fissure, it nevertheless points up the fact that the mutually beneficial relationship cannot be taken for granted and must be nurtured on both sides of the Atlantic if it is to survive difficulties such as these. The future holds the promise of much more severe tests over issues such as the enlargement of the Alliance and NATO's role in implementing a peace plan in the former Yugoslavia. The importance of the question of the nomination of the new Secretary General should not be underestimated, but it is of a different order. At this moment it remains unresolved. Yet, it will be resolved and business will be resumed as usual relatively quickly.

In the same time-frame, at the top of the security agenda for both Europe and North America is the prospect of a genuine peace agreement in the former Yugoslavia and the creation of a NATO-led implementation force to make it stick. A sophisticated implementation plan is ready. A large number of European NATO member countries, NATO Partner

---

[*] Nicholas Sherwen is Head of Publications in the NATO Office of Information and Press. The views expressed in this article are his alone and should not be construed as reflecting the policies or positions of the North Atlantic Treaty Organization.

countries, and non-NATO countries have committed themselves to providing forces. An accommodation has been reached with regard to the role to be played by Russian forces. US participation in the force which will soon be required is a *sine qua non* for its success. The US Administration recognizes this and is pushing ahead on the assumption that a reluctant Congress can be won round. Congress, on the other hand, is sullenly reiterating its willingness to pull the rug from underneath the entire operation unless it can be convinced that US interests are genuinely served by its compliance. The Administration has evoked the disintegration of the Alliance and the emasculation of US influence in the Western world if this were to happen. The retort of Congress could still be 'So what, if the alternative is body-bags and a heavy financial bill? This is a European problem. Let Europeans sort it out.'

The argument has certain resonance and at a time when the US has legitimate preoccupations with its own economic and social situation, it should come as no surprise if voices are raised in Congress against the possibility of a renewed long-term American commitment to the security of another part of the European continent outside the North Atlantic Treaty area.

Yet, the argument is flawed. What will be the consequences if the proponents of the 'stay at home' policy succeed in their campaign? On economic as much as political grounds the case for the US presence in Europe and its participation in Europe's future is overwhelming. The legacy of disengagement to the generation of Americans running the country at the start of the new millennium will be irrevocable; a United States which has undermined its own prosperity, lost global credibility and opted our of the challenge facing the international community to uphold democratic values wherever they are threatened.

Vice-President of the European Commission Sir Leon Brittan addressed the Airlie Conference in Virginia on this theme at the end of October 1995, from the standpoint of the European Union. Quoting Woodrow Wilson, he acknowledged the basis for US involvement overseas not only in terms of altruism and the upholding of the values for which the United States prides itself on standing, but also in terms of the protection of its own interests. He pointed to practical economic and political reasons for the Congress to stand four-square behind successive Presidents in investing in the US' global role: a sharp rise in dependence on international trade and reduction of economic self-sufficiency; increased involvement in dynamic world markets calling for proximity to customers; and the inevitable impact on US companies of the disruption or instability of such markets. Greater interdependence worldwide, he pointed out, means that company boardrooms and constituency parties cannot stand aloof from the events shaping the market place, even if the latter is physically remote. The same growth in interdependence also brings transnational problems into sharper relief, highlighting the need for cooperation, pooling of experience and sharing the costs of finding and implementing remedies, for example in the environmental sector or in the context of major population movements. The willingness of the well-sourced nations of the world to stand by the poorer and smaller goes well beyond altruism, argued Leon Brittan.

It is certainly true that stable markets thrive in stable societies, not hungry, deprived, embittered or war-torn ones. While economic realities have to be faced, scaling down US global interests may become the most expensive course of all. There are also political realities: reliable suppliers and buyers of US goods are viable business partners for other ventures.

Notwithstanding the visionary and magnanimous stance of the US towards the reconstruction of Europe after the Second World War, American foreign policy is now, as it always was, the legitimate defence of national self-interest. In that, nothing has changed. But the world has changed. Countries which, at one time, would have had no voice in international affairs because of their relative size, are now less inclined to align themselves with powerful neighbours unless it is demonstrably in their interests to do so. The early years of multilateralism often meant bi- or even trilateralism with spectators. Today's multilateralism is quite different and in many fields the US will have to work harder to achieve the same level of influence over the course of events. It can only do this successfully from centre-field, not from a role on the touchline. Nor is there the option of setting the course and withdrawing. The dynamics of world affairs, in fields such as information technology, modern communications and financial operations, not to speak of world trade or politics, means that permanent involvement and constant calculation of opportunities is indispensable.

Much has been said in recent months about the nature of the transatlantic relationship. In May 1995, Foreign and Defence Ministers of the Western European Union noted that 'Europe, the US and Canada share a common heritage and are bound by close historical, political, economic and cultural ties... Transatlantic solidarity is essential for the preservation of peace and freedom and for the strengthening of an undivided, free and democratic Europe.' Reviewing developments since the end of the Cold War, they concluded that 'the fuller integration of all European countries into a continent whole and free cannot be successful without the strong and active participation of all Allies on both sides of the Atlantic.'

At the national level, there has also been a new focus on the community of interests which joins Europe to the United States. Speaking at the beginning of October 1995, British Foreign Secretary Malcolm Rifkind told the Conservative Party Conference that the two sides of the Atlantic need each other as much as ever. The economies of the North American Free Trade Area and of the European Union are already closely enmeshed, he said, and it is the ultimate objective of the British Government to see this process extended to global free trade. As a first step, he announced that Britain is committed to working towards the development of a transatlantic free trade area and to securing the benefits that will accrue from this for jobs, trade and economic prosperity. With memories of the Uruguay round of the GATT still fresh, US commentators and policy-makers may need a little more time before they become too enthusiastic.

American observers of the European political process might also be forgiven for entertaining a sense of *déjà vu* as they watch the unfolding debate over the development of Europe's separate identity, whether in the field of foreign policy or security and defence. Once again, this is coupled with assurances that the process will strengthen the European pillar of the transatlantic partnership; and simultaneously voices are to be heard calling for the North American-European relationship to move into a higher gear.

The first post-war manifestation of the European defence identity, in part at the behest of the United States and Canada, was the Brussels Treaty Organization created in 1948. Having fulfilled its initial purpose as a building block for a North Atlantic Alliance, it was then absorbed into NATO when the latter was established in 1949. Vestiges of the Brussels Treaty structure remained, with a separate identity as the Western Union, and later as the Western European Union. However, the embryonic military structure established under the Brussels Treaty, including land, air and naval commands and a fledgling infrastructure programme for the construction of airfields and communications systems, was transferred to NATO. European security had become a transatlantic issue, not only in fact but in institutional and treaty terms as well.

The impetus to establish a unified European defence structure did not stop with these developments. The Pleven Plan adopted by the French National Assembly in October 1951 for the creation of a European army within the framework of NATO was widely discussed. However, the Petersburg negotiations for its implementation were soon to be super-

seded by negotiations on the establishment of a European Defence
Community (EDC). In 1951, specific provisions of the never-ratified
EDC Treaty offered mutual consultations between the projected Council
of the EDC and the North Atlantic Council, as well as joint meetings and
permanent contacts between the two staffs in a process which would
strengthen the North Atlantic Community. During the 1970s and 1980s,
the activities of the informal EUROGROUP and of the more structured
Independent European Programme Group represented the principal
manifestations of efforts to strengthen cooperation and cohesiveness
between the European member countries of the Alliance, albeit in limited
fields (respectively, public relations, communications, logistics, long-term
operational concepts, medicine and joint training, and armaments
procurement). The 1984 reactivation of the Western European Union
once again launched the search for a common European defence identity
which would 'strengthen the European pillar of the North Atlantic
Alliance.' With the signature of the Maastricht Treaty in 1991 came
further affirmation of this goal. In the last few years the WEU Council
of Ministers had reiterated its objective of strengthening the Alliance's
European pillar on many occasions and, for its part, the North Atlantic
Council has restated its support for the process in which its European
member countries are engaged.

In the light of this history, the perception of a newly-discovered
complementarity between the aims of the European pillar of the Alliance
and the Alliance itself, and particularly of deep-seated rivalry and
competition between the Western European Union and NATO is
manifestly absurd. They are, after all, separable but not separate parts of
the same security-related process.

The central mechanisms for sharing responsibility and benefits in the
security and defence field between Europe and North America is well-
established and readily available. Through NATO, a forum for consultations and decision-making exists and a unique structure for putting
decisions into effect has been developed over a period of nearly fifty
years. Yet outside this vital but limited sector of activity, despite the
shortening of distances and the ease of modern communications
worldwide, the distance across the Atlantic seems just as great and as
difficult to bridge as ever. A promising new factor is the emergence of
the embryonic World Trade Organization, which offers to provide an
additional institutional link. Sir Leon Brittan sees prospects for this
process to develop further, especially in non-governmental fields, in the
area of justice and home affairs, in the business world through the
expansion of the Transatlantic Business Dialogue, and among legislators,

through the creation of a forum for transatlantic parliamentary contacts. This is reminiscent of the 1962 Atlantic Convention of NATO Nations' call for 'a true Atlantic Community which must extend to the political, military, economic, moral and cultural fields.' On the one hand, this appeals for a stronger and more comprehensive transatlantic relationship to be transformed into a fully-fledged Atlantic Community; on the other, it seeks assurances that the European process will reinforce the European side of the transatlantic equation.

In the parliamentary sphere, the North Atlantic Assembly provides and interparliamentary forum independent of NATO which brings together European and North American legislators concerned with transatlantic security issues. It constitutes a link with national parliaments which ensures that concerns relevant to the Alliance are aired when national legislation is being framed. Moreover, it serves as a permanent reminder that intergovernmental decisions taken in the NATO forum are ultimately dependent on political endorsement by elected parliaments. The basis for transatlantic inter-parliamentary contacts is therefore already available and could perhaps be expanded to embrace a broader political agenda addressing subjects of common interest in fields such as those enumerated above.

Clearly, if the transatlantic process is to have any meaning, it must be enjoined at all levels – governmental, parliamentary and trade certainly, but also cultural and academic. Unless our seats of learning and teaching are part of the process, it has a limited chance of getting very far. And so to this book. It has an unusual curriculum vitae. It was partly the recognition of the paucity of existing academic contacts between North America and Europe that led the Graduate School of International Relations at The University of Kent at Canterbury and the Lyman L. Lemnitzer Center for NATO and European Community Studies at Kent State University, Ohio, to accept a challenge to launch a new dialogue on transatlantic issues at the academic level. Exploiting a happy coincidence of names and the first-class reputation of both universities for taking initiatives, a NATO grant was made available for a first, joint publishing project, drawing on the expertise of both establishments, reinforced by contributions from universities and research centres on both sides of the Atlantic. The project had modest objectives but largely succeeded in achieving them. It sought to give an international, transatlantic dimension to otherwise unrelated publishing endeavours, namely the *Occasional Papers* series of the Lyman L. Lemnitzer Centre and *Paradigms: The Kent Journal of International Relations* (now *Global Society*) published at Canterbury.

The resulting special edition on the Transatlantic Relationship resisted the temptation to enter into a debate about the perceived disarray in NATO (who was it who said that he had not been aware that it was ever 'in array'?). Instead, it sought to engender a more fundamental discussion about the relevance of different manifestations of the relationship in the post-Cold War world. That it did so in a way that was novel and effective is demonstrated by the fact that it has given impetus to new initiatives to take the dialogue further. There is plenty of scope for it to develop without digging up the transatlantic bargain once more just to examine its roots. Both sides need the other, says the cliché. What does that mean? What can and can not be taken for granted? What are the constraints and the limitations? How do world events, in which both sides have a vested interest but neither a monopoly of influence, impact on the relationship? Are there separate European and North American agendas for the future relationship with Russia and other independent republics of the former USSR? And where does the relationship have to go in order to ensure that it is not shipwrecked every time there is a stiff breeze blowing across the Atlantic?

Much of the debate will inevitably center on US leadership. Is it needed? Can the US provide it? Should it have to? Certainly it sometimes seems that the US is faced with Hobson's choice and Catch 22 and will be rebuked for taking initiatives as often as it is for holding back. Is there not a better approach? The first task is to understand the problem. By offering new perspectives on some of the main issues from both sides of the pond, this project is a small contribution to such understanding. If it opens doors to other initiatives in the same sphere, so much the better.

Acknowledgements

I would like to thank Nicholas Sherwen, Head of Publications in the Office of Information and Press of the North Atlantic Treaty Organization, for his assistance with this project, both financial from NATO and for his personal interest. Thanks also to Dominic Powell for helping to set the typescript. Marilyn Spice and Nicola Cooper in the secretarial office of the Department of Politics and International Relations at the University of Kent provided valuable administrative support for which I am also very grateful.

Notes on the Contributors

Dan Hiester is Lecturer in International Relations at the Graduate School of International Relations, University of Kent at Canterbury. He is a specialist in pan-European security, nuclear proliferation, and transatlantic relations. His most recent publication is, 'NATO: Approaching the Millennium', in Pàl Dunay, Gabor Kardos and Andrew Williams (eds), *New Forms of Security: Views from Central, Eastern and Western Europe* (1995).

Lawrence S. Kaplan is University Professor Emeritus of History and Director Emeritus of the Lyman L. Lemnitzer Center for NATO and EC Studies at Kent State University, Ohio, USA. He is currently Adjunct Professor of History at Georgetown University. Professor Kaplan's books include *The United States and NATO: The Formative Years* (1984) and *NATO and the United States: The Enduring Alliance* (1988).

Sean Kay is an American specialist in European security, American foreign policy and post-Soviet affairs and a Lecturer at the University of Massachusetts at Amherst. He has been a Researcher at the North Atlantic Assembly of NATO and a Research Fellow of the North Atlantic Treaty Organization (co-recipient). His more recent publications includes 'NATO and the CSCE: A New Russian Challenge?,' in S. Victor Papacosma and Mary Ann Heiss (eds), *NATO in the Post-Cold War Era: Does it Have a Future?* (1995).

Juliet Lodge is Professor of European Studies ad Director of the Centre for European Studies at the University of Leeds. She is Director of the Jean Monnet Group of Experts on the 1996 Intergovernmental Conference, and a specialist on the EU, institutional reform, judicial cooperation and foreign and security policies. Professor Lodge is author of several books, and she is currently completing a book on the JHA.

Robert O'Brien is Lecturer in International Relations in the School of English and American Studies at the University of Sussex. He has studied at Carlton University (Canada), the University of Haifa, the London School of Economics, and York University (Canada). He was a Parliamentary Intern for the Canadian House of Commons, where he acted as an assistant to the Chair of the Defence Committee. Dr. O'Brien has published in the area of Canadian defence policy, international political economy, and North American integration.

Jarrod Wiener is Lecturer in International Relations at the Graduate School of International Relations, University of Kent at Canterbury. He is a specialist in International Political Economy, and has a particular interest in transatlantic trade relations. He is a former editor of *Paradigms*, and is the founding editor of *Global Society: Journal of Interdisciplinary International Relations*. His most recent book is *Making Rules in the Uruguay Round of the GATT: A Study in International Leadership* (1995).

Stephen Woolcock is Senior Research Fellow at the Centre for Research on the United States at the London School of Economics. He was previously Senior Research Fellow at the Royal Institute of International Affairs and has been a Visiting Professor with the Institute of European Studies, Cornell University and Paul Henri Spaak Fellow at the Center for International Affairs, Harvard University.

1 The Transatlantic Partnership in the 1990s

Jarrod Wiener and Dan Hiester

The transatlantic partnership in the 1990s consists of a complex web of institutions wherein the Unites States and Europe cooperate in the spheres of politics, security, economics, and culture. These institutions have shown a greater dynamism in the 1990s than perhaps at any time since their creation. Responding to changed security realities, the North Atlantic Treaty Organization (NATO) was enlarged to encompass the states of Central and Eastern Europe through the North Atlantic Cooperation Council (NACC) in December 1991 and the Partnership for Peace (PfP) programme in January 1994. The main transatlantic partners are also the main players in the economic organizations of the United Nations, the International Monetary Fund (IMF), World Bank group (IBRD), and were the dominant forces behind the transformation of the General Agreement on Tariffs and Trade (GATT) into the World Trade Organization (WTO) in January 1994. These actors also consult through the Group of Seven (G7) industrialized states and the Organization for Economic Cooperation and Development (OECD). To these was added the Declaration on US-EC Relations of 23 November 1990, which established a framework for regular and intensive consultation. Recently, there have been calls for a further institutionalization of an 'Atlantic Community,' and proposals for a comprehensive agreement on foreign direct investment and a transatlantic free trade area.

Having said that the transatlantic relationship is complex and that its institutional expression is expanding, it must quickly be added that both the relationship and the modalities for its expansion have often proved problematic. Throughout the history of the Alliance, even from its very inception, there have been voices inside the United States Congress which have opposed the scale of US military commitments to Europe through NATO. Some also opposed the economic aid given to Western Europe. The passage of the Marshall Plan was no easy affair, as the Administration was forced to work with much diligence to convince Congress of the military and economic threats to the security of the

1

United States if the states of Western Europe had 'gone Communist.'[1] To some in the US, the defence of Europe was a mere extension of the defence of the United States. But, since the 1970s, distributive conflicts increased within the Alliance as these voices questioned whether the US should continue to bear disproportionate costs for western defence, and for the maintenance of the international economy, when Western Europe, it was believed, was benefiting proportionately 'more' than the US.[2] The issue of 'burdensharing' came on the agenda of some US legislators as Western Europe recovered economically, and began to compete with the US in a number of industries.

By the 1980s, as the US experienced mounting trade deficits, this disinclination to bear a high cost became an outright antagonism against 'free riders.' At the same time, Western Europe accelerated the implementation of its programme for further integration. The Single European Act (SEA) gained momentum to harmonize vast areas of activity in the European Community, ranging from immigration and border controls, to monetary union and competition policy. Significantly, the member states of the European Union (EU) began to debate a Common Foreign and Security Policy (CFSP), the creation of an European army[3], Eurocorps, with France – having already withdrawn from the NATO integrated military command structure in 1966 – and Germany at its core, and a strengthening of European defence institutions, such as the Western European Union (WEU). The United States, for its part, had always been ambivalent about European integration. A Europe modelled after the US would not contemplate the waging of another European 'civil war' again, which could involve the re-engagement of the United States. On the other hand, a strong, united Europe could pose a formidable political obstacle to the United States if their interests were to become incongruent on fundamental issues, particularly if the machinery for Europe to pursue its own interests, such as the Eurocorps or the WEU, were to be created in such a way that excluded the US.

Indeed, it had become abundantly clear to the US that the Europeans would, on occasion, pursue their own internal project ahead of considerations of importance to the US, and without too much concern for US sensitivities. This was evident from the very first time that the then EEC and the US met in the Dillon round (1960) to harmonize Europe's new Common External Tariff (CET) structure (implemented by the 1958 Treaty of Rome) with the customs union provisions of the GATT. There, the transatlantic Allies came to the brink of their first post-Second World War trade war, the famous 'chicken war,' which had erupted over the quantity of frozen broiler chickens that the US exported to West

Germany. This was the first lesson that a united Europe could prejudice the economic interests of the US. Another came in 1986 when the EC was enlarged to include Spain and Portugal, which brought the EC and US to the brink of a trade war over US exports of feedgrains to the EC. And, as the EC integrated a wider range of political and economic areas through the Single Market programme implemented on 1 January 1993, the US felt that its exporters were prejudiced in a number of areas, such as public utilities, television broadcasting, telecommunications, and standards and certification, thus leading to fears of a 'Fortress Europe.' Acrimonious bilateral disputes threatened to escalate into trade wars.

More significantly, of all of the trade partners that the United States has targeted on its annual list of 'unfair traders',[4] the US has been most cautious about naming Europe. Indeed, the US has been careful during sensitive negotiations either to remove it at the very last minute, or to place it on a secondary list of partners 'to watch.' This is most likely because the EC has been the only trade partner of the US to institute a list of its own[5], to consistently implement counter-sanction retaliatory measures, and to defend its interests by proactively escalating trade conflicts. Perhaps the then European Commission President Jacques Delors foreshadowed the implications of a more economically and politically independent Europe in the context of the escalation of trade tensions over the export of US feedgrains to Spain and Portugal when he stated in 1987: 'Je ne serais pas effrayé par la perspective d'un conflit ouvert avec les Etats-Unis.'[6] In November 1992, in the midst of the bitter agriculture dispute of the Uruguay round, Delors stated that 'it is important for an adolescent Europe to say No to Big Brother.'[7]

Perhaps this experience in international trade relations, an area which had been given supranational authority from the start of European integration, could foreshadow difficulties to come in the area of security.[8] If saying no to Big Brother were to be the attitude of a mature area of common European policy, where would this leave the interests of the United States vis-à-vis an EU with a CFSP and Eurocorps in the post-Cold War system?

TURNING POINT, OR POLITICAL VACUUM?

There can be little doubt that transatlantic economic and political relationships have been at times problematic. Viewed within an overall historical progression as outlined above, it is evident that there have been 'turning points.' Some have been evolutionary, such as the growth of

Europe and the relative decline of the United States. Interspersed along the historical continuum have been a series of 'crises' within the Alliance. Among the major ones were in 1956, when the US forced Britain and France to withdraw their troops from the Suez; in 1966, as France withdrew from NATO's integrated military structure; in 1977, when the US neutron bomb project caused much anxiety among the European Allies; and in the early 1980s, when there were bitter transatlantic disagreements over the construction of the Soviet gas pipeline and the negotiations leading to the Intermediate Nuclear Forces (INF) treaty. More fundamentally, as one of the present authors has written elsewhere, Europe has always felt an 'insecurity-reassurance-resentment syndrome'[9] wherein the European Allies persistently sought reassurance when they felt that the US was less than fully committed because of interests elsewhere, but complained of US high-handedness and insensitivity if the US acted decisively. This began with the US involvement in Korea and Vietnam and the intervening debate over the stationing of nuclear weapons in Europe, the détente between the superpowers in the 1970s and the announcement of the Strategic Defence Initiative (SDI) in the 1980s which was initiated without consulting the European Allies.

But in the background of such 'crises' had been the threat of a common enemy, literally at one's door – at Europe's arguably since 1948, and at the United States' since the deployment of intercontinental ballistic missiles in the 1950s and 1960s. This had concentrated the Allies' minds, and served as a strong incentive to smooth over any political, strategic, or distributive disagreements.

Perhaps the ending of the Cold War is not so much a turning point as it is a vacuum. In the 1990s, the Soviet army was not the overwhelming source from which security threats emanated, and as such threats became more diffuse a presence of over 300,000 US troops in Europe became difficult to justify to disgruntled forces in Congress. At the same time, while the US and the EU remained deadlocked in the acrimonious agriculture negotiations of the GATT in February 1992, many Congressmen, ominously, for the first time linked publicly the progress of the GATT negotiations to the number of US troops in Europe. Then Vice-President Dan Quayle warned, 'we will see the Cold War replaced by a trade war.'[10] This could not have occurred during the Cold War.

Perhaps the Cold War was a mere aberration of an historical process, one that would be resumed after its ending. The renewed discussion of a common European defence structure was gaining momentum just at the time that NATO had lost its mission. History is replete with turning points, but nature abhors a vacuum. Perhaps the institutions of the transatlantic partnership, born of American hegemony, and driven by the imperatives of post-Second World War security and economic reconstruction, are no longer suited in the 1990s to a post-Cold War international system? This is the question that concerns the contributors to this book.

SECURITY INSTITUTIONS

Post-Cold War difficulties between the Allies over security have centred on three main issues. The Bosnian conflict has persisted as a thorn in the side of the Alliance. The enlargement of NATO to Central and Eastern European states has proved to be the focal point for disagreement over NATO's new mission. Finally, whilst the prospect of an independent European security identity has been welcomed by the US, an unsure foreign policy of the Clinton Administration and a more assertive Congress have raised questions about a return of American isolationism, or worse, of unilateralism.

Lawrence Kaplan, who opens the discussion of security issues with 'NATO After the Cold War,' argues that the conflicts in the former Yugoslavia have strained the Alliance. The United States has viewed it as a European problem, which European states should have taken the lead to resolve by activating European security organizations. The European states, on the other hand, were not inclined to take direction from the US so long as it refused to contribute troops to the UN peacekeeping effort. With troops on the ground, European states have been more cautious about the prospect of enforcing a no-fly zone and conducting air-strikes to force the Bosnian Serbs to comply with cease-fires and to respect safe-havens. These concerns proved well founded when UN peacekeepers were taken hostage by the Serbs. Following the seizure of safe-zones by the Serbs in mid-1995, the prospect that the US would be forced by Congress to lift the arms embargo proved most contentious.

The issue of NATO enlargement also has been a difficult one. Central and East European states began to demand membership in NATO almost as soon as they had become independent. Having rhetorically supported for decades the freedom of those states from the clutches of the 'Evil Empire,' there was moral pressure to welcome them into the fold of the pacific union of democratic states. There was also a pragmatic desire to spread the institutional benefits of cooperation, including democratization and transparency in the civil-military relationship in these states. As is elaborated in greater detail by Lawrence Kaplan and Sean Kay in this volume, the response was the creation of the NACC in December 1991, and the Partnership for Peace in January 1994. However, this raised problems of how to proceed. The legitimate security concerns of the states of Eastern Europe needed to be accommodated within the new security architecture in such a way that would not upset the new, and still delicate, relationship with Russia by extending the Alliance to its borders. Moreover, there was some concern to extend guarantees to Russia that would assure its great power status.

The NACC was developed as a forum for consultation and joint projects between the 16 NATO members and the Central and Eastern European states through a number of NATO Committees. The North Atlantic Council (NAC) and NACC cooperate in such areas as regional conflicts, including an ad hoc group on peacekeeping; economic development, including the conversion of defence industries and the democratization of the military; and in scientific and environmental affairs.[11]

However, the Central European states, in particular but not exclusively, desired a more organic relationship that would lead to full membership of NATO. The result was the Partnership for Peace. As described by NATO's Assistant Secretary General for Political Affairs, it is 'an invitation to these countries to deepen and intensify their ties with the Alliance through practical cooperation.'[12] This would be accomplished through the creation of individual programmes suited to each state 'to promote transparency in defence budgeting, promote democratic control of defence ministries, joint planning, joint military exercises' and the interoperability of their militaries with those of NATO members, with the ultimate aim being eventual NATO membership.[13]

The PfP became a source of some division between the US and the European Allies. As Kaplan and Kay show in greater detail, the PfP initiative, designed to please everyone, in the end satisfied few. Kay in particular traces the debates surrounding the PfP and NATO enlargement in mid- to late 1994, at a time when Russia was proposing that the then Conference on Security and Cooperation in Europe (CSCE) should serve as an overarching framework for NATO, the NACC and the Commonwealth of Independent States (CIS). The response of the Clinton Administration was a 'dual-track' to strengthen the CSCE, and to hold out to Central and East European states the prospect of eventual NATO membership. However, as Kay points out, the US was ambiguous about both. The Czech Republic, Poland and Hungary were no closer to becoming members of NATO; the requirements for entry are so stringent that their faltering economies will be hard-pressed to meet them. At the same time, Russia felt a loss of prestige as a former superpower and still a nuclear power to be placed on a par with the Visegrad countries, not to mention to have NATO forces on its doorstep.

Worse, while the principle of full NATO membership, including the siting of nuclear forces, was held out to all CSCE members (but especially to the Visegrad countries) this position was denied in discussions with Russia. As Kay argues, this hedging over the expansion of NATO, particularly by the US, which had issued conflicting statements, had not taken sufficiently into consideration the implications for the Alliance, in terms of military commitments, costs, and political responsibilities. He thereby illustrates that without US leadership to provide a 'clear sense of mission and strategy, the Alliance was divided and in crisis.'

In November 1994, the Russian foreign minister Andrei Kozyrev refused to sign an Individual Partnership Plan under the PfP until the Allies' intentions concerning NATO membership for Eastern and Central European states were made more explicit. There followed conflicting statements by members of the Alliance, with the United States stating that the timetable for membership would be speeded up. This prompted Yeltsin to warn of a 'Cold Peace' at the CSCE Summit in Budapest in December 1994.[14] The US subsequently reversed its policy. Although these issues have now been partially resolved[15], leadership problems in the United States, Europe, NATO and Russia mean that the future of the NATO-Russia relationship remains very uncertain. Nevertheless, this episode highlighted a lack of a clear direction in US foreign policy and a divergent view of the European security architecture between the US and its European Allies (who themselves were not of a common opinion).

This is a trend that European unification could intensify. Kaplan suggests that the 'quickening pace of European unification' has been accompanied by 'a diminution of the American connection.' He continues that, '[I]f the European movement ultimately embraces a military component, it could be the final act in NATO's history.'

Through the Single European Act of February 1986, the member states of the then European Community resolved to consider a 'European identity in external policy matters.' In the Treaty on European Union of February 1992 (Maastricht Treaty), member states 'resolved to implement a common foreign and security policy (CFSP), including the eventual framing of a common defence policy, which might in time lead to a common defence, thereby reinforcing the European identity and its independence.'

Yet in her contribution to this volume, Juliet Lodge argues that, far from presenting a well-planned alternative to transatlantic security institutions, the EC member states had been forced by developments, in Yugoslavia in particular, to abandon their image as a 'civilian power' and to act credibly in international institutions. Lodge traces the development of the CFSP and suggests that such episodes as the development of the Eurocorps and the assignment of NATO forces to WEU missions 'highlighted the continuing reliance on the US.' Moreover, there are financial and logistical obstacles to a CFSP, not to mention the willingness of member states to retain freedom of action to pursue national interests – a fact that has been affirmed by the nuclear testing of France, despite the public condemnation of some other EU member states. To be clear, there never has been any doubt that this would be anything other than complementary to the transatlantic Alliance, and the United States welcomed the fact that Europe was prepared to take a greater role in European security. For these and other reasons which Lodge explains, she concludes that 'the big and sensitive matters of security and defence will inevitably remain tied to Atlantic considerations.'

Indeed, the new European security architecture is being constructed within a multilateral framework. The NATO Declaration of the Rome Summit of November 1991 stated that the Allies agree to the 'necessary transparency and complementarity between the European security and defence identity as it emerges in the Twelve and the WEU, and the Alliance.' And, to accommodate a more independent European security framework, NATO conceived of the concept of a Combined Joint Task Force (CJTF) at its summit in Brussels in January 1994. Through this, the Allies:

> ... stand ready to make collective assets of the Alliance available... for WEU operations undertaken by the European Allies in pursuit of their Common Foreign and Security Policy. We support the development of separable but not separate capabilities which could respond to European requirements and contribute to Alliance security.[16]

Unfortunately, what immediately followed was a débâcle where the US Congress forced President Clinton to stop enforcing the arms embargo against the Bosnian government. It became difficult for European NATO members to take seriously the US commitment of 'logistics, command and control operations.' In April 1994, Stanley Sloan expressed the sentiment that 'questions have been raised concerning whether the transatlantic relationship is as central to the interests of the Allies as it once was.'[17] This could lead one to believe that if there is to be a schism between a more comprehensive European military posture and NATO, it most likely will come about because of pressures inside the United States, rather than Europe, a point returned to later.

ISOLATION, TRADE BLOCS, AND THE CALL OF THE PACIFIC

There are several directions in which US foreign policy could develop. One is isolationism, or at least the prioritization of domestic concerns ahead of foreign engagements. Another is that the US could become disillusioned with a 'Fortress Europe' and withdraw into regional supremacy, which raises the question of zones of influence and trade blocs. Finally, the US could turn its attention away from Europe to the Pacific region due to a perceived importance of economic over security interests in the post-Cold War world.

During the 1980s, it seemed for a time that the GATT, whose Uruguay round hobbled at times unconvincingly past one failed deadline after another, no longer expressed a political-economic consensus among the United States and many states of Europe, and that negotiations within the institution, as exemplified over the issue of agriculture, served only to highlight not only divergent national priorities, but increasingly divergent economic ideologies. At the same time, Europe accelerated, and the United States initiated projects for more intensive regional cooperation.

There is some credibility to the argument that the integration of trading zones could lead to a greater polarization of international trade, which would leave a vacuum in the liberal multilateral trade order. The US appears to have changed its opinion of bilateral trade agreements in the mid-1980s, which had been that these prejudiced the integrity of the multilateral system, by pursuing a trade agreement with Israel in 1984, which then US Secretary of State Shultz called a 'landmark piece of legislation, setting the tone for agreements with other nations and eventually supplanting the world order of trade as we know it.'[18] Indeed, in 1988 there followed a Free Trade Agreement with Canada, which was extended to Mexico in 1993 through the North American Free Trade Agreement (NAFTA). The danger, as expressed by *The Economist* is that: 'the passing of the Cold War will allow the irrepressible nation-state to return to its natural game of jockeying for national advantage... success in this game will now be measured in market share rather than in territory... trading blocs will replace alliances [and] commerce will be the continuation of warfare by other means.'[19]

In 'Manifest Destiny and the Pacific Century: Europe as No.3?,' Robert O'Brien argues that 'European policy makers will increasingly face competition for US attention and efforts will need to be made both to maintain a place on the US agenda and to convince Americans at all levels of the continued importance of transatlantic relationships.' Recent reports that the British government, with the support of the European Commission and some member states of the European Union, is to launch a plan to create a 'transatlantic common market' would seem to indicate that such views as expressed by O'Brien and others are far from being unheeded in Europe. The question is: Is it already too late? O'Brien points to the recently established shifts in United States policy to, on one hand, both continental and hemispheric concerns, and, on the other, giving a clear priority to relations with Japan and China. As evidence for the former he cites the agreements with Canada and Mexico culminating in NAFTA for the continent and the decision reached at the December 1994 Miami summit to work towards a Free Trade Area of the Americas covering the hemisphere. Both economic and political data are cited to underline the central importance of Japan and China to the United States' Pacific focus.

The presentation is not one-sided, however, and O'Brien demonstrates that US economic influence in the Asia-Pacific area is much less than that of Japan except as a market for its products. But this does not detract from his central argument that US attention is focused more across the Pacific than the Atlantic because Asian societies pose a broad challenge to US competitiveness whereas European activity in sectors such as agriculture, aerospace, and entertainment are largely peripheral to US concerns (a perspective that is not shared by Wiener's contribution to this volume). Even more controversially, moving on to the security field, O'Brien argues that the United States has already shifted its security focus to the Pacific and that, 'European security matters could take second or even third place to US interests in other parts of the world.'

The assertion that with the Cold War behind us, the United States is more concerned with first, its own backyard, and second, the Asia-Pacific region, with Europe coming a potentially poor third, is not uncontroversial in a volume concerned with the future of transatlantic relations. But, perhaps more ominous than the threat of continual escalations of frictions between the US and EU *is* that the US could simply turn its attention away from Europe. The assumption that participation and leadership in the Second World War and the international institution building that followed ended once and for all the principle of isolationism in American foreign policy may have been misguided. The 1990s may be witness to the end of a brief period, historically, of US internationalism and a return to a more traditional American foreign policy of non-involvement. Indeed, the US Congress, on the whole – not only the self-proclaimed isolationists – seems more preoccupied with domestic matters than with foreign affairs. And, there has been pressure from Congress to limit the ability of the President to deploy US troops on UN peacekeeping missions, such as the January 1994 approval in the House of Representatives of the National Security Revitalisation Act. Indeed, Lawrence Kaplan argues that a level of 100,000 troops in Europe demonstrates that to the US, Europe is neither seen as a vital security interest, nor one that the Americans should take the lead in dealing with. He states: '[T]he disillusionment with European behaviour in Bosnia, a preoccupation with domestic problems, and a rise in aggressive unilateralism, if not isolationism, under resurgent Republicans in 1995' could all lead to 'an American military withdrawal from Europe.'

The US could turn its attention to the Americas or to the Asia-Pacific Region to the detriment of Europe. Traditionally, the Western debate on European security was centred on NATO and carried out as a dialogue between North America and Western Europe. The question needs to be asked whether this relationship, based on the security requirements of a divided Europe, is still relevant, not only because the Cold War is over, but as issues of economic security are seen to be as important as issues of military security. The Asia-Pacific region is an area of remarkable economic dynamism, with markets experiencing exceptionally rapid rates of growth. The US has always been a Pacific power as well as an Atlantic one, and Secretary of State Warren Christopher did state on the eve of the Asia-Pacific Economic Cooperation summit in November 1993 that the US hosted in Seattle that, 'Western Europe is no longer the dominant area of the world.'[20]

SOME CAUSE FOR (GUARDED) OPTIMISM

Having put forth the worst possible scenarios, there are some good reasons to be optimistic about the future of the transatlantic partnership.

Balkans – Débâcle?

The Bosnian conflict is not one such security threat. The present writers each have argued elsewhere that Bosnia should not to be taken as a test case for the ability of the international community to police the so-called 'New World Order.'[21] Some conflicts may simply be insoluble, at least by outside parties, whatever their individual or collective power, military or economic. Bosnia may be just such a conflict. It has attracted much media attention – more so than other contemporary conflicts of its kind. That the United States and Europe have allowed the Bosnian conflict to sour the transatlantic partnership is a failure of leadership on both sides of the Atlantic. But the debates have shown that there has been as much of a lack of consensus within Europe as there has been between Europe and the US. The history of efforts to deal with the conflict shows that there has been a lack of a unified European, American – indeed, public – view. While this is not to deny that there have been transatlantic disagreements, especially since there have been European forces on the ground in the absence of American troops, the Bosnian conflict illustrates that when the decisions that have to be made are moral, rather than strategic, reasonable people can hold to quite different, even opposite, yet still perfectly defensible positions.

The debate over Bosnia has been essentially a moral one. As Mervyn Frost has written, '[d]uring the long period of the Cold War there was, both among scholars and practitioners, a well settled discourse on International Relations' in terms of its frames of reference and the kinds of questions that were debated, and that '[r]ecent developments in Eastern Europe have brought some fundamental questions to the surface.'[22] In terms of sheer *raison d'état*, a contained conflict in the former Yugoslavia does not present security threats to the Alliance. Some of the vocal public, which had been assaulted periodically with live pictures of atrocities there, has held to more cosmopolitan and utilitarian views. The political leaders' failure was not that they were unable to come up with a successful plan of action, nor that the US failed to 'lead,' nor that Europe would not 'follow,' nor even that Europe would not assume a leadership role. It was not, in classic style, a 'crisis in the Alliance.' In fact, the frames of reference within which one could reasonably discuss the security issue seem not to be applicable. Where there has been failure, it has been on the part of both the US and European governments who have lacked the courage to stand up and say to an understandably concerned public that there are situations where intervention, beyond the humanitarian, is unlikely to work. This realism may be unpopular and morally unpalatable to some, but far more dangerous has been the error at all levels, and by all leaders, to allow Bosnia to become the defining crisis for the future of NATO, Atlantic relations, Europe, and the so-called 'New World Order.'

Yet, regardless of whether the Balkans are worth the bones of a single Pomeranian grenadier – to borrow a phrase from Bismarck – for many politicians, in the US Congress for instance, the conflict in Bosnia *has* often been taken as a yardstick of the effectiveness of security organizations. This is dangerous, if for no other reason than that the conflict in Bosnia may not be the last of its kind. If other issues like it accumulate they are likely to lead to this fundamental question being debated in the US Congress, as Sean Kay points out, during the ratification process of new members of NATO if this should come to pass. In the context of NATO enlargement, one former Clinton Administration official stated: 'This isn't NATO expansion – it's a US implosion. These guys want to show you their designs for a new addition to the house while the living room is on fire.'[23] Thus, whilst the crisis in Bosnia is not an immediate danger to the transatlantic Alliance, by not stating so the Allies have allowed it to become one.

Moreover, even assuming that one is justified in laying blame for prevarication in Bosnia, it is imperative that it is placed on the doorstep of the right institution. It is not NATO, strictly speaking, that is dithering and has lost credibility, but the United Nations. As François de Rose understated: 'it is obvious that the current experience of collaboration in the Balkans between the organization which can state the law and that which could enforce it, has not been satisfactory.'[24] One could argue that this is mere semantics, since the main players in NATO also sit on the UN Security Council.[25] This would be quite correct, and that organization, too, has also suffered a blow to its credibility as a result of the conflict. But the loss of credibility has been mainly in the eyes of international public opinion (as well as, of course, the Bosnian Serbs), and as has been astutely observed, public opinion of the UN is only as old as its most recent failure.[26]

It is important to recognize, though, that the differences of opinion – over the no-fly zone, the lifting of the arms embargo and the blockade in the Adriatic – did not escalate, but were settled through political accommodation. It could be, as Lawrence Kaplan alludes in his article, that the governments on both sides of the Atlantic recognized that the conflict did not jeopardize the stability of the world, continent, or even of the region as did the Cold War. That the differences of opinion, whilst very real, were able to be overcome is testament to a realization that fundamental national interests have not been at stake. The logical progression of this argument is that if a real security threat were to erupt, one could expect NATO and the UN Security Council to spring into action.

Indeed, the NATO operation in September 1995 in which the US was quite actively involved demonstrated a number of things. Not least, it reaffirmed the principle that 'diplomacy without force is like an orchestra without a score.'[27] The success of 'Deliberate Force' in bringing the warring parties to the negotiating table showed that, even if the conflict itself may not be of vital interest, the maintenance of the credibility of the international security institutions is. Importantly, the military operation illustrated that the transatlantic partners *would* take action to preserve the credibility of NATO and the UN, and that the United States would be on hand to extricate European troops on the ground in the event of a non-permissive withdrawal.

Trade Blocs?

Fears about the US and the EU retreating into regional trade zones must be balanced against the successful completion of the Uruguay round which reaffirmed their commitment to multilateralism. Not only that, as Wiener outlines in his chapter on transatlantic trade relations, the Uruguay round brought new issues previously excluded from multilateral attention into the orbit of multilateral oversight, such as trade in services, trade-related investment measures, and agriculture, and strengthened commitments to the protection of trade-related intellectual property rights. Moreover, the Uruguay round created an overarching institutional framework of the World Trade Organization, and imparted greater coercive force to the mechanisms for dispute settlement. What is important to recognize is that the expansion and strengthening of the multilateral trade institution came about as a *result* of adverse economic conditions and heightened trade conflicts, the very things that some pessimistic commentators believed would fragment the multilateral trade system.[28]

The NAFTA project does not necessarily have to be seen as an exercise in bridge-burning. It is true that the EU has found valuable leverage in some of its common policies when negotiating with the US, such as the European Public Procurement Directive which served to direct attention towards the US Buy America Act. To be sure, once the WTO has concluded its assessment of NAFTA in 1996, there will be similar policies which the EU may find objectionable. Whereas the trade diversion from the creation of the EU has been estimated to be only 2.5% of extra-EU trade, the NAFTA is expected to produce up to 5%.[29] One such area is the domestic content requirement of the NAFTA in certain sectors which can be considered to be prejudicial. The tariff classification for some goods changes according to the 'regional value content' of between 50 and 60% in some cases.[30] Textiles, for instance, are subject to a 'triple transformation test,' in that they have to be cut and sewn from fabric spun from North American fibres to qualify for NAFTA preferences[31]. There is also a requirement that when assembled, an automobile cannot receive NAFTA duty-free treatment unless it contains 62.5% North American content.[32] Such sourcing requirements, admittedly, were intended to guard against 'screwdriver' assembly plants, but can set a poor precedent in principle for future regional programmes.

However, regional integration can be seen as setting a precedent for future areas of multilateral regulation, and even as providing incentives to do so. While not denying the inherent economic benefits of North American trade liberalization, and the political benefits to the US of an economically secure southern neighbour, the NAFTA has provided the United States with the means to threaten the EU with exclusion from a larger market. Another fear is that the NAFTA is in reality an 'investment bloc.' For instance, whereas each party of the NAFTA has agreed to accord national and most-favoured-nation treatment to each other's financial institutions, there is no such provision for outside parties.[33] However, it is important to recognize that so long as these trade 'blocs' continue to negotiate, the danger that they will become exclusionary diminishes. On past performance, regional integration in trade has been an impetus to multilateral negotiations. The Dillon round of the GATT was convened in response to the Treaty of Rome, and the enlargement of the EC was a factor for the launching of the Kennedy and Tokyo rounds.[34] And, at the beginning of 1995, the European Commission has called for cooperation between the WTO and the OECD to create a global framework of investment rules to enforce at the multilateral level the principles of most-favoured-nation, national treatment, and transparency to foreign direct-investment related policies, as well as to guarantee the free transfer of funds, dispute settlement and compensation in the case of expropriation.[35]

Not only is the fear of exclusion fuelling multilateral rule creation, but the process is being driven by the globalization of capital and foreign direct investment. International trade is increasingly less important relative to international investment. From 1983 to 1990, for example, the volume of foreign investment grew at a rate three times that of world trade. The stock of direct investment between Europe and the US stands at $460 billion, which is increasing at an annual rate of $35 billion.[36] More tellingly, US firms earned approximately $10 billion in profits on $96 billion worth of merchandise exports to the EC in 1990, but earned $32 billion on $446.5 billion of investment there.[37]

While it is undeniable that regional trade agreements are coalescing in Europe and in North America, to invoke an image of 'protectionist blocs' of a 1930s genre, or of futuristic 'Orwellian Superzones,' is to overstate the extent to which demarcations drawn on the map of the international economy with a political marker are able to interrupt the forces of the global economy which can supersede their boundaries. The very reference to 'trading blocs' is another example of misapplied historical imagery. The protectionist 1930 US Smoot-Hawley Act had signalled to a post-October 1929 international economic system that the US would safeguard its own interests at the expense of others, against which Britain and its Commonwealth retaliated in 1932 with the Commonwealth System of Imperial Preferences – an exclusive trading arrangement that prejudiced the interests of the US.[38]

Yet there is no inherent reason for the globalizing forces of capital to respect trade demarcations, which are of decreasing relevance to the global economy. This is not to suggest that with increasing interdependence there will no new sources of potential friction, as the transatlantic dispute over standards and certification has shown. And, at the same time, globalization is raising its own difficulties. As Wiener outlines, the turning of attention to the trade in agriculture and cinematographic films in liberal trade fora has raised non-economic security concerns relating to the preservation of core values, such as 'culture,' and a 'way of life.' Europe has argued that liberalization should not extend so far as to destabilize social structures, whereas the US has maintained that Europe's arguments are mere excuses to protect inefficient industries. Wiener considers that these issues could represent a fundamental divergence over economic ideology. But, irrespective of whether these arguments are genuine, they are likely not only to continue, but to escalate as information technology brings the societies of Europe and the US into closer contact, and the high-tech industries of the EU and the US into more intense competition in the building and content of the global information infrastructure.

Stephen Woolcock's chapter on 'EU-US Commercial Relations and the Debate on a Transatlantic Free Trade Area' expands on and enhances arguments in the areas just discussed, highlighted by a close examination of the issues raised for both sides of the Atlantic by the debate over the

Transatlantic Free Trade Area (TAFTA). While it is assumed that the security imperatives of the Cold War suppressed many potential transatlantic commercial disputes, some commentators expected that with these preoccupations removed, the situation would change. As a way of examining this possibility, Woolcock puts forward three broad scenarios for commercial relations in the 2000s: a continuation of the status quo, drift at a greater or lesser pace, and a deepening of economic ties. The broad conclusion is that the continued growth of transatlantic commercial interdependence has replaced the security imperative as the major restraining influence on underlying EU-US commercial contradictions breaking out into open, damaging, long-term disputes, a view which fits well with other ideas developed in this volume. While there has been an obvious decline in US commercial leadership, this is not the major problem. The biggest danger that could arise is if attempts to deal with commercial difficulties by transatlantic bilateral trade liberalization are carried out at the expense of a commitment by both sides to the joint promotion of the multilateral trade system. Woolcock is reasonably sanguine that this will not happen, however, as he rules out the extreme scenario of commercial integration because of embedded transatlantic and domestic restraints. The opposite extreme scenario of a trade war is ruled out by commercial interdependence. The US approach supports the status quo as it has showed continued concern for third country commercial relations that must not be jeopardized by bilateral transatlantic arrangements. All this leads Woolcock to conclude that while drift may be the most likely scenario, this is not necessarily a negative outcome as long as multilateral liberalization continues to be promoted.

Isolationism?

Turning to US isolationism, fears of the US 'returning' to a more 'traditional' foreign policy after the aberration of the Cold War may also be overstated; though the alternative to isolationism – unilateralism – is perhaps just as damaging to the transatlantic partnership. Fears of a resurgence of isolationist tendencies are based on a particular, and perhaps faulty reading of the history of American foreign policy and the current international situation. The roots of American isolationism are usually traced to President George Washington's Farewell Address warning against involvement with foreign powers. The 1823 Monroe Doctrine, which stated that the American continent should remain free from further European colonization, also clearly stated America's intention to remain neutral, indeed aloof, from Europe's internal squabbles. The United States of America was an anti-imperial power. The extreme reluctance to enter the First World War, and despite the spate of Wilsonian internationalism, the refusal to join the League and the isolationism of the 1920s completed the picture. The story was repeated in the period up to, and the beginning of, the Second World War. Although President Roosevelt was seen as having an internationalist perspective, he was hampered by an isolationist Congress, especially the Senate, in a seeming repeat of the Wilsonian experience. The events of the war and its aftermath, particularly the 'iron curtain' that descended upon the continent of Europe changed this dramatically, and America's role in the world. Those who now fear (or in some cases welcome) a return to American isolationism base their concerns on this perceived history of American foreign policy. There are other possible interpretations.

History very rarely repeats itself, but irrespective of whether the past can be a reliable guide to the future a misperception of the past is no help at all. An alternative thesis would be that America never has been isolationist, at least in the manner described above. As with all foreign policy analysis, the domestic context must never be ignored. George Washington was speaking at a time of fierce internal political debate, much of it focusing on external issues but having a great deal to do with the struggle for political dominance among emerging political parties. The argument was not that America could and should remain isolated from external events, but that in a time of national weakness the United States should aim to remain neutral in foreign conflicts, avoid alliances, and so build its strength to act unilaterally when US interests so required it. Although having a background in Anglo-American discussions, the Monroe Doctrine was a unilateral statement of American policy. An analysis of this trend, including America becoming an overtly imperial power in the Pacific in 1898, could be continued throughout the nineteenth and into the twentieth century. If this is a more accurate portrayal of the development of American foreign policy behaviour, then a return to a more traditional stance could mean more American unilateralism rather than isolationism, an equally gloomy prospect for those who seek a continuation of partnership with the United States.

Recent debate over foreign policy in Washington is unlikely to lift this gloom. US foreign policy may be at a fundamental point of change. The tradition was that 'politics stopped at the water's edge' and that, in modern times at least, Congress and the President pursued a bipartisan foreign policy. This may have been more apparent than real, but certainly throughout the Cold War a loose consensus existed, even over contentious money issues such as troops in Europe or contributions to the United Nations. Even the Vietnam war, which marked a watershed of sorts, was fought by an establishment consensus, albeit one constantly under attack. It was begun and reached its height under 'liberal' Democratic presidents, but was vigorously pursued and then ended under 'conservative' Republican presidents. The breakdown in this long postwar history of American foreign policy consensus has a great deal to do with domestic factors. 'It's the economy, stupid' (reputedly Bill Clinton) may tell us more about the current state of US foreign policy than the fall of the Berlin Wall.[39]

In 1996, we are faced with a Presidential/Congressional split on foreign policy, with the President trying to play the internationalist (Presidential Decision Directive 25 notwithstanding) and the Congress trying to get a foreign policy with minimal cost to the US. However, it is a weak Presidency and a weak Congress facing a declining domestic consensus and an increasingly interdependent world where political economy rather than military strategy increasingly appears to dominate. It is the breakdown in domestic consensus that puzzles America's partners. What is sometimes forgotten is that despite its size and impact abroad, America remains a quintessentially insular country. Rightly or wrongly, for many Americans it is time to put America first in order to maintain the strength which is necessary for the continued independence of the United States, which brings us back to George Washington's Farewell Address. Just as then:

> It's not isolationism. Unilateralism is the major feature. It is a more nationalist foreign policy, a much more selective use of military engagement, asking the question: What is the US interest here? What's in it for us?
> ... We want to benefit from our engagement in world affairs and from our leadership, but at the same time we are reluctant to pay the costs in the way we once did.[40]

The implication is that the US in future will be less of a partner, and potentially, at least in economic terms, an adversary. However, there are those who are worried that unilateralism is simply a step on the way to isolationism. Charles William Maynes, editor of *Foreign Policy*: 'There is now more danger of the US returning to the pure isolationism of 1920-25 than I have ever seen. At the moment, the current is unilateralist rather than isolationist, but it will lead to isolationism, because we will not be able to carry the Allies with us.'[41]

As for the shifting of United States attention eastward, it is important to recognize that East Asia is a region of great diversity, and with historical animosities among the states of the region that make the Bosnian crisis look tame by comparison. Some observers have warned that the area could soon be characterized by 'political fragmentation and hostility.'[42] Moreover, American trade conflicts with Japan have been perhaps even more protracted as those with Europe, and these appear to be debated with greater fervour in the US Congress. When US legislators spoke of 'burdensharing' in the context of Europe, there was an outright 'bashing' of Japan. As one Congressman put it in 1982, 'we work our tail off so that the Japanese can have a stable international economic environment which they can use to put Americans out of work.'[43] Finally, the strategic timing of the Seattle summit of the Asia-Pacific Economic Cooperation (APEC) in November 1993 should be appreciated. Convened just when Europe was deliberating the final Uruguay round package, threats of exclusion could have been an additional incentive for Europe to ratify the deal, or at least to provide pro-GATT member states with a weapon to use in the internal European Council deliberations.

CONCLUSION

The transatlantic relationship is the 1990s is not unproblematic; but then, it never has been. Hardly any of the difficulties touched upon above are, in essence, new. The Alliance was always faced with the problem of accommodating differences. The trick was to resolve them without self-destructing. The ending of the Cold War could, quite rightly, lead some to believe that NATO's military mission has come to an end and, perhaps less rightly, to assume that the political alliance itself would dissolve.

However, the ending of the Cold War does not represent a 'vacuum' as it was referred to above. This was deliberately overstated. For, the 'New World Order' of the 1990s is not like its predecessor 'New World Orders' of 1919 or 1945 which did mandate the creation of new organizations, and which did demand leadership. Historically, political vacuums have been filled by the ebbing and flowing of alliance systems, and, more recently by the leadership of a predominant state. But while much has changed after the Cold War, there is also much continuity between the old order and the 'new.'

At the structural level, the transformation from bipolarity to more diffuse patterns of power is undeniable. However, other political relationships, such as the transatlantic one, are more fluid. What makes the enlargement of NATO, for instance, different from previous alliance reconfigurations is that whilst the Warsaw Treaty Organization has dissolved, NATO, despite having some trepidation about how to confront the new order, and with member states often disagreeing publicly about it, nevertheless endures. The NACC and the PfP have not been unproblematic, and, admittedly, they have raised differences of opinion on how to proceed. But, it is important not to lose sight of the grand project. The Allies recognize that while the character of the insecurities in the post-Cold War system have changed, the fact that there are insecurities has not. Extreme nationalism, intolerance, nuclear proliferation, and the resort to arms to settle political conflicts are among the few that were enumerated by former NATO Secretary General Willy Claes.[44] As Nicholas Sherwen has said elsewhere, the 'Alliance ... has provided fixed points of reference in an uncertain world – a handrail up an obscure staircase, to which member counties have been able to cling without knowing exactly where the stairs would ultimately lead.'[45] To the extent that NATO is a central reference point, its importance has been only reinforced by the fact that the footing on the staircase has become less certain.

We should not become mesmerized by the past in our attempt to peer into the future. The institutional expression of the transatlantic relationship is expanding, and it is doing so in a way that is inclusive. Security institutions are evolving in a way this is compatible with regional security complexes, and supportive of former adversaries. In economic matters, the forces of globalization also seem to be creating pressures for convergence. As the division between trade and investment becomes increasingly blurred, the institutional arrangements for dealing with these issues may respond through initiatives ether in the OECD or the WTO, and will likely not be at the expense of multilateralism. Moreover, it may be too traditionalist/realist to concentrate on the nation-state as the only actor. Global interdependence, as discussed elsewhere in this introduction, means a genuine interdependence, horizontally and vertically. There has long been a vast literature on the growing international role of international organizations, both governmental and nongovernmental. More recently there has been a growing awareness of and interest in the role of intra-state actors in both shaping national foreign policies and acting independently in the international arena. This is an increasingly important phenomenon in the United States. State governments, for instance, have for a long time been active in seeking overseas investment and promoting overseas sales. This type of activity has increased considerably in recent years and now encompasses local, state, regional and even ethnic group activities in both influencing US foreign policy and pursuing their own agendas abroad.[46] These developments do not fall within any of the categories of isolationism, unilateralism, or internationalism as traditionally defined, but they fit well within the concept of growing global interdependence, or for lack of a better term, 'globalization.'

Where does all of this leave the subject of transatlantic partnership in general and the future of NATO in particular? Clearly, in a state of uncertainty. But the main argument developed here is that while we need to examine carefully the past in order to comprehend the historical context of current debates and developing trends, we also need to break free of the traditional categories in which we try to place developments in an attempt to try to understand them. The *Strategic Survey 1994/95* provides an apposite note on which to end:

> Just as likely as nostalgia for an era when Americans did not deal with the rest of the world is nostalgia for an era when they largely ran it. The American temptation today is unilateralism as much as isolationism: international engagement on American terms and in American interests, or no international engagement at all. The unpleasant reality is that neither course is good for the rest of the world, nor for the United States itself.[47]

Neither course is likely, however. Complex global interdependence will probably not allow it to happen.

NOTES

1. See Clair Wilcox, *A Charter for World Trade*, Macmillan, New York, 1949; and Richard N. Gardner, *Sterling-Dollar Diplomacy in Current Perspective: The Origins and the Prospects of our International Economic Order*, Columbia University Press, New York, 1980.
2. See Joseph Lepgold, *The Declining Hegemon: The United States and European Defense, 1960-1990*, Praeger, London, 1990.
3. As Nicholas Sherwen pointed out in the Preface to this volume, this was for the second time. The original European Defense Community and European Army proposal did not come into being due to the absence of the UK and the decision of the French Assemblée Nationale not to ratify the treaty.
4. The National Trade Estimate of the US Trade Representative, as required by the 1988 Omnibus Trade and Competitiveness Act.

5.   For instance, Services of the European Commission, *Report on US Barriers to Trade and Investment*, Doc. No.I/194/94 (April 1994).

6.   Translated: 'I would not be afraid of the prospect of an open confrontation with the United States.' *Le Monde*, 2 January 1987.

7.   'Leap Into the Unknown for Nervous EC Leaders,' *Financial Times*, 5 November 1992, p.8. Such a statement, however, may show a inclination to overlook a debt owed to 'Big Brother.'

8.   Article 113 of the 1958 Treaty of Rome had transferred from individual member states to the European Commission the power to negotiate trade matters in the GATT forum. This is not to say that this authority has not gone unchallenged, or that some member states have not been able to influence the process.

9.   See Dan Hiester, 'NATO: Approaching the Millennium,' in Pàl Dunay, Gabor Kardos and Andrew J. Williams (eds.), *New Forms of Security: Views from Central, Eastern and Western Europe*, Dartmouth, Aldershot, 1995; and Hiester, 'The United States as a Power in Europe,' in Robert Jordan (ed.), *Europe and the Superpowers: Essays on European International Politics*, Pinter, London, 1991, pp.22-47.

10. 'Quayle Warns on EC GATT Talks,' *Financial Times*, 10 February 1992, p.1.

11. See NATO Heads of State and Government Declaration on a Transformed North Atlantic Alliance, London, 6 July 1990; NATO Ministerial Statement on Partnership with the Countries of Central and Eastern Europe, Copenhagen, 6 June 1991; and NATO Heads of State and Government Declaration on Peace and Cooperation, Rome, 8 November 1991. See also 'The 1994 NACC Work Plan,' *NATO Review*, No.6, December 1993, pp.30-33.

12. Gebhardt von Moltke, 'Building a Partnership for Peace,' *NATO Review*, No.3, June 1994, p.3.

13. See NATO, *Partnership for Peace*, Framework Document of the NATO Summit in Brussels, 10 January 1994.

14. For a discussion of this and its impact on the CSCE Budapest summit, see 'Yeltsin's "Cold Peace" Warning Shivers NATO,' *The Guardian*, 8 December 1994, p.15. It was at this meeting that its name was changed to the Organization for Security and Cooperation in Europe (OSCE), which is used hereinafter.

15. Russia did sign an Individual Partnership Programme on 22 June 1994, of course, which led to a 16+1 formula. See 'Areas for Pursuance of a Broad, Enhanced NATO/Russia Dialogue and Cooperation,' *NATO Review*, July 1995, p.35.

16. Declaration of the Heads of State and Government Participating in the Meeting of the North Atlantic Council Held at NATO Headquarters, Brussels, on 10-11 January 1994. Press Communiqué M-1 (94) 3, 11 January 1994, p.3.

17. Stanley Sloan, 'Transatlantic Relations in the Wake of the Brussels Summit,' *NATO Review*, Vol.42, No.2, April 1994.

18. 'Israel Free Trade Bill Clears House Easily,' *Congressional Quarterly Weekly Report*, 11 May 1985, p.880.

19. 'The World Order Changeth,' *The Economist*, 22 June 1991, p.13.

20. *The Guardian*, 18 October 1993.

21. Dan Hiester, 'Introduction: The Future of the Transatlantic Relationship,' *Paradigms: The Kent Journal of International Relations*, Vol.7, No.2, 1993, pp.vi-xi; Jarrod Wiener, 'Leadership, the United Nations, and the New World Order,' in Jarrod Wiener and Dimitris Bourantonis (eds.), *The United Nations in the New World Order*, Macmillan, London, 1995, pp.41-63.

22. Mervyn Frost, 'Constituting a New World Order,' *Paradigms: The Kent Journal of International Relations*, Vol.8, No.1, 1994, pp.13-22. See also Chris Brown (ed.), *Political Restructuring in Europe: Ethical Aspects*, Routledge, London, 1994.
23. 'R.I.P The New World Order,' *Time International*, 12 December 1994, p.29.
24. François de Rose, 'A Future Perspective for the Alliance,' *NATO Review*, No.4, July 1995, p.12.
25. Of course, Russia also sits on the UN Security Council.
26. Adam Roberts and Benedict Kingsbury (eds.), *United Nations, Divided World: The UN's Role in International Relations*, 2nd. ed., Clarendon Press, Oxford, 1993.
27. Reputedly Frederick the Great. See Adam Watson, *Diplomacy: The Dialogue Between States*, Routledge, London, 1991, p.53.
28. See Jarrod Wiener, 'Endgame for the GATT, or the End of the GATT? The Uruguay Round and the US-EC Relationship,' *Paradigms: The Kent Journal of International Relations*, Vol.7, No.2, 1993, pp.94-118.
29. See Richard Harmsen and Arvind Subramanian, 'Economic Implications of the Uruguay Round,' *International Trade Policies: The Uruguay Round and Beyond, Vol.I, Principal Issues*, IMF, Washington, 1994, pp.4-5.
30. North American Free Trade Agreement, US Government Printing Office Publication 1992-330-817/70635, Art.401 (b) and (d).
31. NAFTA. Annex 300-B, Section 2; Art.404.
32. NAFTA, Art. 402, 403.
33. NAFTA, Art. 1401(2).
34. This point is made by Kym Anderson and Richard Blackhurst (eds.), 'Introduction,' *Regional Integration and the Global Trading System*, Harvester-Wheatsheaf, London, 1993.
35. See: 'Commission Strategy: FDI Rules Needed in EU,' *Business Europe*, Economist Intelligence Unit, 30 January 1995; 'Address by Sir Leon Brittan: Smoothing the Path for Investment Worldwide, Washington DC, 31 January 1995,' Commission of the European Communities, *RAPID*, 31 January 1995 (speech 95-7).
36. 'Commission Proposes Worldwide Investment Instrument,' Commission of the European Communities, *RAPID*, 1 March 1995 (Press Release: 95-197).
37. Cynthia Day Wallace and John M. Kline, *EC '92 and Changing Global Investment Patterns: Implications for the US-EC Relationship*, The Centre for Strategic International Studies, Washington DC, 1992.
38. See, for example, H.W. Arndt, *The Economic Lessons of the Nineteen-Thirties*, Oxford University Press, Oxford, 1944.
39. More eloquently, Presidential candidate Clinton stated: 'We must understand that foreign and domestic policy are two sides of the same coin. If we're not strong at home we can't be strong abroad. If we can't compete in the global economy, we'll pay for it at home.' Remarks of Governor Bill Clinton, Los Angeles World Affairs Council, 13 August 1992.
40. Ted Galen Carpenter, quoted in 'Ancien Regime Fights for the Old Order and America Firsters Look to their Own,' *The Guardian*, 20 February 1995. p.9.
41. *Ibid.*
42. Barry Buzan and Gerald Segal, 'Rethinking East Asian Security,' *Survival*, Vol.36, No.2, Summer 1994, p.7.
43. Rep. Duncan L. Hunter, quoted in 'Trade, Defense Issues Fray US-Japan Ties,' *Congressional Quarterly*, 27 November 1982, pp.2903-2908.

44. Willy Claes, 'NATO and the Evolving Euro-Atlantic Security Architecture,' *NATO Review*, Vol.42, No.6, December 1994/No.1 January 1995, pp.3-7.

45. Nicholas Sherwen, 'Introduction,' in Jamie Shea, *NATO 2000: A Political Agenda for a Political Alliance*, Brassey's, London, 1990, p.2.

46. See The Stanley Foundation *Reports*: 'Global Changes and Domestic Transformations: The Midwest and the World,' September 1993; 'Shaping American Global Policy: The Growing Impact of Societal Relations,' October 1993; 'Shaping American Global Policy: The Growing Role of the Pacific Northwest,' October 1994; 'Latinos, Global Change, and American Foreign Policy,' October 1994; and 'The Changing Face of American Foreign Policy: The New Role of State and Local Actors,' November 1994.

47. International Institute for Strategic Studies, *Strategic Survey 1994-1995*, May 1995.

2 NATO After the Cold War

Lawrence S. Kaplan

It has been a quarter of a century since the Johns Hopkins scholar, David Calleo, wrote that 'the Supreme Allied Commander has never been the first servant of the Council, but the viceroy of the American president.' The North Atlantic Treaty Organization itself, he asserted, was 'the rather elaborate apparatus by which we have chosen to organize the American protectorate in Europe.'[1] This was the language of revisionism in 1970, articulating a judgement that NATO was little more than an instrument of America's imperial power. Whether that power was exploitive, as the foregoing statements imply, or benign, as the United States and many of its Allies believed, the Alliance under American leadership was a success.

From the time that the Alliance was founded in 1949, Europe's fear of communism spreading under the wings of the Soviet Union kept it intact and gave meaning to the military organization it had created. Although less fearsome in 1970, Soviet power still sent shivers down the collective spine of Western Europe. And, even though détente between East and West had been in the making since the end of the Cuban missile crisis in 1962, it was a fragile co-existence always subjected to such shocks as the brutal snuffing out of the 'Prague spring' in the summer of 1968. At the same time that the Soviet Union accepted the Federal Republic's *Ostpolitik* and engaged in confidence-building SALT talks in the 1970s, it accelerated its nuclear capabilities and challenged the Western European Allies with medium-range missiles targeted on their major cities. The result was what Norwegian historian Geir Lundestad has labelled the American 'empire by invitation.'[2] Only France was prepared to revoke the invitation – for itself but not for its Allies; France was not unhappy with American troops remaining in neighbouring countries. Notwithstanding mutual displays of annoyance, Europeans regarded the American commitment to the Alliance for almost two generations as a guarantee of stability in the West.

It was on the strength of this assumption that over 300,000 Americans enjoyed a welcome in Europe that deserves more attention than it has received in the past. These forces enjoyed favours and concessions which in other circumstances would have been insults to national sovereignty. American villages blossomed in Germany, Italy, England, and even in France before 1966. Germany in the 1960s allowed gasoline stations on the autobahns to serve only American servicemen, with signs in English along the highways. While there was increasing restiveness as time went by over the American economic presence in Europe in the form of soft drinks, automobiles, or computers, these were acceptable while the Soviet menace loomed large. As long as the Soviet arsenal of nuclear weapons and superior manpower on the ground remained in place NATO's solidarity was assured.

The disbanding of the Warsaw Pact and the subsequent dissolution of the Soviet Union in 1991 seemed to remove almost overnight NATO's *raison d'être*. It no longer had the mission to defend the West from the communist East when the latter ceased to exist. To bowdlerize Dean Acheson's words, which so aggravated the British in 1962, NATO had lost its 'empire,' and had not yet found a new role.[3] The sudden self-destruction of the adversary instantly made irrelevant much of the Allies' military planning. As late as September 1989, six weeks before the Berlin Wall collapsed, NATO planners were concentrating on the most pressing problem of the day, namely, the modernization of the Lance nuclear missile in Germany. This had been a sensitive issue with Germans, since the tactical weapon would be usable only on German soil, East or West. West Germany's reaction was part of its growing rebellion against NATO's intrusions on the quality of life from noise pollution by low-flying planes to tanks on manoeuvre ripping up arable fields. But no matter how much distress these activities caused and no matter how much assurance Gorbachev-inspired reforms in the Soviet Union gave to the Western Allies, the reality of Soviet power dividing Europe continued to be a centripetal force holding the Alliance together. Had the unexpected events of the following year not occurred the Allies in all likelihood would have accepted the improved missile. Instead, President Bush cancelled without fanfare the Lance Program on 3 May 1990.

What was left for NATO to do when the enemy had left the field? Even if the 'end of history,' in the words of State Department official Francis Fukuyama,[4] had not been cancelled almost as soon as it was proclaimed, the future was expected to be one of harmony between former enemies, and consequently of stability in a world formerly caught up in the rivalry of the superpowers. There were hopeful auguries in 1990 and 1991. The new Russia seeking entry into capitalist society looked to the West for support, and in turn appeared prepared to be part of a consensus in the Security Council. The immediate results of this dramatic change was the empowerment of the United Nations to fulfil peacekeeping functions which had been hampered by the Cold War. There was even a prospect of a UN police force to keep the new world order. The Gulf war of 1991 was an example of the kind of co-operation, although at a minimal level, that could have set a precedent for suppressing disorder around the world. If this was to be the future, what need was there for an alliance directed against a threat that no longer existed? Any threats to European security should be managed by Europeans themselves through one or more of the military agencies associated with the European Union. In light of the expectations of the European Union after its meeting in Maastricht in 1992, there hardly seemed to be a need for an American-led alliance to defend the West.

There were other serious after-effects of the collapse of NATO's former mission. The most immediate from an American standpoint was the size of the American presence in Europe, or even the very existence of an American military presence. This was not a new issue. Pressure to reduce American forces in Europe had been building over time, in large measure as a by-product of Congressional unhappiness over burden-sharing in the organization. For years complaints had been raised over the contrast between American costs and the European contribution, particularly in light of Europe's prosperity in the last generation. The Europeans retorted that the costs of supporting American troops had increasingly become part of the host's responsibility. In addition, the Germans were more frequently asking the question that the French had always raised: How reliable was the American commitment? Would the end of the Cold War mean the departure of American troops from the continent?

There was some justification for Europe's uneasiness. The figure of 326,414 American troop strength which SACEUR General John Galvin had identified when he took office in 1987 was deemed too high even before the disbanding of the Warsaw Pact. The minimal cuts begun by President Bush in 1989 culminated into a 20% reduction in Army and Air Force personnel, from 305,000 to 270,000. The reductions continued. In May 1991 the Congress called for a troop reduction from 250,000 then in place to 100,000 by 1995. This remains the figure under the Clinton Administration. At this size at least a 'medium' army corps could be formed in place of a 'large' corps, according to a Congressional Research Service (CRS) study in September 1992.[5] While this would be a lesser combat force it could be supplemented by contingency units airlifted from the United States.

Will the momentum be checked at 100,000? The CRS survey observed that at 50,000 the most that could be extracted would be an army division, much like the force currently on the line in South Korea. Below this figure the United States would have to think solely in humanitarian terms, or, more likely, to leave Europe to the Europeans. If the reduction of US forces in Europe should come to pass, the assumptions of France and the hopes of the Soviets would finally be realized. There has always been a strain in French thinking about NATO which held that the United States was an alien presence in Europe, at best only a temporary one. America would leave when its interests changed. The Soviets as early as the 1950s worked to convince Europe that the continent could enjoy peace and security if only the American troops departed, as the Rapacki proposals of 1958 had postulated. An American military withdrawal from Europe is not beyond the realm of possibility. The disillusionment with European behaviour in Bosnia, a preoccupation with domestic problems and a rise of aggressive unilateralism, if not isolationism, under resurgent Republicans in 1995 could lead to this. If the US were to withdraw, NATO in all probability would cease to exist.

There would be no need for NATO without the United States (or Canada, which would follow the American lead). Any potential security threats to Western Europe should be manageable by the European security organizations, such as the Western European Union (WEU) or Organization for Security and Co-Operation in Europe (OSCE). The onset of the 1990s had witnessed a quickening of the pace of European unification, and with it a diminution of the American connection. With the Maastricht agreements of 1992 the Europeans appeared ready to go beyond the economic framework of the Treaty of Rome and to move into a political unity symbolized by the change of name from European Community to European Union.

Although the expectations of Maastricht were extravagant, the aspirations of a United States of Europe have not disappeared. Divisions between those members who want immediate expansion and those who want to deepen existing ties have slowed the movement. Nevertheless, the enlistment of new members such as Sweden and Austria as well as the anxiety to join on the part of a waiting list that includes Turkey and Poland attests to the EU's vibrancy in 1995. If the European movement ultimately embraces a military component, it could be the final act in NATO's history. Not only was there no superpower to frighten Europeans in the mid-1990s, but in the event of a potential threat Western Europe had the power and equipment to cope with it. The US and NATO would be irrelevant to the security of Europe.

Not surprisingly, France has been the leader in furthering both the removal of the United States and the empowering of Europe as it presses its campaign for an 'independent' Europe. One French commentator saw the Brussels meeting of the North Atlantic Council in January 1994 which featured the American sponsored Partnership for Peace, as 'la dernière fois, sans doute – that the United States would impose its will on the Council.'[6] In place of the American superpower, indeed, in place of NATO itself, there would be a variety of alternatives available for the defence of the West. They ranged from the Franco-German Eurocorps to the incorporation of the WEU as the military arm of the EU.

THE BOSNIAN CONFLICT

The Bosnian war seemed to possess all of the foregoing elements which should have attended the imminent demise of the Atlantic Alliance: the transformation of the Soviet Union into a quasi-ally of the West, the decline of American military power in Europe, and the assertiveness of the European partners. Serbian aggression was a challenge that the Europeans could meet alone. But from its inception the major European Allies, Britain and France, regarded the Bosnian conflict as a civil war in which neither side was blameless. While conceding the aggressive designs of Serbian leaders, the Allies saw their primary role as helping the United Nations to maintain a neutral presence, and supporting innocent civilians – but not the warring parties – of either side. Indeed, if there was a bias it was not against the Serbian aggressor but against a Muslim state in the Balkans. Opposing this position, the United States made an effort to aid the Bosnian government by asking for an end of the arms embargo which had only served the well-armed Serbs and for the use of NATO air power to protect Bosnian enclaves. The American refusal to accept Serbian territorial conquests was undergirded by its moral revulsion against Serbian behaviour, particularly its ethnic cleansing policies that forced thousands of Muslims from their homes in the course of the war.

Europeans and Americans had not been so divided since the Suez débâcle of 1956. While Americans pointed to Europe's unwillingness to take charge of a matter in its own backyard, Europeans refused to accept lectures from a country which would not provide troops for the UN mission. Reluctantly, the Allies accepted in principle the use of NATO air power to enforce UN safe zones, but then did as little as possible to make the threat credible to the Serbs. The principle of consensus in NATO appeared to be failing as America's authority dwindled and as Europe failed to take up the leadership that the United States seemed to have been abdicating. Three years after the Bosnian war had begun the only bond holding together the Alliance over the Bosnia issue was the common ground of the 'contact group', and with it the concept of a federal Bosnia. Under this arrangement the Muslims would receive 51% of the territory, which required considerable concessions by Serbs who held 70% of Bosnia-Herzegovina. How firm would this 'contact group' be, consisting of Russia along with NATO members United States, Britain, France and Germany?

Superficially, the problem lies with the role of the United Nations, to which the Alliance seemed to defer. The reason for this may be traced to the Gulf war when the UN, with the moribund Soviet Union reluctantly agreeing, gave its sanction to the war against Saddam Hussein. Among other consequences of the end of the Cold War was the potential for a united Security Council to exercise a military function which had eluded it for two generations. While peacekeeping missions had been conducted in the Middle East and Cyprus during the Cold War, it appeared in 1991 that an expanded mission was possible and that NATO could be an instrument in achieving the UN's objectives. Correspondingly, the UN could serve NATO by legitimizing out-of-area operations which otherwise might be open to criticism. Although the Gulf war was not a NATO action, there were enough NATO nations engaged – the United States, Britain and France in particular – to offer that impression to the world at large.

What worked in Iraq was a dismal failure in the Balkans, however. The Allies' inability to act together undermined NATO's new mission as crisis manager which had been a vital part of the 'Strategic Concept' developed at the North Atlantic Council meeting in Rome in November 1991. By invoking Article 4 of the North Atlantic Treaty,[7] they did have a reason to be involved in this particular out-of-area region, which was neighbour to more than one member. What better example of the Rome message than in Bosnia where the threat could arise not from 'calculated aggression against the territory of the Allies but rather from the adverse consequences of instabilities.'[8] Moreover, the Allies had ample warning of trouble in Yugoslavia ever since the death of Tito in 1980. Slobodan Milosevic, the former communist apparatchik turned nationalist, foreshadowed his intentions to convert multiethnic Yugoslavia into a greater Serbia by his repressive policies towards the formerly autonomous region of Kosovo, which was populated mostly by ethnic

Albanians. The United States did, however, take the preventative step of
stationing an army battalion in Macedonia to prevent a potential intra-
NATO conflict between Greece and Turkey.

Notwithstanding, the extent of European involvement was to offer
peacekeepers under a United Nations umbrella, and to provide safe-
havens to shelter civilians caught between the Bosnian Serb aggressors
and the Muslim-controlled Bosnian government forces. NATO was
brought into the picture, only to make a travesty of its potential role as
a military arm of the United Nations. Its plans for enforcing a 'no-fly
zone' were never implemented. The confused lines of communication
between the UN and NATO inhibited decisive action and encouraged
Serb resistance. The British and French were unwilling to jeopardize
their peacekeeping forces in Bosnia and were ambivalent about supporting the territorial integrity of Bosnia.

As these events unfolded, the position of the United States was in
sharp contrast to that of its European Allies. Aroused by televised scenes
of Serb brutality the Clinton Administration initially demanded a NATO
response. Here was an opportunity for Europe to exercise a leadership
role. The fruits of unification could have been displayed through the
EU's activation of one or more of the European security organizations
to manage the problem without major American involvement. Such a
solution would have fitted the Clinton Administration's agenda in 1993
when domestic issues were its first priority. This explains Secretary of
State Christopher's missions to Europe in 1993 to urge the Europeans to
act, if not by sending forces into Bosnia alongside the Bosnian government, at least by lifting the embargo on arms which was only serving the
Serbian side. These missions failed, and in their failure underscored the
loss of status that the United States enjoyed in the Alliance during the
Cold War. The US position was further undermined by its persistent
unwillingness to station its own troops as part of the UN's peacekeeping
force. The memories of loss of life in the Somalian operation in October
1993 seemed to inhibit an American initiative in Bosnia. Europe's
rejection of American advice caused the US Congress to sound a
unilateralist if not isolationist note. The American action in removing its
ships from a naval embargo in the autumn of 1994 was an important
answer to Europe's obdurate refusal to heed American advice.

Actually, NATO had used air power against Serb positions in Bosnia
and with apparent effect in February 1994 when it was first exercised
after international outrage over deaths in a crowded market-place. This
intentionally consisted of only a warning strike, and it succeeded in
deterring Serb attacks temporarily. When the Serb leadership recognized

the extent of the disarray between the UN and NATO and between the United States and the European Allies, subsequent strikes lost even symbolic value. The Bosnian Serbs rejected the 'contact' group's division of the nation with impunity. Not even the putative influence of Milosevic or his Russian ally made a difference.

Granting that Yugoslavia is not Czechoslovakia, the scene in Europe in 1995 resembles the 1890s more than the 1930s, when Western Europeans moved towards the creation of the Triple Entente. The European parties are the same, particularly as Russia finds common ground with Britain and France. The object of their attention, however, is different; it is the United States, not Germany. But despite the differences over the Balkans, the war is regional, not continental or global. There are centripetal forces countering the American impulse to withdraw and Europe's annoyance over American behaviour. There is also room for compromise over the Bosnian tragedy without wholly abandoning the victims of that conflict. The United States refrained from lifting the arms embargo unilaterally, and the Europeans moved toward enforcing access to protected zones in Bosnia. The Clinton Administration's offer to supply up to 25,000 troops to help extricate, if necessary, UN peacekeepers from Bosnia reflected an effort towards accommodation in December 1994 that was not present the month before. And Europe's intention to provide more effective lines of communication and supply to their forces in Bosnia suggests that the 'two-key' rule on use of NATO air power could be changed. NATO remains in 1995 a symbol of stability which none of the Allies wished to risk abandoning.

However, the fact remains that there has been no 'NATO method' to deal with Bosnia, as the Allies pursued their national interests in dealing with that Balkan conflict. In doing so they have inflicted more damage upon the Alliance than any specific Soviet measure in the years of the Cold War. The mid-1995 crisis over the Bosnian Serb aggression against the Britain and French UN peacekeepers risked the dissolution of the Alliance. American pressure for air strikes against the Bosnian Serbs had jeopardized British and French forces whose governments resented an American leadership which demanded action but withheld troops. The United States in turn has never concealed its annoyance over European unwillingness to identify the Serbs as aggressors, and to act accordingly, The outcome could be the end of the Alliance with the United States washing its hand of a 'European' problem, and Europe convinced that American isolationist sentiment had proven the unreliability of the transatlantic partner.

Yet, in the grand scheme of things, notwithstanding the intra-NATO conflict over Bosnia the post-Cold War objective of maintaining the stability of Europe has not changed. No matter how morally repugnant the Allied behaviour – of both Americans and Europeans – has been over war-torn Yugoslavia, that war has not moved out of the Balkans, or spread to Albania or Macedonia (or to Greece or Turkey). NATO solidarity has been in silent agreement on these issues at meetings of the North Atlantic Council. If this has been international, it has been a wise judgement.

Less sensible has been the language of communiqués, both from NATO headquarters and from the White House. As inter-allied tensions flared in the summer of 1994, and as the Bosnian Serbs flaunted their defiance of NATO and the UN more flagrantly, the White House trumpeted NATO's success in ending the Serb shelling of Sarajevo and restoring calm to the capital. A White House press statement read: 'We have led the way in NATO's decisions to enforce the no-fly zone, to protect UN troops if they are attacked, to enforce the economic sanctions against Serbs on the Adriatic and, most recently, to end the Serbs assault on Gorazde.'[9] What is striking about this string of achievements is the general inaccuracy of the claims. Sarajevo continued to be shelled periodically throughout 1994, the no-fly zone had been violated repeatedly by Serb aircraft, and the United States pointedly withdrew its few ships enforcing the blockade in the Adriatic. True, it mentioned the Contact Group and its comprehensive settlement, but this was hardly an American achievement. The settlement represented a scaling down of the Bosnian government's ambitions and a softening of the requirements that the United States had earlier laid down. While some credit may legitimately be taken for the peacekeeping troops in Macedonia the most likely reason why the conflict has not spilled over there is Milosevic's absorption with the Bosnia conflict.

The White House's overstated claims have been matched by NATO communiqués. Of some 30 paragraphs in a lengthy communiqué issued after the ministerial meeting of the North Atlantic Council at Istanbul in June 1994, only three dealt with Bosnia. The Council expressed its concern that the conflict should be settled 'at the negotiating table and not on the support efforts towards an early and durable political settlement.' Words such as 'negotiated compromise' and a 'viable, realistic and reasonable territory' for the 'Bosnia-Croat Federation' may be found as well as the urging of parties to accept a settlement that preserves Bosnia and Herzegovina as a single Union within its inter-nationally recognized borders. These were vague phrases with little meaning. Nowhere was there condemnation of either side for violating the UN/NATO safe zones. Nor was there any identification of the violation of UN/NATO safe zones as a source of aggression. The only mention of Bosnian Serbs appeared in a hope for a settlement 'providing for constitutional arrangements that establish the relationship between Bosnian-Croat and Bosnian-Serb entities.'[10]

What both the United States and NATO did in their public statements was to paper over the differences in the Alliance and to pass off with meaningless phrases the cancer in the Balkans which should have been central to their meetings in 1994. The bulk of NATO's attention dwelled on the commitment to a strong transatlantic partnership through the development of a European Security and Defence Identity. This entity may be as irrelevant to NATO's survival as the OSCE which 'remains central to European security.' How the OSCE can ensure security if NATO itself fails is in no way clear. Too much attention is paid to the Combined Joint Task Force, as if by simply mouthing this term, NATO can put aside the more specific issues that need redress.

Where there has been more substance in NATO deliberations there arose the question of relevance. Among the achievements of the Brussels summit in January 1994 was the establishment of the aforementioned Combined Joint Task Force (CJTF). The very linking of such loaded terms as 'combined' and 'joint' evoked expectations that a panacea had been found. 'Combined' meant that two or more military services would be involved, and 'joint' meant that two or more nations would contribute to the task force. Even the term 'task force' reinforced expectations; it implied a limited operation in the post-Cold War world where NATO's power could be concentrated on contingencies of all kinds, inside or outside NATO borders. The CJTF could be the vehicle for allowing Europe to handle its own problems without America being part of any particular combination.[11]

The trouble with the CJTF is how to put it into effect without conflicting with older NATO institutions. In January 1994 the North Atlantic Council bestowed its blessings on the CJTF, noting that the military capabilities of the WEU and NATO would be 'separable but not separate,'[12] thereby encouraging a flexibility that could be of vital importance in the new function of crisis-management. But what does 'separable' but not 'separate' mean? Some elements of a potential task force, such as the Eurocorps, have shown signs of being competitive with NATO. If the test is in practice, there has been no sign of its presence in the most obvious proving ground – Bosnia. The problem with the CJTF is not with its mechanics; it offers a genuine means of fulfilling the aspirations of the Rome agreements in 1991. Rather, it lies in the lack of consensus on the part of the political leaders of the Alliance. Flaws in the management of the Alliance, not in the composition of CJTF accounted for the failures in the Balkans.

NATO ENLARGEMENT

While it may be too late to manage the Bosnian crisis satisfactorily it is not too late for NATO to act in unison in its relations with Eastern Europe and the Russian Federation. In fact, this may be more significant in the long run than the consequences of the irresolution of the Bosnian conflict. Yugoslavia was, and remains, an out-of-area location. The nations of Central and Eastern Europe may become members of the Alliance, with far-reaching impact on its organization as well as its mission. The key questions revolve around the admission of new NATO members on the eastern flank of NATO, particularly the Czech Republic, Poland and Hungary. Ever since they had won their freedom from the Warsaw Pact they had been campaigning for membership in the Alliance. Their primary champion had been Germany, pressing for early admission much as it had pressed for recognition of Croatia, Slovenia and Bosnia to further its traditional influence in Central Europe. Opposing the German initiative were Britain and France. Those Allies had other concerns as well, ranging from suspicion of German ambitions in Eastern Europe to France's concern that an eastward expansion of NATO could divert attention from the threat of Muslim fundamentalism on the southern flank of NATO. In this instance the Western powers had support from the Clinton Administration, which had its own worries about the admission of former Warsaw Pact states upon the new and fragile Russian-American friendship. Conceivably, precipitate action could arouse Russian fears of NATO intentions, jeopardize President Boris Yeltsin's efforts to westernize and democratize Russian institutions, and push the nation down the road towards extreme nationalism.

As 1994 opened the Clinton Administration felt that it had just the right mix of encouragement for the Eastern Europeans and comfort for the Russians. American enthusiasm for the 'Partnership for Peace,' unveiled at the summit meeting of the North Atlantic Council in Brussels in January 1994, prevailed over the scepticism of the European Allies. The new 'partners' would be 'allies,' but not in the beginning. While they would not be offered membership immediately they would be able to participate in a host of confidence-building activities, such as military exercises, would have access to certain NATO technical data, and would exchange information on defence planning. Full membership is possible only after some major qualifications are met, among which are an irreversible commitment to democracy, civilian control of the military and the development of the nation's military capability to a level of interoperability with those of NATO members. [13]

Such stiff requirements, if enforced, could make the partnership the kind of sham that the Multilateral Force has been in the 1960s. The MLF had promised a nuclear capability to Europeans while keeping the nuclear warhead firmly in American hands. Under the PfP the qualifications for membership might make it impossible for any Central or Eastern European country to fulfil. While the records of NATO's or the US Administration's deliberations are not available, it is likely that the illusion of membership without actually being able to realize it was precisely what the designers of the Partnership had in mind. The Czechs and Poles would have the assurances they wanted, while the Russians would not have NATO immediately at their doorstep. Indeed, the Partnership was held out to Russia itself.

The programme went forward in 1994, but not quite as its planners had envisaged. The Poles among others were not satisfied; they wanted immediate admission to NATO. American friends of the former Warsaw Pact nations were also unhappy. Influential voices, both Democratic and Republican, insisted on the vital necessity of expanding membership without worrying about its impact on Russia. The new Republican majority in the Congress in 1995 made an issue of President Clinton's coddling of the Russians, of being excessively concerned with Russian sensibilities at the expense of its beleaguered neighbours. Within a week of each other Zbigniew Brzezinski and Henry Kissinger, writing Co-Ed columns for the *New York Times* and the *Washington Post*, respectively, in December 1994, urged the Administration to bring the Czech Republic, Poland and Hungary into the Alliance as quickly as possible. [14]

Even as the Central European powers grudgingly went along with the Partnership as at least a first step towards membership, Russia was suspicious of its implications. Yeltsin warily agreed to join provided that Russia was accorded a special status. But this was effectively revoked in December 1994 at the Budapest meeting of the CSCE when Yeltsin denounced the Partnership as the onset of a 'cold peace.' It is obvious that the hopes of the Brussels summit have not been realized. NATO's offer of expansion, carefully qualified as it was, seemed to do precisely what the Administration had hoped to avoid; namely, to tip the balance of power in Russia away from democrats and economic reformers and towards nationalists and supporters of a command economy.

There may be a way out of this dilemma which could quell the anxieties of the East Europeans without stoking the paranoia of the Russians and without inviting the many new problems which the expansion of NATO would bring. Current plans to grant full membership to Czechs or Poles or other East Europeans could be abandoned. The chances that they would fulfil the Partnership requirements are minimal at any event. Given the fragility of their economies, how realistic is it to expect that they could afford to modernize their military establishment to meet NATO standards in the near future? And how sensible is it to ask them achieve this goal? Diverting funds into a military build-up could threaten the modernization of their economies which undergird the strength of their new democracies. One of their major objectives is to make themselves attractive to the European Union which all the countries of the former Warsaw bloc aspire to join.

This course need not mean the scuttling of the Partnership, even if NATO could convince East European States that Russia poses no immediate danger to their future, or that Russian military action against Chechnya would not be translated into a revival of the Soviet empire. Instead, the Partnership could be redesigned to permit early membership under Article 5 of the North Atlantic Treaty. Such an arrangement would offer assurance to new members that an armed attack against any one or more of them 'shall be considered an attack against them all' to be responded to by individual and collective action of other members, 'including the use of armed force' to protect their territorial integrity. There would be no need for joint exercises or the involvement of SHAPE or the creation of a military machine to win this security.

Article 5 represented the 'pledge' which comforted Western Europeans in 1949 when only a guarantee of American membership could ensure security against a Soviet invasion. The Korean War a year later changed NATO's perception of the threat, and opened the way for a military build-up which lasted to the end of the Cold War and remains in place in attenuated form today. But it is unnecessary for armies to be stationed on Russia's borders in 1995 when the Russian military is in disarray. Should this situation change in the future Article 5 should deter aggression as long as NATO's military posture is prepared to meet such a challenge. And if NATO is to survive, with or without new members, the new techniques of crisis management should be able to cope with this possibility. Assistant Secretary of State Richard Holbrooke identified a variation of this model in his statement before the House International Relations Committee hearing on US Policy in Europe. Full membership in NATO, he noted, would mean guarantees under Article 5: 'That doesn't necessarily means American troops on their soil. There are countries in NATO today which have no American troops on their soil but have the guarantee. Is it a nuclear guarantee? Of course, it's a full guarantee. Do I ever see a reason for that to be revoked? No, I don't.'[15]

This arrangement would not set a precedent. The history of the Atlantic Alliance will always make France's departure from the organization in 1966 a traumatic milestone. France left SHAPE but did not renounce the treaty. Article 5 continued to cover France was well as its neighbours in the Alliance even though the French military was no longer involved with the defence of Europe. But the French precedent has its limitations; France was a major military power with its own nuclear component when de Gaulle acted. A more useful precedent would be the examples of Iceland, a charter member of the Alliance, and Spain, a member since 1982. Iceland had no army in 1949, and has none today. Yet it is fully protected by the terms of its membership. Similarly, Spain's army is not integrated into the SHAPE command, and has abstained from troop commitments to the organization. There is no reason why Poland or Hungary or the Czech Republic, or other neighbours of Russia might not enter NATO under the same terms.

What impact, then, would the expansion of NATO to the Russian border under these conditions have upon that former superpower? There would be no reason for Russian leaders to complain, as Foreign Minister Andrei V. Kozyrev did in December 1994, that membership of East European neighbours would place a potentially hostile military on Russia's doorstep. NATO would be no farther east then it had been in the past. And the rapid pace of downsizing NATO's military should give little excuse for nationalist posturing.

Conceivably, this outcome could be the occasion for Russia to return to its earlier interest in potential membership in the Alliance. There would be no specific barrier. But it is unlikely that Russian leaders, Yeltsin or his successors, would accede to this arrangement. Yeltsin's agreement was an aberration, as was made obvious in his insistence on a special status befitting a nuclear power. It is difficult to envision Russia accepting parity with Poland or Hungary. Instead, having given evidence of good faith in its treatment of the East European powers NATO could fashion a new relationship with the Russians that would recognize Russia's special position without arousing alarm once again among its neighbours. The relationship could take a number of forms. One of them might be to exploit the OSCE to serve as a vehicle for a comprehensive treaty between NATO and the Russian Federation. The OSCE embraces both the United States and Russia, and has often been cited by Russian leaders as the instrument they would prefer as a guarantor of European security. Such a mechanism would be preferable to a United States-Russian arrangement that would revive Europe's old concerns over superpower negotiations in the Nixon-Brezhnev mode. If it were adopted, clear understandings would be necessary to clarify the future of the Baltic states and the Caucasian republics. The former could be included under the NATO blanket while the latter would remain inside the Russian Federation. But if Latvia or Estonia should become a member of NATO, the position of the Russian minority would have to be monitored strictly. And there must be no more Chechnya incidents. The Chechens would enjoy autonomy within the federation. The alternative could be the secession of Islamic states along Russia's southern tier which could lead to much instability in Eastern Europe.

The benefits of a stabilized Europe would be substantial. Russian pride would be respected through its role in the 'near abroad.' The smaller neighbours would relax through NATO membership. Rather than looming as a menace the Russian presence in the Balkans could soothe tensions. Most importantly, steps towards democracy and a market economy could proceed without being burdened by dangers of a military coup, a communist revival, or a new wave of imperial expansionism. While there would be many unsettling issues in any grand resolution of Europe's security they need not be insoluble. A small volatile nation such as Moldova, with its breakaway Russian minority could be incorporated into Partnership by establishing ties with both NATO and the Russian Federation. More difficult would be the place of such a large nation as the Ukraine in this new Europe. Conceivably, a special relationship between the two Slavic powers might be an answer. But small signs of cooperation between Russia and the Ukraine were evident in 1994 over Crimea and over nuclear issues. Whatever the Ukrainians may wish, it is difficult to envision them inside the Atlantic Alliance without tipping the delicate balance that a NATO-Russia agreement would create.

If any of these optimistic scenarios should come to pass, one then could make a case for NATO itself to be discarded. Without a revanchist Russia, without fearful Poles and Baltics, and without turmoil in the Balkans and the Caucasus, the European Union with the aid of one or more of the European units currently associated with NATO should be able to maintain the stability of the continent. It is the European Union, after all, which presumably will be the engine of Europe's prosperity. For the former Warsaw Pact nations membership in NATO would be the instrument of their own *Wirtschaftswunder* in the 1990s, much as NATO was for Western Europeans in the 1990s. NATO could disband, and the United States could work out a new cooperative but not necessarily entangling relationship with Europe.

Regrettably, it is unlikely that such happy outcomes will be realized in the near future. There are too many variables that cannot be controlled by even the most solid of arrangements. Given the fluid political and economic condition of Russian society, Russian democracy could be the victim at any time of a military coup or an anti-Western government, coming into power by ballot or by force. The centrifugal currents operating in the old Soviet empire have not run dry, and the potential for more conflicts between Moscow and the former Soviet republics remains alive in 1995. NATO's presence, even in an attenuated military form, is an insurance against a new anti-Western campaign on the part of inflamed Russian nationalists.

CONCLUSIONS

Even if Russia becomes comfortable with NATO next door and accepts a supportive treaty with the Western Allies, security in Europe does not automatically follow. The rising militancy of Islam not only might topple secular Arab regimes but could affect the northern as well as the southern littoral of the Mediterranean. France and Italy may be affected. And it is not beyond the realm of possibility that Greece and Turkey, both members of NATO, might fall out in an even more dangerous fashion than they did over Cyprus in 1974.

But there is another centripetal force undergirding NATO in the mid-1990s and that is the role of a powerful united Germany. While German democracy is as assured as that of any of its neighbours, its very size creates problems. Its dominant role in the European Union is one fact for slowing the unification of Europe. In this context the American component of NATO is a counterbalance to the authority of Germany in the Alliance. The Allies rarely publicize this issue, but the Allies in NATO remember the 'pledge' of 1949, and show no signs of wishing to remove this link. The downsizing of American and European forces in the Alliance is not accompanied by demands for the expulsion of American troops. Nor is there any sign that any member intends to exercize its right to remove itself from the treaty under Article 13.

If the American connection remains important for Europe today, does it follow that the European entanglement is still in America's national interest? While there are voices in the United States which from time to time speak out about the Pacific region replacing the Atlantic, or about the high cost of the Atlantic burden, the consensus of both political parties is that a return to isolationism, even if possible, would be self-destructive. The American stake in European stability is as vital today as it was during the Cold War. The mechanisms within the Alliance may change. It is not unreasonable to assume greater European responsibility in the future, possible symbolized by a European SACEUR, as some American commentators have observed over the past generation. But such changes need not involve an abandonment of Europe. Breaking entangling ties with Europe now would threaten what historian John Lewis Gaddis has called 'the long peace.'[16] There is no longer the balance of terror which had discouraged conflict during the Cold War. What NATO balances today is the threat of disorder that has accompanied the intensification of ethnic and religious conflict in the 1990s.

The American component of NATO gives it credibility to cope with uncertainties of the future. Despite failures regularly thrust onto the front pages of newspapers, there is no evidence that the Alliance will be relegated to the back pages and then be reduced to the small print of an obituary column in the manner of the Southeast Asian Treaty Organization (SEATO) and the Central Treaty Organization (CENTO). NATO is the only institution with the capacity to keep order, if not quite a new world order, as the century comes to an end. But capacity may be an insufficient guarantor of European security if the Allies lack the will to act in concert. A happier outcome of the Bosnian crisis might be NATO's recognition that this sort of out-of-area issue deserves the unified attention of all the Allies. There is an opportunity to demonstrate a European unit that the European Union has been seeking over the years. And, without dissolving the Alliance the United States would recognise a diminished but not insignificant role for the future, not only in southeastern Europe but also across the Mediterranean where the troubles of the Maghreb could spill over onto its northern shores. America's infrastructure in Europe as well as the important psychological impact of a continued partnership would retain its importance, particularly in east-west relations, but the United States would have to identify a new role for its European partners that hitherto neither Americans nor Europeans have been willing to conceive since the end of the Cold War.

NOTES

1. David Calleo, *The Atlantic Fantasy: The US, NATO, and Europe*, Johns Hopkins University Press, Baltimore, MD, 1970, pp.27-28.
2. Geir Lundestad, 'Empire by Invitation? The United States and Western Europe, 1945-1952,' *The Society for Historians of American Foreign Relations Newsletter*, Vol.15, September 1984, pp.1-211.
3. See 'Our Atlantic Alliance: The Political and Economic Strands,' speech delivered at the US Military Academy, West Point, New York, 5 December 1962. Reprinted in *Vital Speeches of The Day*, 1 January 1963, pp.162-166.
4. Francis Fukuyama, 'The End of History,' *National Interest*, Summer 1989, p.4.
5. CRS Report for Congress, 28 September 1992, Edward F. Bruner, 'US Forces in Europe: Military Implications of Alternative Levels,' pp.1-2.
6. See editorial, "L'Otan obsolète, freine la politique européene de défense", *Le débat stratégique*, No.12, January 1994, p.1.
7. Article 4 authorizes members to 'consult together whenever, in the opinion of any of them, the territorial integrity, political independence, or security of any of the parties is threatened.'
8. 'The Alliance's New Strategic Concept,' agreed by Heads of State and Government participating in the Meeting of the North Atlantic Council in Rome on 7-8 November 1991, *NATO Review*, Vol.39, December 1991, p.26.
9. The White House, 'A National Security Strategy of Engagement and Enlargement,' July 1994, p.21.
10. Ministerial Meeting of the North Atlantic Council, Final Communiqué, Istanbul, *NATO Review*, Vol.42, June 1994, pp.25-28.
11. Stanley R. Sloan, CRS Report for Congress, 'Combined Joint Task Forces (CJTF) and New Missions for NATO,' 17 March 1994.
12. Declaration of the Heads of State and Government participating in the meeting of the North Atlantic Council held at NATO Headquarters, Brussels, on 10-11 January 1994, *NATO Review*, Vol.42, February 1994, p.31.
13. Partnership for Peace: Invitation Issued by the Heads of State and Government participating in the meeting of the North Atlantic council held at NATO Headquarters, Brussels, from 10-11 January 1994, *ibid.*, pp.28-30.
14. Zbigniew Brzezinski, 'NATO – Expand or Die?,' *New York Times*, 28 November 1994; Henry Kissinger, 'Expand NATO Now,' *Washington Post*, 19 December 1994.
15. Testimony of Assistant Secretary of State Richard Holbrooke to the House International Relations Committee hearing on US Policy in Europe of 9 March 1995.
16. John Lewis Gaddis, *The Long Peace: Inquiries into the History of the Cold War*, Oxford University Press, New York, 1987.

3 American Strategies Towards the Enlargement of European Security Institutions: Partnership or Cold Peace?

Sean Kay

In 1994 the United States renewed its transatlantic leadership through a strategy that affirms the American commitment to European security institutions and seeks to enlarge a zone of democratic, free-market, militarily stable states to the East. The cornerstone of this policy has been the North Atlantic Treaty Organization (NATO) which has adopted a framework for cooperation with former Warsaw Pact states through the Partnership for Peace (PfP) established in January 1994. As the PfP has accelerated the discussion of enlargement, the US has increasingly supported the role of the Organization for Security and Cooperation in Europe (OSCE) to ease intense Russian opposition to NATO expansion. This dual-track policy is contributing to a broad concept of European security of which NATO expansion is an important, but not the sole, element in a comprehensive security architecture.

Hasty NATO expansion is unwise and potentially very dangerous.[1] Western concerns about NATO expansion include whether NATO could maintain its cohesiveness, the impact on NATO military strategy, whether the US and other NATO countries are willing to take on the military and financial burdens of the diplomatic and political objectives that lay behind NATO expansion, and whether the Alliance can afford other potential Greece-Turkey relationships at a time when the Allies are already divided over how to deal with existing crises. The primary concerns have been not to offend Russia, nor to do anything that might weaken the reform process there. The US has no intention of rushing enlargement but believes that NATO can have an extended dialogue over expansion while keeping Russia happy in the process.

The Clinton Administration is under considerable pressure from many diverse quarters, internal and external, to move faster on enlargement – perhaps to commit to a specified and targeted expansion in 1996 (between the Russian and American presidential elections) or at least by the year 2000. Those in favour of rapid NATO expansion include an awkward alliance of liberal-internationalists wanting to broaden NATO's successful role as an institution for internal stability and traditional realists who would like to encircle Russia and keep it from re-emerging as a major force in European security. Such an approach could create more instability than stability if the effect is to weaken Alliance cohesion or reformers in Moscow. Moreover, the likely candidates for NATO expansion are the Czech Republic, Poland, and Hungary (the three more prosperous Visegrad countries). These states are already stable and are not threatened. What they really need is European Union (EU) membership which appears far off. It is possible that the greatest threat to stability in the Visegrad states may ultimately be French farmers. Finally, NATO expansion could spark a very divisive ratification debate in the US Senate that could ignite a more fundamental discussion over whether the US needs to maintain NATO at all.

NATO expansion should be handled very carefully and should only come in the event of a crisis. It is necessary to use the PfP to accelerate the transformation of civil-military structures in Central and Eastern European states should NATO need to expand quickly. As this process accelerates, the OSCE can be strengthened in ways that should meet some of Russia's concerns about NATO expansion while not diluting the effectiveness of the Alliance as a military and political organization. The best way to accomplish this is to institutionalize the existing Bosnia Contact Group, or something very similar, into the OSCE as a permanent but non-binding 'OSCE Contact Group for European Security.'

THE PARTNERSHIP FOR PEACE AND RUSSIA

Fears of Russian imperialism, regional instability, and an unwillingness or political inability of the European Union to expand quickly into Central and Eastern Europe make the passionate appeals for NATO membership – especially those from the Czech Republic, Poland, and Hungary – impossible to ignore. Sympathetic to these concerns, the Clinton Administration formulated the PfP in late 1993 to provide a perspective for NATO membership and momentum towards reform for all states in the OSCE region – particularly among the former Warsaw Pact members and newly independent states. The PfP provides for a broad range of direct cooperation without granting the collective defence guarantee of NATO – Article 5 of the NATO treaty. PfP establishes 16 plus 1 consultations, permanent offices at NATO installations, and joint training and exercises for all non-NATO European countries which choose to participate. This policy was carefully designed to accelerate a process of cooperation but to delay NATO expansion because of a lack of unanimity within NATO and to accommodate Russian opposition. Should the political and military situation in Russia change or other unforeseen events threaten the stability of Central and Eastern Europe, NATO could be expanded quickly since the states will have had a period of working within the PfP framework.[2]

Assessing Russia's views vis-à-vis US and NATO interests is not the same as conferring a veto over NATO policy. NATO is a defensive Alliance and must be able to act when its interests are challenged. However, on 10 June 1994 at NATO's other forum for dialogue with former Warsaw Pact countries, the North Atlantic Cooperation Council (NACC) meeting in Istanbul Turkey, NATO countries deferred to Russian sensitivities about Alliance expansion to the point of conferring an informal veto for Russia within the NACC, which seriously undermined this forum. For five hours Russian representatives haggled over the final communiqué and forced the NACC to omit a reference to NATO expansion.[3] Shortly following the Istanbul meeting, Russian Foreign Minister Andrei Kozyrev travelled to Brussels, signed the PfP framework document, and agreed to a joint NATO/Russia declaration establishing a special relationship for Russia in its relations with the Alliance. After signing, Kozyrev declared that 'we do not preclude the possibility that we or other countries should join NATO but there should be no haste.'[4]

Concern remained in NATO circles that Russia would use the PfP to prevent NATO expansion and to continue its efforts to dilute NATO's role in European security. At this time Russia was also aggressively advancing proposals to strengthen the then CSCE that would both weaken NATO and enhance the role of Russia within its near abroad. In July 1994 Russia submitted a formal proposal to the CSCE that all interlocking organizations in Europe – including NATO, the NACC, and the Commonwealth of Independent States – be subordinated to the CSCE. Russia suggested that the CSCE should create a formal 'Executive Committee' that would consist of 10-12 permanent and rotating members.

On 9 September 1994, differences arose between the US and Germany over whether or not Russia could be a member of NATO. This discord became public at a conference in Berlin at which German Defence Minister Volker Ruehe rejected Russian membership stating that it would 'blow NATO apart, it would be like the United Nations of Europe, it wouldn't work.'[5] Ruehe added that some former Warsaw Pact countries could join NATO before the year 2000. Speaking at the same meeting, US Secretary of Defence William Perry indicated that he would not rule out Russian membership in NATO but that it would not happen in the foreseeable future – neither would NATO expansion. Complicating these differing views, Vice-President Al Gore told another conference held in Germany the same day that NATO would discuss throughout the autumn of 1994 the modalities and time-scale of bringing in new NATO members.[6] However, on 2 October Secretary Perry cautioned that: 'European security is best based on a practical and cooperative relationship between NATO and Russia, not by closing Russia out,' and that the PfP should be managed carefully 'to avoid drawing new dividing lines in Europe.'[7]

NATO EXPANSION AND THE OSCE

In October and November 1994 the Clinton Administration formulated a dual-track strategy that would accelerate the dialogue over NATO expansion while attempting to accommodate Russia's concerns by strengthening the CSCE. The policy adapted American diplomacy to a growing frustration with the PfP. As a senior Administration official told the *New York Times* on 27 October: 'Much of the rhetoric that was used in the past was empty of substance. Partnership for Peace is like getting guest privileges at the club – you can play golf once in a while. Now we want to send the bylaws and ask, "do you want to pay the dues?"'[8]

The US proposed the creation of a NATO working group to define specific criteria for expansion. This included identifying costs, troop commitments, and regulations to be met – without establishing a timetable or candidates for expansion.[9] A State Department official involved in formulating this approach insisted: 'this policy is not designed to create an obstacle but to begin a process.'[10] However, the policy supported expansion while making it difficult in practice. In accelerating the discussion of expansion, NATO bought itself time.[11]

By stressing the CSCE, the US demonstrated to Russia that there are inclusive opportunities for security cooperation other than NATO.[12] As

a senior Administration official stated in a background briefing on 1
December, the US was:

> making clear that NATO will expand, but this is going to be part of
> a larger European security structure that involves many different
> institutions – the European Union and in particular the CSCE....The
> Russians have in the past set forth a very maximal agenda for CSCE
> whereby it would become kind of the preeminent European security
> organization, effectively dominating over all other organizations,
> including NATO. That, of course, is not acceptable to us. We
> consider, for the United States, NATO still to be the number one
> organization from our point of view, but we certainly want to
> increase the role of CSCE ... this is a strategy that emphasizes our
> desire to have an inclusive relationship between NATO and all the
> Partners for Peace, that when NATO expansion occurs, it's not going
> to be directed against Russia, but part of the broader policy of
> integration. CSCE fits into this larger policy as an institution where
> Russia is a member. [13]

However, despite its well-founded intentions, the CSCE track appeared
to have not considered sufficiently how Russia might respond.

The fundamental weakness of the new American policy was an
unwillingness or an inability to explain the 'why' of NATO expansion
and to express satisfactorily the legitimate reasons for taking a cautious
approach. Instigating a process designed both to accelerate dialogue and
to slow the process could only alienate both the Central and East
European partners and Russia. Moreover, by late November 1994, the US
had not fully explained the 'how' of strengthening the CSCE other than
to support the change of name to the 'Organization' for Security and
Cooperation in Europe. [14] The Clinton Administration was correct to
strengthen the OSCE without giving it too much authority. The OSCE
should be left to do what it does best – to set the standards that ensure
accountability of state behaviour in Europe, to provide a forum for
consultation on security issues, and to serve as a mechanism for
preventive diplomacy. By wanting the OSCE to maintain these primary
functions of the CSCE regime, the American approach had the appearance of being little more than saying nice things about the CSCE/OSCE
to make the Russians happy and hoping that it would work.

IMPLEMENTATION: FROM PARTNERSHIP TO COLD PEACE

The dual track NATO/OSCE approach was not well received by Russia. Though Foreign Minister Kozyrev had signed the PfP framework agreement in June 1994, Russia had yet to agree to an Individual Partnership Programme for specific cooperation. When Kozyrev travelled to Brussels in December to approve the more detailed cooperation agreement, he declined at the last minute declaring shock and surprise at NATO's discussion of expansion. This was in spite of the fact that the US had briefed Russia in late November as to its plans for the Alliance and the OSCE.

America's NATO Allies were also not immediately comfortable with this new policy. As one report indicates, the US sought to complete the review of NATO expansion criteria in the spring of 1995 but this was rejected by the European members of the Alliance as moving too fast.[15] Also on 1 December *Suddeutsche Zeitung* reported the leak of a confidential cable from German NATO Ambassador Hermann von Richthofen to his foreign ministry of 22 November. The cable asserted that the PfP would be ineffective in convincing the states it is aimed at of NATO's sincerity to expand 'thereby discrediting a piece of Alliance policy.'[16] The cable complained that: 'the US Administration is moving quickly to expand NATO without consultations on the ... consequences for the Alliance.'[17] Von Richthofen concluded that without a clear sense of mission and strategy, 'the Alliance is divided and in crisis.'[18]

Intra-alliance differences over NATO expansion were papered over on 1 December when NATO foreign ministers stated that:

> We expect and would welcome NATO enlargement that would reach to democratic states to our East, as part of an evolutionary process, taking into account political and security developments in the whole of Europe. Enlargement, when it comes would be part of a broad European security architecture based on true cooperation throughout the whole of Europe. It would threaten no one and would enhance stability and security for all of Europe.[19]

The NATO ministers qualified this by asserting that while no country could veto NATO expansion:

> [I]t is premature to discuss the time-frame for enlargement or which particular countries would be invited to join the Alliance. We further agreed that enlargement should strengthen the effectiveness of the

Alliance, contribute to the stability and security of the entire Euro-Atlantic area, and support our objective of maintaining an undivided Europe. It should be carried out in a way that preserves the Alliance's ability to perform its core functions of common defence as well as to undertake peacekeeping and other new missions and that upholds the principles and objectives of the Washington Treaty.[20]

The ministers approved the US plan for a NATO working group to review expansion and to provide an initial report to the next North Atlantic Council ministerial meeting in May 1995 and a final report by the end of the year. They also endorsed the continued strengthening of the CSCE.

On 5 December President Clinton attended the Budapest CSCE summit to advance the second track of US policy. In his formal presentation President Clinton reasserted the NATO position that no country is excluded from potential membership and no country outside will have a veto over expansion. Clinton added that:

We must not allow the Iron Curtain to be replaced by a veil of indifference. We must not consign new democracies to a grey zone ... We seek to increase the security of all, to erase the old lines without drawing arbitrary new ones, to bolster emerging democracies and to integrate the nations of Europe into a continent where democracy and free markets know no borders but where every nation's borders are secure.[21]

Russian President Boris Yeltsin responded that:

[A] system of blocks, that is to say something we have left behind, is now coming back – the NATO bloc on the one hand – and Russia on the other ... Without compromise on this issue between NATO and Russia, there would be no point in continuing a partnership ... Otherwise we will go our own ways, and why have partnership at all – after all, it presupposes mutual support of the sides for each other ... Americans do not wish to see Russia in NATO and that is the crux of the matter.[22]

Yeltsin added that if the West were to expand NATO it risked bringing a 'Cold Peace' to Europe after the Cold War.

Returning the same day to Washington, President Clinton was described by an Administration official travelling with the President on

Air Force One as expressing 'concern and a state of perplexity about what the Russians were up to.'[23] More rueful in his assessment was the Georgian leader and former Soviet Foreign Minister Eduard Shevard-nadze who lamented that: 'The Cold War is over. Beware of the peace.'[24]

A NEW APPROACH

By the end of 1994 the dual-track approach appeared to have failed. Russia had withdrawn its participation in the PfP and had begun a major war in Chechnya. The American position was clarified by US Assistant Secretary of State Richard Holbrooke writing in *Foreign Affairs* in March 1995. Holbrooke stressed that NATO had agreed at the 1994 Brussels summit to expand and now the Alliance was merely exploring the modalities of the process. He articulated seven key points about NATO's objectives:

1. The goal remains the defence of the Alliance's vital interests and the promotion of European stability. NATO expansion must strengthen security in the entire region, including nations that are not members. The goal is to promote security in Central Europe by integrating countries that qualify into the stabilizing framework of NATO.

2. The rationale and process for NATO's expansion, once decided, will be transparent, not secret. Both Warsaw and Moscow, for example, will have the same opportunity to hear exactly the same presentation from NATO later this year, and both should have access to all aspects of the Alliance's thinking in order to understand that NATO should no longer be considered an anti-Russian alliance.

3. There is no timetable or list of nations that will be invited to join NATO. The answers to the critical question of who and when will emerge after completion of this phase of the process.

4. Each nation will be considered individually, not as part of some grouping.

5. The decisions as to who joins NATO and when will be made exclusively by the Alliance. No outside nation will have a veto.

6. Although criteria for membership have not been determined, certain fundamental precepts reflected in the original Washington treaty remain as valid as they were in 1949: new members must be democratic, have market economies, be committed to responsible security policies, and be able to contribute to the Alliance.

7. Each new NATO member constitutes of the United States the most solemn of all commitments: a bilateral defence treaty that extends the US security umbrella to a new nation. This requires ratification by two-thirds of the US Senate.[25]

Holbrooke added that the US would make more vigorous use of the OSCE's consultative and conflict prevention mechanisms to establish the OSCE as an integral element in the new security architecture. Within this context he stressed that 'if the West is to create an enduring and stable security framework for Europe, it must solve the most enduring strategic problem of Europe and integrate the nations of the former Soviet Union, especially Russia, into a stable European security system.'[26]

What was new about Ambassador Holbrooke's article was a concluding statement addressing a proposal by former National Security Advisor Zbigniew Brzezinski that Moscow should be offered a formal treaty of cooperation between NATO and Russia.[27] Holbrooke noted that there would be numerous difficulties in doing so but that the US was not ruling it out. Such an arrangement would require negotiation over a broad range of issues including the pace of NATO expansion, the state of other Russian-NATO ties such as the PfP, the degree to which the OSCE has been turned into a more useful organization, and the implications of events such as the fighting in Chechnya. 'Notwithstanding this array of issues,' wrote Holbrooke, 'the US government as well as its major allies have supported development of this important *new track* [emphasis added] in the European security framework.'[28]

In February 1995 Russia approached the US through diplomatic channels to indicate that it might be willing to accept a slow and limited expansion of NATO under certain circumstances. On 11 March *The Washington Post* reported that Russia wanted a guarantee that the process of expansion would not be rushed, that there would be no nuclear weapons stationed on the territories of new members, that Russia could be a member of NATO eventually, and that the end result would be a formalized forum for East-West cooperation on security issues. According to the press account, Russia was also suggesting the creation of a non-aggression pact with NATO.[29] NATO officials characterized the

Russian position as a substantial change from the dialogue of late 1994 though it remained unclear if Russia was seriously altering its stance on NATO expansion. The US saw this as an opportunity to renew the discussion of NATO expansion within the context of a new Russian relationship. As Vice-President Al Gore said in Estonia on 14 March:

> It is important to understand that the process by which NATO expands is a process that must take place at the same time the relationship between NATO and Russia is deepened and clarified. Both processes must take place simultaneously and both processes must take place in full open, public view with no surprises and no sudden movements. This is the correct way to proceed.[30]

The same week, EU foreign ministers meeting in France agreed that NATO should 'consider an agreement, treaty or charter between the Atlantic Alliance and Russia in parallel with the enlargement of NATO to show Russia that we are not neglecting it,' said French Foreign Minister Alain Juppé (summarizing the EU position). It was necessary in order to 'find something to reassure Russia,' Juppé added.[31]

The US and its Allies were too eager to accept the new Russian flexibility on NATO expansion. On or around 15 March Boris Yeltsin sent a directive to Kozyrev castigating the foreign ministry for being too consenting on NATO expansion. Yeltsin ordered Kozyrev to take a hard line on the issue. Thus Kozyrev said in Paris on 20 March: 'Why rush things if we run the risk of creating new lines of division?'[32] US Secretary of State Warren Christopher pondered the statement and asserted that Kozyrev seemed to believe that 'there had been some change in the position of the United States or NATO, that we were going at a different pace than before... That is not correct.'[33] Nonetheless, following a meeting in Geneva on 23 March between Christopher and Kozyrev to arrange for President Clinton's forthcoming trip to Moscow, Kozyrev declared to the press that: 'The honeymoon has come to an end.'[34]

After a Moscow meeting with US Secretary of Defence Perry on 3 April Russian Defence Minister Pavel Grachev linked Russia's compliance with the Conventional Forces in Europe Treaty (CFE) to NATO expansion and insisted that should NATO expand: 'Countermeasures could be taken... [W]e might create necessary military groups in the most threatening directions and set up closer cooperation with other CIS countries.'[35] The next day, the speaker of the upper house of the Russian parliament told Perry that the parliament was unlikely to ratify

the START-2 Treaty if NATO were to expand.[36] Russia's first Deputy
Defence Minister Andrei Kokoshin was quoted by *Nevazismaya Gazeta*
as saying that the expansion of NATO would create instability in Europe
by removing the 'semi-demilitarized zone which has now emerged in
Central and Eastern Europe.' He added that 'it is necessary to abandon
the false impression that NATO expansion is inevitable and unavoid-
able.'[37]

Russia's concerns were intensified by a series of public statements
from Visegrad and NATO countries suggesting that the process of
expansion was accelerating. For example, on 3 April Czech President
Vaclav Havel said: 'There are a number of indications that we are
seeing a new momentum on the subject of future membership of the new
democracies in the North Atlantic Alliance... One year ago, NATO
membership did not seem likely.'[38] Poland also continued its public
pressure on the West. On 4 April 1995 President Lech Walesa told the
BBC that, as during the Second World War, Poland was being let down
by the West and that Russia was a challenger to European security. The
next day Polish Prime Minister Jozer Oleksy travelled to NATO
Headquarters in Brussels. Prior to his departure from Warsaw, Oleksy
told reporters that in the debate over NATO expansion 'Russia has no
significance... Poland defines its own aims and goals. Other countries can
have their opinions on the subject, but they cannot have any influence.'
Oleksy told NATO ambassadors that: 'Our answer to the question when
NATO should open up to new members is – as soon as possible.'[39]

NATO refused to grant Poland (or any country) the time-table that
it sought.[40] Nevertheless, British Foreign Secretary Douglas Hurd met
with Polish Foreign Minister Wladyslaw Bartoszewski in Warsaw on 12
April and stated that: 'We in Britain are convinced that Poland will join
as a full member of NATO and the EU, and that these are irreversible
processes.'[41] On 14 April Robert Hunter, the US Ambassador to
NATO, travelled to Prague and said that the first round of the NATO
expansion study had been completed and that a second version would be
prepared for NATO foreign ministers meeting in the Netherlands from
30 to 31 May, for a final draft to be provided for December. Hunter told
reporters that the decision to expand NATO 'is made, now it's just a
matter of doing it right.'[42]

Though NATO's timetable had not changed, American officials
sought to clarify the situation. On 24 April, Secretary of State
Christopher said that: 'The processes of NATO expansion has proceeded
on precisely the same timetable that we decided on last December... This
timetable has not been altered because of other events since that time. It

is a deliberate timetable.' Christopher added that 'NATO is not a social club. Any decision on enlargement will be taken with great care and deliberation and precision.'[43]   In Brussels two days later, NATO Secretary General Claes refused to commit to expansion by 1998 (a date pushed hard by the Polish foreign minister in Washington earlier that week) and insisted that: 'The European security architecture is not possible without Russia... It is not possible to give an answer on the timing of expansion.'[44]   Yet the same day a somewhat contradictory message was given by a State Department spokesman who said that: 'One of our most important foreign policy objectives in Europe is to see NATO expand, and no country outside of NATO has the right to a veto over that process or will veto that process... [W]e have a very clear and consistent position on this.'[45]   In an indirect response, Russian Foreign Minister Kozyrev said that if NATO expands, nationalists could devour him and that he would have to write his memoirs 'from the Gulag.'[46]

These public tensions over NATO expansion set the background for the meeting between Presidents Clinton and Yeltsin celebrating the 50th anniversary commemoration of the end of the Second World War in Moscow. Prior to the meeting, Yeltsin summarized the Russian position on European security in an interview with *Time* magazine. Yeltsin said that:

> We do not think the real problems of European security can be resolved by expanding NATO to the east... The creation of a model of mutual and comprehensive security should become our common aim in Europe. The dialogue on such a model has already begun in the Organization on Cooperation and Security in Europe. I think diplomats should focus their efforts on this, rather than discussing terms for the expansion of NATO.[47]

To this Russian Defence Minister Grachev added on 6 May that: 'The expansion of NATO does not correspond with the interests of creating a new Europe without military blocs.'[48]

The Clinton Administration was prepared to assure Yeltsin that Russia could be a member of NATO and that it would be willing to give Moscow written assurances to that effect as well as on the non-deployment of nuclear weapons on new member territory. On 7 May *The Washington Post* reported that such a concession was being held as a reserve policy to bring Russia into the PfP and for negotiating a special NATO/Russia relationship.[49]   On 8 May a senior US official travelling with President Clinton to Moscow told reporters that: 'It is very import-

ant that the Russians understand that in this process there are no
surprises, that it will proceed at its own natural pace, and we will not
accelerate the pace.'[50] The US never expected Yeltsin to make concessions on the NATO issue but worked tirelessly to get him to commit to
full participation in the PfP.

Security issues dominated the summit and the NATO issue was
discussed at length. In a joint statement both leaders made it clear that
differences remained but that they were not sufficient to harm the US-
Russian relationship. Yeltsin stressed that the US and Russia understood
each other better but that their positions remained unchanged. The
meeting provided Yeltsin with a politically important appearance that
NATO expansion was slowing by getting President Clinton to agree that
the discussion of the issue should continue throughout the coming year.

From an American perspective the meeting was a success. President
Clinton attained a firm commitment by Yeltsin to enter into the PfP by
agreeing to a special NATO-Russia dialogue at the upcoming North
Atlantic Council meeting from 30 to 31 May. On NATO expansion,
President Clinton said that:

> I made it clear that I thought that anything done with NATO had to
> meet two criteria. Number one, it must advance the interests of all
> the Partners for Peace, the security interests of all of them, including
> Russia. And number two, it must advance the long-term goal of the
> United States, which I have articulated from the beginning of my
> presidency, of an integrated Europe, which I believe is very
> important, and I think Russia shares both of those objectives.[51]

In answering questions from the press Clinton offered a forthright
clarification as to what NATO had and had not decided:

> [T]he important thing for me was not that Russia and the United
> States would agree today on the details of NATO expansion. Indeed,
> it's important for all of you to understand, NATO has not agreed on
> that. NATO has not agreed on that. This whole year, 1995 was to be
> devoted for the rationale for expanding NATO and then determining
> how it might be done, with no consideration whatever of who would
> be in the included membership and when that would be done. That
> was the plan ... not only have we not agreed on that, as far as I know
> there may be significant differences among the NATO partners
> themselves.[52]

This was an extremely important clarification for the Russian audience given that the Administration had told a number of PfP countries that the US was committed to expansion. NATO as a whole had *not* decided to expand. The Clinton Administration may have decided internally to push its Allies to enlarge NATO, but the process would have to be agreed by the 16 Allies and approved by 16 parliaments – something that was by no means certain.[53]

At the 30 to 31 May foreign ministers' meeting, NATO renewed its commitment to the principle of expansion and welcomed the decision of Russia to implement an Individual Partnership Programme and to begin a new NATO/Russia dialogue. NATO Secretary General Willy Claes was specific in assuring Russia that the Alliance had nothing but peaceful intentions in enlargement by stating that:

> The admission of new members to the Alliance is aimed at enhancing security and stability in all of Europe. It is not directed against Russia nor does it diminish the national security interests of Russia. When the Alliance decides to invite new members to join, it will be part of our effort to build cooperative security structures in Europe to which we hope Russia will contribute its share. The objective will be to enhance security for all countries in Europe, including Russia, without creating dividing lines. Enlargement will be part of a broad European security architecture based on genuine partnership and cooperation in the whole of Europe.[54]

Russia's Foreign Minister Kozyrev placed the new relationship with NATO in a positive framework. However, he reminded the NATO ministers that:

> Russia's position regarding NATO expansion has remained unchanged. We continue to believe that it does not meet either the interest of Russia's national security or the interest of European security as a whole. Furthermore, the hasty resolution of the issue may threaten the establishment of truly mutually advantageous and constructive relations between Russia and NATO and the usefulness of Russia's involvement in the PfP. It will not create greater stability and security either.... [W]e suggest to halt and think rather than act hastily and blindly.[55]

The apparent change in Russian views towards cooperation with NATO was a major success for the Clinton Administration's and NATO's efforts vis-à-vis Russia. Nevertheless, many problems remained – especially an ongoing danger that Russia would use its special relationship with NATO to dilute Alliance policy and use its leverage against NATO enlargement. In a letter to NATO prior to his speech to the North Atlantic Council, Kozyrev wrote that: 'A decision about the enlargement of NATO to the East would create for Russia the need for a corresponding correction of its attitude toward the Partnership for Peace.'[56]

Having breathed a sigh of relief that Kozyrev did not back out of PfP as he had the previous December, NATO officials remained cautious about further alienating Russia. Speaking on background to reporters following the ministerial meeting, NATO officials. suggested that after the completion of the expansion study in the summer of 1995, the issue of new members would be placed on a back-burner. 'Something like this has to be driven through and there is not much drive in NATO at the moment,' said one NATO source.[57] The entire discussion of NATO enlargement at the May ministerial was muted by the crisis facing the Alliance in the Balkans which raised more fundamental questions about the future of European security. There would be little point in an enlarged NATO or a stronger OSCE if neither could act to resolve Europe's worst crisis since the Second World War.

TRANSATLANTIC LEADERSHIP AND THE FUTURE OF EUROPEAN SECURITY

The institutional strategy implemented by the Clinton Administration in 1994 and 1995 had a sound foundation with its core purpose to keep reform advancing in both Central and Eastern Europe and the former Soviet Union. However, by the summer of 1995 (the time of this writing) it was clear that the policy needed refinement. In April 1995 American officials told Central and East Europeans that the decision to expand NATO had been made. Within a matter of weeks Boris Yeltsin was told that it had not. The US needs to clarify its position on NATO enlargement. This can be accomplished by making a clear statement that in current circumstances, NATO will not expand to the borders of the former Soviet Union. As German Chancellor Helmut Kohl said on 9 May 1995, to manoeuvre Russia into a corner would be 'fatal stupidity.'[58]

The US and NATO should use public and private diplomacy to state in no uncertain terms that if Russia violates the agreed limits of the CFE, takes aggressive or threatening actions in its near abroad, or democracy collapses there – NATO will expand. Such linkage can be a useful tool to prevent an extreme nationalist from coming to power in Russia. This would tell the Russian people and government officials that a vote for despotism or neo-imperialism is a vote for NATO expansion. NATO can expand rapidly under such circumstances because the candidate states, having worked through the PfP, will be near or at NATO standards. If NATO is forced to enlarge, it should expand all the way to the Ukraine and not risk committing the Ukraine and other European former Soviet republics to a grey zone of Russian influence.[59]

US Ambassador to NATO Robert Hunter suggested that the best way to respond to Russian fears of NATO expansion is to assure them that NATO is a defensive alliance and poses a threat to no one.[60] The best way to show this is for NATO and Russian militaries to have direct, close, and regular contact, consultation, and cooperation via PfP and a comprehensive NATO/Russia dialogue. The West must understand Russian concerns and adopt a strategy that neither heightens nor accommodates them. American officials regularly insist that Russian statements against NATO enlargement are designed to appeal to fluctuating domestic politics in Moscow. However, no matter how one looks at it, enlarging NATO means expanding the military responsibility of Germany and the United States – Moscow's two twentieth century enemies – closer to Russia.

For this reason, the US should support giving more substance to the OSCE but retain the general objective of empowering it in a way that does not undermine NATO. By placing the existing Contact Group (the five power consultation over the Balkan crisis) within the OSCE as a non-binding 'OSCE Contact Group for European Security' or something similar, the OSCE could attain a higher profile without changing anything.[61] According to one American official, the US does not currently support institutionalizing the Contact Group, but might favour using it as 'an example of a new sort of ad hoc group that might be formed within the OSCE framework for addressing regional security problems.'[62] Such an institutional change should be presented to Russia as a good faith effort to meet Moscow half-way while clarifying that this is as far as the US is willing to go. This might be sufficient to satisfy Russia as it will allow Moscow to claim significant influence on European security issues in a way that does not fundamentally alter European security institutions or the existing balance of power on the continent.

Since the Visegrad countries have made such remarkable efforts at reform and because they still have fears of Russian imperialism and other Central and East European states need further incentive for internal political, military, and economic reform, NATO should make a good faith offering to these countries. If these states need assurances that they can eventually join NATO and if the West feels that acting is better than doing nothing, then it should place the Czech Republic on a fast-track to NATO membership and admit it as soon as possible. The Czech Republic is well advanced as a democratic free-market country and, most significantly, shares no common border with the former Soviet Union. Czech membership could serve as a test for NATO enlargement. This should be done with full transparency and by explaining to other Central and East European countries that it shows that NATO can expand quickly if necessary and that they should continue to use the PfP to aid their entrance should things go wrong in Russia.[63]

When Czech President Vaclav Havel addressed a conference of NATO military leaders at SHAPE Headquarters on 27 April 1995 he stressed that NATO must redefine its aims and purpose before admitting new members. 'The expansion of NATO should be preceded by something even more important, that is, a new formulation of its own meaning, mission, and identity,' said Havel.[64] Specifically the post-Cold War role of the US in Europe needs clearer definition. The debate over the US role in Bosnia and the expansion of NATO may expose a more serious problem in transatlantic relations after the Cold War. The US is experiencing a strong resurgence of a vocal and influential isolationist sentiment. It is very likely that a debate over NATO expansion in the US Congress could lead to a more dangerous discussion of the future of NATO itself. While many observers of the US Congress point out that the Contract With America legislation encourages the expansion of NATO, the bottom line costs and commitments that this would require have created a growing unease about expansion. On 7 May 1995, Speaker of the House Newt Gingrich said that the US must carefully weigh the implications of NATO expansion to avoid 'giving a commitment which we have no intent to keep.'[65]

Perhaps Speaker Gingrich had also looked at a new poll by the Chicago Council on Foreign Relations which showed that a plurality of the American public favoured NATO expansion but that a majority would not defend Poland if attacked by Russia.[66] Though Speaker Gingrich has contributed considerably to the problems surrounding the NATO expansion debate by politicizing it in his Contract With America, he is correct. Article 5 of the NATO Treaty is a very serious commitment by the US. If Americans are not willing to equate Warsaw with Boston – or any other American city – then NATO simply cannot afford the loss of credibility that would come in the event of some (unlikely) attack on Poland or any other new member.

The Republican Congress is serious about reducing American commitments abroad and there is a danger that the question of NATO expansion will become a major issue in the 1996 US presidential election.[67] President Clinton should avoid the temptation to use NATO expansion as a means of showing that he is a committed internationalist. Transatlantic leadership means doing nothing that might endanger the core foundation of American involvement in Europe – Article 5 of the NATO Treaty. Specifically, President Clinton must reject criticisms that by not expanding NATO quickly the Administration has been soft on Russia. This can be avoided by stating clearly the conditions under which NATO will expand and using them to link NATO expansion to continued democratic and market reform in Russia.

Finally, both the United States and Russia must get past their lingering Cold War distrust. Tensions between the two have shown that Cold War suspicions persist. President Clinton summarized this problem well in his 10 May 1995 speech at Moscow State University celebrating the end of the Second World War. Clinton thoughtfully observed that:

> Because our alliance with you was shattered at the war's end by the onset of the Cold War, Americans never fully appreciated ... the true extent of your sacrifice and its contribution to our common victory. And the Russian people were denied the full promise of that victory in World War II, a victory that brought the West five decades of freedom and prosperity. Now the Cold War is over. Democracy has triumphed through decades of Western resolve, but that victory was also yours through the determination of the peoples of Russia, the other former Soviet Republics, and the countries of Central and Eastern Europe to be free and to move into the 21st century as a part of, not apart from, the global movement toward greater democracy, prosperity, and common security.[68]

The Cold War is over. The Cold Peace may be coming but it is not here yet. President Clinton has instigated a process that can facilitate broad European integration through the a multi-institutional strategy for attaining European security into the twenty-first century. Success will require a willingness to go slow and to proceed with caution in a way that does nothing to harm the most important commitment in American foreign policy – a solid and lasting transatlantic relationship.

NOTES

1.   For a survey of the arguments surrounding this debate see Michael E. Brown, 'The Flawed Logic of NATO expansion,' *Survival*, Vol.37, No.1, Spring 1995 and Geoffrey Lee Williams, 'NATO's Expansion: The Big Debate,' *NATO Review*, Vol. 43, No. 3, May 1995. Also see Michael Mandelbaum, 'Preserving the New Peace: The Case Against NATO Expansion,' *Foreign Affairs*, May/June 1995, Vol.74, No.4; and Senator Sam Nunn, 'The Future of NATO in an Uncertain World,' speech delivered to the SACLANT Seminar '95, Norfolk, Virginia, 22 June 1995. For a summary of the arguments in favour of NATO expansion see Strobe Talbott, 'Why NATO Should Grow,' *The New York Review of Books*, 10 August 1995, Vol.XLII, No.13, and William E. Odom, 'NATO's Expansion: The Critics are Wrong,' *The National Interest*, No.39, Spring 1995. For an early argument for a pragmatic partnership between NATO and the CSCE see Sean Kay, 'NATO and the CSCE: A Partnership for the Future,' *Paradigms: The Kent Journal of International Relations*, Vol.7, No.2, Winter 1993.

2.   On 27 May 1994 a senior American official speaking on background asserted that 'should the situation deteriorate in the East and Russia, and it became necessary at some step to draw the line between Eastern and Western.... [T]he Partnership for Peace would put us in a better position to do that.' *White House Information Service.*

3.   See Sean Kay, 'NATO and the OSCE: A New Russian Challenge,' in Victor S. Papacosma and Mary Ann Heiss (eds), *NATO In The Post-Cold War Era: Does It Have a Future?*, St. Martin's Press, New York, 1995.

4.   *Ibid.*

5.   *Reuters.* 9 September 1994.

6.   *Associated Press.* 9 September 1994.

7.   *Associated Press.* 2 October 1994.

8.   'US Wants to Expedite Entry of Eastern Nations into Alliance,' *New York Times*, 27 October 1994.

9.   According to US Undersecretary of Defence Walter Slocombe: 'NATO should only want new members who have passed beyond ambitions toward the territory of their neighbours, who have accepted the rights of their minorities, and who have established real and working democratic systems.' Presentation to the Defence and Security Committee of the North Atlantic Assembly. North Atlantic Assembly Annual Session, November 1994, Washington, DC. The US has directly pushed potential new NATO members with historical territorial disputes (such as Hungary and Romania) to sign formal bilateral treaties settling such disputes before they could be considered for membership in NATO. *Reuters*, 14 June 1995.

10.   Interview conducted by the author in November 1994.

11.   More details of the dual-track approach were made public prior to the December NATO foreign ministers meeting and CSCE Heads of State summit. After the proposed working group completed an 'owner's manual' of the requirements for membership, NATO would provide a non-discriminatory brief to all PfP countries – including Russia – on the results. Apparently the standards for NATO expansion pushed by the US would be sufficiently stringent that if Russia ever did meet the criteria, it will be a very different place – a true and permanent Western democracy.

12. This was a substantive change in US views toward the CSCE. While recognizing that the CSCE played an important role in stimulating post-Communist change in Central and Eastern Europe, the US historically has viewed the CSCE as cumbersome and as a means through which the Soviet Union – and then Russia – could cast a veto over European security policy.

13. *White House Information Service.*

14. The US did propose a 'beefing up' of CSCE capabilities to include non-proliferation, peacekeeping within the CIS, preventive mechanisms for addressing ethnic conflict, economic development, and to involve the CSCE more directly in the resolution of long-term problems in the Balkans.

15. See John Borawski, 'Partnership for Peace and Beyond,' *International Affairs*, Vol.71, No.2, 1995, p.245.

16. *Associated Press.* 1 December 1994.

17. *Ibid.* Richthofen specifically noted existing differences within NATO over expansion that included Greece and Italy favouring the inclusion of Romania, Bulgaria, and possibly Malta while northern NATO countries wanted to prioritize admission of Poland, Hungary, and the Czech Republic.

18. *Ibid.*

19. *NATO Office of Information and Press*, 1 December 1995.

20. *Ibid.*

21. *White House Information Service*, 5 December 1994.

22. *Reuters.* 5 December 1994.

23. *Reuters.* 5 December 1994.

24. *Reuters*, 6 December 1994. For a survey of the decisions made at the Budapest Summit, see Victor-Yves Ghebali, 'After the Budapest Conference: The Organization for Security and Cooperation in Europe.' *NATO Review*, Vol.43, No.2, March 1995. At the summit the most significant concession to Russia was acceptance of a Russian proposal to conduct an ongoing review of the ingredients for a European security architecture in the twenty-first century. This was not a major concession, as the review group would only give a report to the OSCE leadership at the next summit meeting.

25. Richard Holbrooke, 'America, A European Power,' *Foreign Affairs*, Vol.74, No.2, March/April 1995, pp.45-46.

26. *Ibid.*

27. Zbigniew Brzezinski, 'A Plan for Europe,' *Foreign Affairs*, Vol.74, January/February 1995, No.1.

28. *Ibid*, p.51.

29. 'Russia Intends to Pursue Guarantees from NATO,' *The Washington Post*, 11 March 1995, p.A21.

30. *Reuters*, 13 March 1995. Vice-President Gore was invoking the language of Russian Foreign Minister Kozyrev from June 1994 who agreed to sign the PfP while insisting on first negotiating a detailed and signed cooperation programme that would formalize a relationship based on what he called "no mutual vetoes or surprises."

31. *Reuters*, 18 and 19 March 1995. Following this meeting the British Foreign Secretary Douglas Hurd stressed that while Russia would not have a veto over NATO policy, such an agreement would be based on the principle of 'no vetoes and no surprises' borrowing even more directly from Kozyrev's language. At this meeting, differences were aired among the European members. France supported a formal NATO-Russia Treaty while Germany pushed for a 'charter' that would not require ratification by all

members and would be less legally binding.

32. *Ibid.*
33. *Ibid.*
34. *Associated Press*, 23 March 1995. At the Geneva meeting, Secretary Christopher delivered a letter to President Yeltsin outlining the US approach to NATO expansion.
35. *Reuters*, 3 April 1995. Actually the Russian military had been pushing for a renegotiation of the Conventional Forces in Europe Treaty since at least early summer of 1993. The NATO linkage may have simply offered the Russian armed forces an excuse to push their case.
36. *Interfax*, 3 April 1995. In *OMRI Daily Digest*, 4 April 1995.
37. *Nezavismaya Gazeta*, 4 April 1995. In *OMRI Daily Digest*. 5 April 1995.
38. *Reuters*, 3 April 1995.
39. *Associated Press*, 5 April 1995.
40. *Gazeta Wyborcze* cited unnamed NATO sources in Brussels as expressing concern over Poland's delay in establishing structures for democratic control over the military (6 April 1995), in *OMRI Daily Digest*, 7 April 1995. The appearance of new momentum towards NATO expansion continued when the Czech Foreign Minister Joseg Zieleniec travelled to Washington DC and met with Secretary of State Christopher and other senior US officials on 7 April. According to *Lidove noviny*, the Czechs were given the impression that during the forthcoming summit between Presidents Clinton and Yeltsin in Moscow, the Americans would tell Russia that the expansion of NATO has already been decided. *Lidove noviny* (8 April 1995), *OMRI Daily Digest*, 10 April 1995.
41. *OMRI Daily Digest*, 13 April 1995.
42. *Associated Press*, 14 April 1995. Ambassador Hunter said that NATO rules would be applied strictly to each new member and that each would have to join and contribute to the NATO integrated military command structure. 'An ally is an ally is an ally. You join the alliance and you do what allies do ... if necessary, countries joining NATO will accept deployment on their territory of whatever is required for security,' he added. Also see Robert Hunter, 'Enlargement: Part of A Strategy for Projecting Stability into Central Europe,' *NATO Review*, Vol.43, No.3, May 1995. Pressure from Central and Eastern Europe on NATO continued the following week when Polish Foreign Minister Bartoszewski met with US officials in Washington on 24 April and insisted in a speech to the Center for Strategic and International Studies that: 'I would not find it discriminatory if the European Union specified the year 2000 for our membership. However, I strongly believe NATO membership should come at least two years earlier.' He also endorsed the dual track approach of using the OSCE to 'avoid isolating Russia.'
43. *Reuters*, 24 April 1995.
44. *Associated Press*, 26 April 1995.
45. *Ibid.*
46. *Izvestiya*, 27 April 1995. In *OMRI Daily Digest*, 28 April 1995.
47. 'Heading for the Summit,' Interview with Boris Yeltsin, *Time*, 8 May 1995, p.75.
48. *Reuters*, 6 May 1995.
49. 'US Offers Assurances on NATO,' *The Washington Post*, 7 May 1995, p.A1.
50. Associated Press. 8 May 1995.
51. *Ibid.*
52. *Ibid.*

53. Assurances by Clinton may not have been enough for the Russians. As Sergei Karagonov, a senior advisor to President Yeltsin, told reporters on 11 May: 'These pieces of paper mean nothing if there are no political conditions for its [a special NATO/Russia relationship] implementation...You cannot build up a special relationship with Russia when you are talking about enlargement at the same time.' To this Andrei Androsov, head of the Russian Foreign Ministry's NATO Department added: 'We need NATO to change its attitude from expansion to real partnership...If the same treatment continues, I fear cooperation will be affected.' *Reuters*, 11 May 1995.
54. NATO Office of Information and Press, 31 May 1995.
55. *Ibid.*
56. *Associated Press*, 30 May 1995. Also on 31 May, *Segodnya* quoted a high ranking Russian defence official as saying that: 'A set of measures have been approved that should prevent NATO expansion.' The report stressed that Russia's decision to join the PfP was conditional on NATO not expanding. *OMRI Daily Digest*, 1 June 1995.
57. *Reuters*, 31 May 1995. On 20 August 1995 the German magazine *Der Spiegel* reported that the draft plan for NATO enlargement included neither a timetable nor precise criteria for admittance of new members and that the forthcoming briefings to NATO aspirants would be left intentionally vague. The report quoted a German diplomat as saying, 'No one should be able to say "we fulfil all the criteria so now you have to take us in".' Finally the article indicated that while the US was pushing for new members to be fully integrated into the NATO military command, France was opposed to this stipulation. Reported in *Reuters*, 20 August 1995.
58. *Reuters*, 9 May 1995.
59. For a discussion of these and related issues see Michael Mandelbaum, *Foreign Affairs*, Vol.74, No.3, May/June 1995. The phrase 'European former Soviet republics' is used intentionally to distinguish them from the Asian or Central Eurasian former Soviet republics. The latter are not part of Europe and should not be part of the PfP or even the OSCE – let alone NATO. Nevertheless in the spirit of 'Vancouver to Vladivostok' several are in the PfP and all are OSCE members. While clearly not part of Europe, it should be made clear to Russia that its behaviour there will be used by the West as a barometer for assessing Russian objectives in its near abroad and will thus be part of the calculation as to whether and when NATO should expand.
60. *NATO Review*, Vol.74, No.3, May 1995.
61. The Contact Group is a consultative forum between the US, the United Kingdom, Germany, France, and Russia.
62. Interview conducted by the author, November 1994.
63. For further discussion of Czech membership in NATO, see Sean Kay, 'European Security: With or Without the United States.' Paper presented at the NATO Seminar on the Future of European Security, 1-6 November, 1994, Cesky Krumlov, Czech Republic.
64. *OMRI Daily Digest*, 28 April 1995.
65. *Associated Press*, 7 May 1995.
66. John E. Rielly, 'The Public Mood at Mid-Decade,' *Foreign Policy*, No.98, p.89, Spring 1995. According to the Chicago Council on Foreign Relations study of public opinion, 24% of the American public support NATO expansion to include the Czech Republic, Poland, and Hungary. However, when the issue of sending troops to resist a Russian invasion of Poland is raised, 50% of the public is opposed and only 32% in favour. On the costs of NATO enlargement, the Rand Corporation has estimated

a necessary expenditure of 20 to 50 billion dollars over a 10 year period to be shared in an unspecified manner between current and new members. See 'Enthusiasm for a Wider Alliance is Marked by Contradictions,' *The Washington Post*, 7 July 1995, p.A1.

67. For example, see the American Interests Abroad Act of 1995, legislation introduced on 23 May 1995. President Clinton appropriately described this legislation as the most serious isolationist threat to the US international role in the last fifty years: White House Information Service. 23 May 1995. Former Republican Secretary of State Lawrence Eagleburger described it in a 24 May interview with National Public Radio as 'immature.' For a summary of similar domestic pressures, see Stanley Sloan, 'US Pressures on NATO's Future.' *International Affairs*, Vol.71, No.2, 1995, pp.217-231. In addition, it is important to note that NATO enlargement is viewed as a means of gaining votes in the 1995 elections from voters with ethnic heritage tied to potential NATO members. According to Eugene Iwanciw, a founder of the Central and East European Coalition, there are 23 million Americans who trace their heritage to Eastern Europe and there are a dozen states where they constitute more than 5% of the electorate. 'Taking an Expansionist Position on NATO is a No-Lost Way of Appealing to These Voters,' *The Washington Post*, 7 July 1995.

68. White House Information Service, 10 May 1995.

4 The EU: From Civilian Power to Speaking with a Common Voice – The Transition to a CFSP

Juliet Lodge

The idea that the European Union should speak with one voice in line with its emerging, but not sought after, status as an international power in the making confronts head-on the issue of just what kind of organization the EU is and what that means for the sovereignty of its component members. Foreign affairs, being the sole preserve of sovereign governments, was deliberately excluded from the EC's competence. However, its economic influence, the rapidly changing and turbulent international agenda, and the member states' recognition of the inseparability of external relations from foreign policy and security, and latterly the inseparability of internal and external security issues, resulted in the mid-1980s in a reappraisal of what international role, if any, the EC should pursue. As a result, not only were its internal mechanisms reformed but as its potential policy scope and domain widened, its long-professed self-image as a civilian power was contested. This paper briefly explores the question of the EC's image, the breaking of the security taboo, the impact on the debate as to its image of enlargement in the context of widening and deepening, and the evolution of the common foreign and security policy (CFSP). It begins by placing the developments in their international and regional context and concludes that the move towards European Union, as exemplified in the Inter-Governmental Conference (IGC) process leading up to the Maastricht Treaty on European Union (TEU), formed an essential pre-condition for the emergence of a European system based on interlocking institutions.

THE EU IN THE REGIONAL AND GLOBAL ENVIRONMENT

The EU faces numerous problems in defining, practising and asserting a credible role in line with the kind of image of itself that it wishes to project. At present, even the definition of its image is confused. On the one hand, it expects to be a relatively assertive player, rather than a mere presence, in the regional setting. On the other hand, it is concerned about its image – whether it has made the transition from a somewhat passive, beneficent 'civilian power' devoid of imperialistic intent to a pro-active organization capable of credibly initiating, following through and executing a 'common foreign and security policy' leading towards an ill-defined concept of a 'common defence' with all that that implies organizationally, politically, economically and financially.

A high-level group of experts of the CFSP was convened at Commissioner Hans van den Broek's request in 1994. Their first report focused on the ways and means of establishing genuine credibility for the EU in its international dealings.[1] This began by assessing not only the EU's relationship with WEU but also the escalation in new threats against a background of geopolitical change and an alleged crisis in the EU's system of beliefs and values. It stressed that doubts about the viability and credibility of the CFSP damaged the EU's credibility, made the notion of 'partnership in leadership' with Washington untenable, and underscored the need to address fundamental weaknesses imperative to avert irreversible damage to the West. While many of the proposals advanced to combat such deficiencies could be adopted without any amendments to the existing treaties, reconciling a credible CFSP and military and defence issues with effective and credible action by the Union remains problematic and probably impossible without treaty reform. Not surprisingly, therefore, the EU has begun to take more seriously the question of what kind of an image (and operational capacity) it wishes to project in the international system. This, in turn, requires it not merely to be clear about the values it wishes to uphold but to confront the operational barriers to achieving effectiveness that arise out of the pillar structure of the treaties and the contradictory and untenable positions that surface as a result of them.

Between November 1994 and March 1995, the EU managed to adopt eleven common positions (such as sanctions, embargoes and similar reactions to crises) under article J2 of the Maastricht treaty (of which four related to former Yugoslavia) and 16 joint actions under article J3 (of which eight related to former Yugoslavia). Confusion between EC/EU matters and those under the jurisdiction of the CFSP inhibits effective policy implementation. For example, a political decision to implement a trade sanction affects trade, finance and cooperation schemes and all activities under Community jurisdiction. Similarly, ad hoc joint actions have been randomly adopted on a range of issues (observing elections in Russia, and South Africa); regulatory work (export of dual purpose goods); sensitive security issues (Stability Pact and Non-Proliferation Treaty) and the mobilization of human and financial resources (humanitarian aid to Bosnia, etc). Article J4(1) provides for the EU to 'request' the WEU to elaborate and implement decisions and actions having implications for defence, but so far no formal use has been made of this and it has been dismissed as immature. [2]

Many observers as well as the various reports of the European Commission and European Parliament (EP) and its political groups put forward an idea for improving the decision-making capabilities and effectiveness of the EU's institutions with a view to enhancing the EU's capacity to act credibly. It was significant that the Commission report for the Reflection Group on the IGC scheduled for 1996 agreed in principle with the high-level expert group in identifying the need for early analysis of long, medium and short term external developments (though it stopped short of advocating the establishment of a central forward planning or policy analysis unit).[3] Equally, the issue of improving the European Parliament's role vis-à-vis the CFSP was noted along with the question of what role, if any, should be given to the European Court of Justice (ECJ), currently excluded from any role in CFSP or defence matters) and whether or not foreign policy decisions should be justiciable. That these issues should have been raised owed something both to the attempts to improve (preferably by abolishing) the pillar structure and the artificial divisions and problems arising out of it and something to the underlying value system and normative beliefs embedded in what might very loosely be termed the 'EU mind-set.'

It was generally accepted that EU behaviour should uphold humanitarian values, human rights and fundamental liberties and that it should act in a moral way in the international system. How this was to be translated into practice posed problems largely because the pillar structure undermined consistency and operational effectiveness. While it was generally understood that EU members should support one another given their mutual dependence, this was often eroded in practice. Consequently, attention had to be paid to defining what might constitute unacceptable behaviour by the member states. Unilateral action was and is certainly frowned upon, and sometimes vociferously condemned, but remains an option open to the member states. Opting-out from EU obligations is therefore possible. However, the treaty imposes obligations on the member states which the European Council is duty bound to uphold: it has a continuing *droit de regard*, for example, in respect of member states who abstain. But non-compliance with the Union's external and security policy can be much more damaging than abstention.[4] Could an ECJ role enable the EU to cope more effectively with unacceptable behaviour on the part of a member state? Could it be taken to task for infringing the treaty obligation to support the Union's external and security policy 'actively and unreservedly in a spirit of loyalty and mutual solidarity' and to 'refrain from any action which is contrary to the interests of the Union or likely to impair its effectiveness as a cohesive force in international relations'? Is this compatible with the high degree of discretion Council presidencies have? Is it compromised by the principle of executive prerogative in foreign and security policy and by the member states' continuing right to preserve essential national interests? These are all organizational and political issues which constrain the ability of the EU to act coherently, cohesively, effectively and credibly in the international system. If too much leeway persists in the implementation of a common (note, not a single) foreign policy, credibility will continue to be sacrificed to national expedience. Even so, the EU is attempting to project a more unified image of itself. The lack of credible, independent military force to back up its policy positions and commitments has inevitably meant that it has had to re-appraise the utility of the concept of itself, possibly too readily abandoned, as a civilian power.

THE IMAGE – BEYOND A CIVILIAN POWER

The self-professed image of a 'civilian power' was devised at a time when not only did the EC lack the military wherewithal to conduct a defence policy but when the notion that the EC as such should have any military capacity was taboo. It represented a rejection of power politics[5] (and stressed Western Europe's economic and cultural contributions). The notion was exemplified in the idea that international relations could be domesticated and subjected to the kind of contractual responsibilities associated with domestic rather than foreign affairs.[6] The notion of civilian power also extended from a period of de-colonization and a changing political relationship between EC states and their former dependant territories and colonies. That this did not always translate into a relationship of equal partnership, as espoused during various phases of the Lomé deliberations was neither surprising in view of the asymmetric economic realities of continued colonial dependence on outlets in EC states, nor was it realistic given the nature of the international political economy and competition for market access from developed, developing and under-developed states who lacked a special relationship with the EC.

However, the ideal of equality was advanced by the EC not for cynical reasons but because there was a genuine conviction that newly-independent states had an equal right to be heard as the older states. It is true that it was part and parcel of the EC's image as an emergent economic force. But the EC was at pains to dispel the idea that it wished to dominate and dictate terms to the rest of the world. Ideals and illusions apart, international trade is not so easily manipulated by governments as to dispel the realities of continuing asymmetries. Moreover, the EC could not claim, even after the common commercial policy had taken root, that it had a homogeneous, uniform trade policy that was not susceptible to the vagaries of the member states' national interests and those of their private sector commercial concerns. History and high politics intervened then as now. That the situation has changed owes much to factors beyond the EC's control. It is a product of globalization trends, changing expectations, circumstances and regional turbulence at the end of the 1980s.

The cliché has always been that the EC is an economic giant but a political dwarf. This implied a division between politics and economics which cannot be sustained. But it does and did correspond to the reality of the EC in the earlier decades when the artificial distinction between the two was most sharply epitomized by the division of competence over foreign matters (at the heart of national sovereignty) between the Commission and the emergent system of European Political Cooperation. The different structures reflected the view that external relations – focusing on trade – was a politically neutral activity (over which the Commission could be given competence) whereas foreign affairs and diplomacy were the stuff of national politics and amenable only to intergovernmental discourse. The impossibility of sustaining this dichotomy was repeatedly highlighted, no more so than when trade sanctions were suggested as punitive measures against specific states outside the EC (as in the Falklands war and during the break-up of Yugoslavia) or against states believed to be sympathetic to terrorism or guilty of flagrant abuses of human rights. In addition, US policy on the export of sensitive goods to the former Soviet bloc also sharply politicized trade issues. More recently, the discussion over defence industry issues, the production and export of arms, ammunition and war materials has highlighted difficulties and led to the call, in some quarters, for a review of article 223 of the Rome treaty. This allows member states to take any measure they deem necessary for the protection of the essential interests of its security connected with production and trade in armaments.

Allied to these developments was the evolution of European Political Cooperation (EPC) and gradual collaboration and coordination among EC states' diplomatic missions abroad. Structural elements of EPC served to intensify cooperation short of the development of a common foreign policy. The American policy of burden-shedding and continued problems within GATT also heightened sensitivities to the degree of divergence between the EC and the US over issues of crucial interest to EC states at a time of economic recession. Third states' expectations of the EC speaking with one voice became more pronounced and coincided with developments internal to the EC to expedite the transition to a European Union. All served to underpin the idea of the EC's transformation into an international actor that had come of age.

The problem remained, however, one of excessive expectations of unity at a time when the EC had little idea of what its new identity on the international stage should or could be, let alone any clear conception of the parameters and structures governing its advocacy of a common (but not a single) foreign and security policy. Instead, commentators variously condemned the apparently more self-assured EC as confirming the stereotype of a hegemonic power within a pyramidal system bent on the exploitation of the southern hemisphere[7], as 'Fortress Europe' bent on mercantilism, or as a nascent capitalist power in search of a regional role predicated on regional dominance. Others viewed the EC as a bastion of stability in a turbulent world and as an example worthy of emulation of how cooperation among former enemies could cement longer term peace and stability. Exaggerated expectations of economic flows from the EC to states on its eastern flanks soon gave way to a more sober assessment. However, the push towards the realization of the Single Market by 1 January 1993 provided a further stimulus to states seeking to safeguard a privileged relationship with it or to join it.

There was a clamour for admission by former members of the European Free Trade Area (EFTA), Central and East European states and others in the Mediterranean basin, many of whom wanted to inject their view of what image and identity the EC should develop during the 1990s. There can be little doubt that some were spurred by fears of exclusion and a desire to ensure that if a defence dimension became part of European Union, it should not compromise those wedded to the spirit of intergovernmentalism and/or neutrality. If the EC did have an image, it was not an entirely positive one: seen as a 'pot of gold' by outsiders and insiders alike, it was bound to disappoint. Unclear about its goals and political and financial capacity to meet undertakings outlined in statements and treaties, and confronted with the unfolding crisis in Yugoslavia and domestic problems over the ratification of the Maastricht treaty, ad hocery became inevitable.

This ad hocery contributed, however, to the realization that the civilian power posture had been sustained primarily by the EC's refusal to become involved in any way in military matters and by tacit continued rejection of the primacy of power politics.[8] Once the security taboo had been breached by the Franco-German brigade and talk of reviving WEU, possibly as the military arm of the EC and then explicitly by the Single European Act, however, the precise parameters of the EC's international posture and image had to be redefined: the civilian power imagery remained important but it was unclear how it fitted with the increasingly typical security/military responsibilities and activities into which the Community was being drawn.

The early 1990s accentuated this confusion. Relations with WEU were redefined in line with operational necessities arising out of the EU's role in Yugoslavia both as an actor in its own right and as a contributor to UN peace efforts. The rhetoric of independence was unmasked. The imperative of maintaining a close integral relationship with NATO, and therefore with the US, was confirmed. The contradictions in postures were exposed, and the diplomatic inadequacies and operationally contingent capacity of the EU revealed – in terms of its nascent infrastructures, reliance on member governments, and the reality of independent authority and capabilities of key member states, such as France, the UK and Germany. All exposed the EU's aspirations, tested its profession of unity; strained the emergent CFSP system, and underscored the reality of Anglo-French military supremacy and capabilities, including the military muscle to translate political decisions into practice. It also exposed the impossibility of preserving the notion of the quintessential equality in status and power of the individual member states within the EU, notably when hard international issues demanded responses requiring the mobilization of human, financial and military resources in order to give expression to common policy lines that lacked the whole-hearted support of all the member states. The problems were compounded, moreover, by the fact that some EU member states were outside WEU or seemingly unable and unwilling to participate militarily in out of EU-area operations but yet were the most vociferous advocates of changing the role and membership of NATO to admit Central and East European states likely to fragment NATO unity, shake WEU and EU cohesion and contest their objectives in a less than constructive manner.

In short, it became clear that the civilian power image had much to offer, that it should be resurrected both to provide the EU with a breathing space in which to reappraise and determine its actual international and regional aspirations as well as the premises underlying the development of the CFSP, and to permit new member states with histories of non-alignment or neutrality to accommodate themselves to the financial and political realities of being full members of an organization having foreign policy commitments that needed to be funded and rendered credible. The EU could not realistically supplant either the WEU or NATO operationally. Politically, it was dependent – if political statements were to retain credibility – on the cooperation of WEU and NATO members, as well as on the WEU and NATO themselves. Internally, the need for hierarchy to be accepted in respect of engagements requiring the mobilization of military resources had to be reconciled with small member states' fears that the big states would drag them into operations they would rather resist. The EU retains the abilities of a civilian power. Should it aspire to be anything more than this? If so, what are the imperatives behind such endeavours? Are they overwhelming? What would be the consequences for the EU of it explicitly stating that its objectives are limited to civilian power-type engagements?

IMAGE AND CAPABILITIES

The image and capabilities of the EC in the international and regional milieux do not neatly coincide. Nor do external expectations of the extent to which the EC should 'speak with one voice' match its actual ability and will to do so. This is partly because of inadequate financial, administrative, logistical and structural resources at the EC's disposal. It is also partly a result of the lack of political direction, political infrastructure and continuing uncertainty and disagreement over the parameters of EC competence in this field among the member states. Tension persists between an arrangement serving national interests geared towards broadly agreed common objectives and the pursuit of a single foreign policy.

Jacques Delors differentiated between a *single* foreign policy and a *common* foreign policy. To put it crudely, it is the difference between a regulation and a directive. Broad parameters of a common policy would be set out and states left to interpret them in the light of domestic traditions and interests. Such a flexible approach was not simply expedient in view of anxieties over the implications of a common policy for national sovereignty but was in line with existing treaties and practice which left states to interpret, in a manner compatible with overall goals, the broad guidelines already agreed. While this approach dealt with the issue of flexibly implementing commonly agreed broad objectives, it did not necessarily significantly enhance the EC/Union's capacity to act proactively or to prevent third states from exploiting internal differences to the EC's disadvantage. That is why Delors went on to advocate the EC strengthening its participation in international organizations whenever the Twelve's and EC interests could be better protected by a cohesive approach.[9] Taylor addressed this question and distinguished between a federal and a quasi/partial federal or supranational capability. Supranationalism, he suggested, helps states to adapt to new needs and problems whereas federalism challenges their existence fundamentally.[10] Germane to a functioning, independent supranational system is the ability of states to take decisions by a 'fluid majority which initiates new policies and structures.'[11]

The lack of fit between the outside world's perceptions of how the EC should act and its actual capabilities is most marked in the defence and security fields. While this is not the place to engage in a discussion as to the relative merits of different theoretical perspectives on security communities, mature anarchy, security complexes[12], complex interdependence and regimes, for example, it must be recalled that among scholars there is a broad agreement that the EC has a dual identity as an international actor (or at least a partially developed international actor)[13] and as a regional regime.[14] When these typologies are applied to the EC, one of the aspects that is commonly stressed is the normative one and the EC's projection of a set of values and norms which, theoretically, guide its actions and conform to its civilian power self-image, with its commitment to the upholding of human rights and liberal democratic values. Ideally, therefore, trading partners, for example, are expected to uphold democratic norms and respect human rights.[15] Practice is often at variance. (Indeed, Galtung has scathingly dismissed the EC's patrimony and values and castigated its attachment to what he sees as a European Christian cosmology.[16]) Beyond trade, however, further common features of these typologies include an evaluation of EC performance. EC foreign policy behaviour is typically characterized as responsive or reactive rather than proactive and defensive. Political difficulties and anxieties over national sovereignty are central to this. But a contributing factor lies with structural deficiencies.

There is no effective system of supranational crisis management, forward and contingency planning, mobilization of appropriate independent administrative, or political, financial or military resources. Rudimentary resources coupled with continuing dependence on the independently controlled resources, and hence goodwill of the member states, inhibit the evolution of a genuine, supranational EC foreign and defence policy capability. Small and significant steps to remedy this were formalized through the establishment of the EPC secretariat in the mid-1980s, and through its subsequent expansion. However, the arguments over the precise scope of an EC CFSP showed the extent to which this remained an essentially contested arena. As such, aspirations and expectations will continue to outstrip the capacity to deliver. The gap between them could prove damaging in the defence arena, broadly conceived. Even then, statements of intent by the EC acting through the Troika, the European Council or EPC, should not be dismissed merely as rhetoric. The aspirations are gradually being matched by political and economic resources. The statements provide at the very least, therefore, a clue as to the direction the EC expects to take. Its civilian power image will not readily be forfeited despite increasing pressure for it to become both a more unified and a more politically strident actor on the international scene.

Defence: The Complicating Factor

The disintegration of the Soviet bloc and, to a lesser extent perhaps, the US policy of burden-shedding, provided potent stimuli for reappraising policy direction in a recession hit Western world. While EC member states were under no illusion that European security was multi-faceted and rested not just on the maintenance and preservation of the Western Alliance but also on the extension of economic prosperity to Central and Eastern Europe, initial euphoria spawned an interest in so-called 'new European architectures.' Preoccupation with such ideas masked the failure to establish a strategic culture which might have made the transition of the EC from its civilian power mind-set to a credible foreign and security policy player more credible and attainable.

As it was, many of the ideas were reminiscent of those for a pan-European and Central European security pact mooted within West Germany and the USSR during the 1950s. They were predicated on the abolition of existing military pacts and either the creation of a nuclear-free central European security peace zone, or on some geographically amorphous but ill-defined neutral security zone. However, political reality meant that these ideas had to give way to a realization (and even relief) that the traditional systems of the West were not to be so readily superseded. Consequently, the role of existing alliance arrangements was reappraised. The concern that an expansion in the EC's competencies would inevitably compromise its relations with WEU and NATO and might even result in competition between the EC and NATO for military supremacy and leadership in Europe led to more sober assessments.

By the early 1990s, a multi-organizational web of interlocking, predominantly functional and complementary arrangements was foreseen. Once again, however, and probably inevitably, the precise parameters of each organization's responsibilities developed from their existing competencies. A civilianization of all their activities seemed to attract policy-makers who felt that the end of the Cold War meant that military preoccupations could be seriously pruned to allow the organizations to focus on the socio-economic, political/civilian rather than purely military functions. This inevitably made for potential overlap and contradictions among them.

For its part, the EC began to contemplate the operational consequences of its seeking to develop a CFSP. The rapidly changing regional milieu, however, meant that its views constantly had to adapt. New architectures lost some of their initial magnetism. The old certainties, as seen in the continuation of traditional structures like NATO, then seemed increasingly attractive, and not necessarily only as medium term arrangements.

Simultaneously, the EC confronted internal and external expectations of it assuming a leading role in the regional milieu in establishing fora to discuss and promote issues of common concern. In 1990, for a short time, the EC had a preponderant weight in the rapidly expanding CSCE which, following the UN lead, ceded such a role to it in respect of Yugoslavia. The UN Secretary General was initially persuaded that regional organizations, in cooperation with the UN, should have an extended role in the maintenance of international peace and security and that the EC and CSCE were obvious candidates for such a role, especially since the UN had severe budgetary problems and rival claims on its resources to sort out. Some member states, notably France, concurred that the CSCE had explicitly delegated the role to the EC as it had itself failed to promote consensus based on shared norms and goals.

The 1990 Paris Charter was an interesting illustration of the tension between reconciling security demands perceived in terms of defence and military insecurities and those seen in terms of promoting normative values and attachment to freedom of expression, tolerance, liberal democratic values and respect for human rights – all of which went under the loose banner of a 'civilianization of security' and its projection via a concept of a human face to security. There were unmistakable echoes of the 1970s' preoccupations both at Helsinki and within the EC when a Community with a human face temporarily assumed prominence. The need to shift from defence to dialogue also partly impelled the establishment of the NACC in December 1991. Seen as an alternative to NATO membership for the new states of the CIS and Central and Eastern Europe, it was designed to foster dialogue through the cultivation of civilian, humanitarian objectives. As such it was seen as a forum for socializing the nascent democracies into Western liberal democratic ways of thinking about international affairs. Confronted by a clamour for membership by the same states, the EC also sought alternative ways of involving them in deliberations on matters of common interest without conceding full membership of the Community. This indicated an arrangement based on the Norwegian formula of 1982 (whereby Norway had observer status in EPC). Only much later, in early 1993, was the EC prepared to add a further rider to the list of criteria it had outlined as preconditions for membership of the European Union, namely that enlargement should not dilute integration.

In the meantime, the EC was faced with the problem of defining a military/defence capacity for itself. Much time was spent trying to determine whether the WEU should be seen as a bridge between the EC and NATO or as the putative military wing of the EC. Clearly, the idea that the WEU could be the EU's defence arm and provide a security guarantee for countries unable or unwilling to accede to the WEU and NATO was both questionable and disingenuous. Equally, talk of partial accession to the CFSP/WEU or NATO for Central and East European states (as, for example, Associates Partners under WEU) not yet admitted to the EU was fraught with difficulties. Moreover, it raised excessive expectations among them of what the Western states might be willing to deliver and increased tension within the disintegrating former Soviet Union. The ill-understood differences between the promotion of 'a common defence' following the eventual framing of 'a common defence policy' foreseen under the Common Provisions of Title I of the Maastricht treaty within the EU also exacerbated confusion. Article J1(2) assigned five principal objectives to the CFSP: i) safeguarding common values, fundamental interests and the independence of the Union; ii) strengthening its security; iii) preserving peace and strengthening international security; iv) promoting international cooperation; and v) developing and consolidating democracy and the rule of law, and respect for human rights and fundamental freedoms. The terms defence/defence policy and security were used often unwittingly interchangeably. As Commission President Santer stated: 'European identity is not a simple fact of life. It is based on the intuitive certainty of a joint destiny, but it is also the product of a slow process of diplomatic negotiation.'[17]

The EC, WEU and NATO: A Human Face to Security?

The EC's main concern was how, in the absence of a treaty base giving it precise military competence and responsibilities, it was to deal with the new security agenda which had both internal (asylum, immigration, refugees, illegal movements of people) and external dimensions. Its preoccupation with finding a framework within which to elaborate and pursue security, and especially defence, matters was both necessary and, to some extent, a distraction. It was necessary since several EC members were neither in NATO nor in WEU and the highly sensitive question of their role in determining policy and financing its implementation, when they were not prepared to provide logistical/manpower support had to be solved. It was a distraction in that it meant that debate on the potential relationship between the EC and its putative defence arm – a revived WEU – deterred contingency planning within the EC and EPC at a time of acute regional turbulence. In short, it put off the day when the EC would have to decide whether and precisely how it was going to engage as a military player in the security realm. (This was even underscored in the Maastricht deliberations and ensuing TEU by the fact that the terms of reference for any future defence policy were made subject to another IGC.) That the EC was being viewed as a pole of stability and security in an increasingly insecure regional milieu also had implications for its organization, agenda and competencies. These required bold responses but conflicted with its civilian power image. However, at the start of the decade, the military dimension dominated public discussion and the EC seemed almost in a haphazard fashion to become attracted to projecting a civilian or human face to security. Yet such a construct for itself tied in with an expansion of its external responsibilities into the security sector and fitted its civilian power pretensions.

Equally, however, it must be recognized that the EC members did have genuine reasons for wanting to project the EC's regional and international interests as distinct and independent. The civilian power/human face to security imagery matched this aspiration and fitted in with the EC's intrinsic financial, logistical and political weaknesses in this area. The question was how to achieve a security potential of sorts without developing a full-blown supranational defence capacity which remained anathema to most EC members. Arguably even those committed to the Euro-army might have found their rhetoric tested had supranationalization really been on the cards.

The effect was to raise the potential importance of WEU as the forum through which relevant European states could assert an independent policy-line from that of the US and, formally, from NATO, although operational tasks tended to be subsumed within NATO. Indeed, during the Gulf war, WEU had been used for operational cooperation. However, few laboured under the illusion that European security could be maintained without NATO's shield. Moreover, the Gulf war and the escalating crisis in Yugoslavia served to highlight the discrepancies between the member states, the extent to which an EC defence capacity remained illusory, and the need for existing organizations to reform their rules in such a manner as to develop a capacity to enable them to take rapid action on NATO's flanks.[18] WEU took this on board publicly only relatively late in the day when in February 1993, van Eekelen mooted the development of an out-of-area rapid reaction capability.[19]

While there was some discussion about the propriety of EU members accepting the Atlantic commitments of the NATO and WEU members, it soon became clear that there was no viable alternative to the EU pledging its support, under the CFSP, for the continuation of respect for Atlantic commitments entered into in 1949. How this is to be squared with independence in policy making remains to be seen. Events precipitated changes in the often fragmented and confused EU mind-set.

The operational needs for a trouble-shooting and peace-keeping capacity in the regional milieu outpaced the ad hoc structural reforms and thinking of European politicians. This is not to suggest that these needs were not recognized. Rather, they conflicted with the rationale behind national policies dedicated to cutting defence expenditure in line with official perceptions of the decline of the Soviet military threat. Moreover, the EC/EU members were overwhelmed by the exponential increase in the competing number of demands facing them.

Yugoslavia proved a severe test of the EC's potential as a regional security actor with a human face able to invoke and implement a CFSP able to deliver on its commitments and meet the operational requirements of any obligations that it undertook. Not only was it was necessary simultaneously to fix rules of engagement but the newly emerging states had to be encouraged to accept and agree on codes of conduct, norms, values and common rules. More importantly, from the EC's point of view – and from that of the UN – it was essential to assert a new principle, namely, that the use of force, for the purpose of humanitarian intervention, could be legitimate. The latter principle was novel and could not be established overnight. It breached the fundamental principle of non-intervention in the domestic affairs of sovereign states. The interaction between the UN and EC/EU, and those two and WEU, NATO, and CSCE on this theme was particularly significant. The development of the Eurocorps, the 'Petersburg tasks' agreed by the WEU and NATO, the EUROFOR and EUROMARFOR decisions of May 1995, and the assignment of NATO forces to WEU missions, highlighted the continuing reliance on the US.

LIMITED CAPABILITIES: ROLE AS A REGIONAL ACTOR?

The prospect of enlargement to the north, south and east posed innumerable problems for the EC. Key issues included i) the impact on a CFSP of the accession of states (other than traditional neutrals) not sharing common preoccupations and recent history with the EC; ii) the need to create a sense of 'community' without dissipating the Union through too rapid a widening without simultaneous deepening; iii) the economic and trade implications for the EC and for the rest of the world of an enlarged EC becoming potentially more self-sufficient and possibly less vulnerable to the vicissitudes of international trade; iv) the ready abandonment of the artificial distinction between external relations and external security; and v) the willingness of the EC to meet the challenges of enlargement by radical internal institutional reform genuinely designed to enhance its capacity to act domestically and internationally. Reconciling these different elements accentuated the EC's need to achieve a balance between what Delors called the EC's essential common interests and the level of ambition. Improving the capacity to act in the short to medium term remains the *sine qua non* of the EC/Union achieving balance in its international dealings.

The pressure for enlargement precipitated a debate on deepening and widening the EC but became irresistible with German unification following the collapse of the Berlin wall. Central and East European states were anxious to prevent the former GDR from stealing a march on them and gaining what they saw as preferential treatment and early accession to the EC. The position was complicated by the GDR's pattern of trade flows which, until then, had resulted in two-thirds of its exports going to COMECON, and by its bilateral agreements with Comecon members for exchange of goods exempted from customs duties, and by investment agreements with the USSR, Poland and Czechoslovakia which included zero rates of duty on some goods. Its integration into the EC was, therefore, likely to cause a number of political, economic and legal problems. The GDR's earlier *de facto* participation in EC trade through its special relationship with the Federal Republic of Germany, however, coupled with unification via accession to the FRG resulted in a widening of the scope of the EC's territory without a concomitant enlargement of its members. Legislation was pushed through within six months[20] and apart from pressure to increase the size of Germany's representation in the European Parliament from 81 to 99 Members of the European Parliament (MEPs), the political weight of Germany's representation remained static, at least officially. No other would-be member could conceivably be absorbed into the EC in a similar way. This left the way open for speculation as to the changing architecture of the new Europe.

Within months of the 1989 Euro-elections, Commission President Delors and French President Mitterrand canvassed the notion of a Europe of concentric circles: at the hub was the EC ringed by EFTA/European Economic Area (EEA), the Council of Europe, the CSCE and the North Atlantic Assembly. Initial suggestions that the outer rings formed a 'waiting room' for incipient new democracies seeking EC membership gave way to a more sober assessment of the functional arrangements between them. It quickly became clear that the competence and aspirations of the different rings overlapped and the potential for contradictory policy among them was large. Moreover, the end of the Cold War precipitated a rethink within NATO as to its future role and an attendant re-focusing on its potential for promoting economic and socio-political cooperation. Of all these institutions, however, only the EC clearly had the capacity routinely to legislate in a manner binding on all its members. It inevitably occupied a special position in all the scenarios presented at this time.[21] By 1992, there was much less optimism that any of the other institutions could match their aspirations. The CSCE was too diffuse and organizationally weak to constitute a genuine and credible policy-making and policy enforcement agency for devising, constructing and regulating a new security order. Increasingly, Central and East European countries turned to and sought membership of NATO as the security guarantor. The Council of Europe was useful as an organization to socialize the emergent democracies to West European political norms and behaviour but was no substitute for full membership of the EC. The emerging EEA, once seen as a half-way house to EC accession, began to disintegrate from within as its own members clamoured for rapid EC membership. In brief, there was a sense in which the concentric circles vision of the new European architecture implied competition between them: the prize was EC membership. Whereas, economically, this was understandable, the EC lacked the political clout or desire to assume a key position at the apex of such a structure.

As a result of the erosion of confidence in the idea of the concentric circles, the need for a concept of interlocking institutions with complementary functions was gradually appreciated. While such a vision was broadly accepted by 1993, in the interim the EC had to adjust to the prospect of rapid enlargement. As in the past, when confronted by enlargement, it reacted by contemplating both the internal, institutional and organizational consequences of enlargement, and appraising the implications for its external relations and role in the international environment. In so far as crude parallels may be drawn between enlargement rounds, the wave of enlargement to the north was comparable in its anticipated internal effects to the first EC enlargement in 1973, whereas that implied by the continuing pressure from Central and Eastern Europe was seen as roughly analogous to the Mediterranean enlargements in posing greater economic, as well as significant political, problems for the EC. There can be little doubt that the prospect of enlargement affected the IGC deliberations on the level and scope of further integration and encouraged the member states both to be more audacious in the short to medium term and implicitly to set a further target for consolidating a deepening of the Community by the mid-1990s.

Widening and Deepening: The EC and EFTA, Towards the EEA

Preoccupied with realizing the Single Market, the EC raised the stakes of membership (as it had done on the eve of every previous enlargement) by deepening integration and expanding its scope through the deliberations on European Union. As in the case of the Single Act deliberations[22] the member states advanced political union by focusing on institutional reforms essential to augmenting the EC's capacity to act.[23] Old taboos were abandoned and the realities of the new security dilemmas recognized. The incompatibility of neutrality with adherence to the European Union with its explicit dependence on the Atlantic Alliance was proclaimed and neutral applicants had to weigh up the advances of full EC membership against the abandonment of absolute neutrality.[24]

When two founding members of EFTA, the UK and Denmark, joined the EC in 1973 free trade agreements were concluded with remaining EFTA members to avoid the re-establishment of tariff barriers. A duty- and quota-free European space for industrial products was created and gradually extended.[25] However, a fully functioning genuine free trade area between the EC and EFTA had not materialized. The EC's commitment to realizing a single market worried EFTA states that new barriers would be created which would preclude that goal. This was seen by them as indicative not only of a Fortress Europe mentality but as imperilling their future prosperity. The reasons for this were clear: the EC is EFTA's principal trading partner. Between 1985 and 1991, EFTA's share of the EC market rose from 8.9% to 22.4%. Denmark's imports were almost equally balanced between EFTA and the EC. In 1991, 25% of EC exports went to EFTA.[26] In an EC-EFTA economic zone, 70% of trade would be conducted among its members. The idea, therefore, of advancing such an economic arrangement, devoid of political commitments to supranationality, was attractive to many EFTA states.

The rapidly evolving situation in Europe outpaced EC-EFTA arrangements and by the beginning of 1993, the EC's position on the potential of EFTA and the EEA (which Switzerland had refused to ratify) had come a full circle. Whereas only months before, the EC had greeted the Central Europeans' quest for early EC membership with suggestions of lengthy transition periods, by February 1993 it indicated that it accepted such a quest as legitimate and the eventual outcome of developing relations with Western Europe. It added the proviso that enlargement could only be considered if it did not dissipate the Union's commitment to further integration. The EC strongly implied that given the set of preconditions set out in the TEU and in numerous Commission speeches, membership would be the culmination of a stepped process which would first involve participation in other European fora, including the EEA. The desire for participation in political deliberations was met by a suggestion that the Norwegian-EPC formula (whereby Norway had enjoyed observer status in EPC since 1982) be adapted to permit Central and Eastern European states to observe and participate (but not vote) in EPC deliberations. Significantly, similar developments were occurring in respect of their links with NATO bodies and the WEU.

Above all, what this indicated was a reappraisal by the EC of the desirability of pressing ahead with enlargement in line with the pace of applications for membership. With the EC's new set of association agreements with Poland, Hungary, the Czech and Slovak republics set to expire in 2002, early accession to the EU or recognition of special status for them began to be mooted. However, there can be little doubt that the EU wanted to impose a more realistic timetable on enlargement to the North and to the East and saw its new criteria as a means of coping with the accession bids of Turkey, Malta, Cyprus and others. The prospect of numerous small states becoming EU members and asking for representation in EC institutions on a par with Luxembourg severely tested the ingenuity of constitutional lawyers and worried EC officials that the whole system would become too fragmented, divided, disparate and unworkable. However, until 1993, the EC had refrained from contesting the timetable being foisted on it by applicants as any demurral was seen as diplomatically insensitive and politically unacceptable, especially if couched in terms of the EC's self-interest. After all, many would-be members were relatively poor and the EC was rich. Moral considerations behoved, it was thought, the EC to embrace the less fortunate. Experience of integrating the five new *Länder* had, however, tempered this idealism with realism.

THE EC, INTER-REGIONALISM AND A CFSP

The EC-EFTA negotiations illustrated an emerging trend in the EC's relations with other states in the regional and international system, namely an increasing preference for structured group-to-group links and inter-regional cooperation. Initially, Germany saw the EC-EFTA arrangement as a model for the development of EC relations with Central and Eastern Europe. While bound by the Interlaken principles as to the priority attached to EC integration, decision-making and autonomy, some in the Commission clearly favour inter-regionalism.[27] Moreover, pressures outside the narrowly defined trade and commercial sectors also seem to push in that direction, at least where European links are concerned. Experience with the Gulf Cooperation Council and with ASEAN superficially supports structured group-to-group links but it cannot be inferred that this is either the only or the optimal way of developing effective relations. It may simply be that this is a way of coping administratively given limited personnel and financial resources to manage relations with diverse states around the world. Political realities and sensitivities can, however, militate against such an approach. While predictability may be injected into such relationships for all parties, and particularly by third country actors facing complex intra-EC bargaining, multilateral cooperation is not simply a means of managing

global interdependence. [28] It establishes and structures and continuing
political dialogue and creates sets of, sometimes unrealizable, expectations. This in turn affects the member states' foreign offices' deliberations and bilateral interactions with states in the corresponding region.
Overall, there is an effect on policy-making both within the EC and EPC
which leads towards the pragmatic evolution of the rudiments of a CFSP.
Deepening is being consolidated in part through the cumulative impact
of long-standing relations with states in the international system. This is
cemented by the Single European Act which, by codifying EPC, imbued
it with a personality in international law and associated its outputs with
the EC's legal order. [29] The TEU, therefore, consolidated and made more
transparent a process that demanded a commitment to the attainment of
a common foreign and security policy. However, the symbolic importance of such a commitment outweighs the actual ability of the EC to
deliver. Operational and military constraints inevitably inhibit its
evolution: the EC's locus of political authority has yet to be adequately
clarified in such a sensitive arena which impinges on the heart of
member states' sovereignty.

THE CFSP

The CFSP is not a sudden break with past practice. It represents a
refinement and a limited rationalization of EC external activities
including trade, aid and diplomacy. The TEU embraces three concept-
ually distinct, if operationally intertwined, key elements that potentially
will have a cumulative impact on the CFSP's shape. The three are:
external trade with its own chapter on common commercial policy
(corresponding to past practice); development cooperation subject to EPC
(appearing for the first time and a throw-over from the Single European
Act (SEA) negotiations when the Dutch were persuaded to drop it from
the short term agenda); and the coordination of foreign policy (formerly
Title III of the SEA and now consolidated in new provisions on the
CFSP under a new Title V; like Title III of the SEA, Title V escapes the
ECJ's control.) This section remains strictly intergovernmental though
subject to the general exhortation in Article C of the common provisions
to ensure consistency in the Union's 'external activities as a whole,' and
to assertion of the Union international identity in the preamble, common
provisions and Article B.
   The CFSP is to include all questions of security, including the
eventual framing of a common defence policy 'which might in time lead

to a common defence' (Article J4). How soon that may be is open to conjecture and to circumstance. But it is telling that the same Treaty article refers to the possibility of revision in the light of the 1998 expiry of WEU (Article J4(6)). The Member States are to support the Union's external and security policy 'actively and unreservedly in a spirit of loyalty and mutual solidarity' (Article J2(4)). To that end, they are to refrain from any action contrary to the Union's interests or likely to impair its effectiveness as a cohesive force in international relations.

The aspirations, as is typical of the EC, are worded in a way open to expansive interpretation. They are not yet matched by sufficient supranational decision rules to permit the development of a restrictive CFSP. Nor is such intended. It is instructive that commitment to a single foreign policy is absent. The intergovernmentalism of the SEA is retained.

The Presidency is to represent the Union in CFSP matters. It is to be responsible for its implementation, and for the expression of the Union's position in international organizations and international conferences. The Troika is to assist in this and the Commission is to be 'fully associated.' That phrase is open to varying interpretation but it is obvious that as with EPC, Commission participation at the table will be essential for operational reasons.

The member states have specific obligations vis-à-vis each other. As with EPC, consultation and information exchange are paramount, especially in instances where only some of the Union's members are members of international organizations where decisions that potentially affect the Union may be taken. UN Security Council member states are to 'concert and keep the other Member States fully informed' (Article J5(4)). The permanent members are, in the execution of their functions, to ensure the defence of the positions and interests of the Union, without prejudice to their responsibilities under the UN Charter's provisions. Diplomatic and consular missions of the member states and the Commission delegations in third countries and international conferences and international organizations are enjoined to cooperate in ensuring that the Council's common positions and measures are complied with and implemented. There may be further steps towards joint missions between member states and the Commission although to date the experimental Franco-German joint representation in Mongolia has not been copied.[30] Cooperation is to be strengthened by information exchange, the execution of joint assessments and in the protection of 'EC citizens' (Article 8c).

The European Council is to define the CFSP's principles and general guidelines. On a day-to-day basis, the EPC Secretariat, to be subsumed in the Council's General Secretariat, will play a prominent but supportive role. The locus of action remains the Council. The Council takes decisions necessary for defining and implementing it in line with the general guidelines. The Council is enjoined to ensure 'the unity, consistency and effectiveness of action by the Union'(Article J8). It acts unanimously except for procedural questions and when, in the process of developing and adopting joint action which is normally subject to qualified majority voting, it decides that unanimity is required (Article J3(2)).

Any member state or the Commission may refer any questions on the CFSP to the Council. The states' autonomy is further enhanced by giving them the right, alongside the Commission, to make proposals to the Council on the CFSP. The Political Committee (of Political Directors) also has a right of own initiative and may contribute to the definition of policies by giving opinions to the Council at the Council's request or at its own initiative. It also falls to it to monitor the international situation in areas covered by the CFSP and to monitor the implementation of agreed policies without prejudice to the responsibilities of the Presidency and the Commission (Article J8). CFSP expenditure is to be financed either from the EC's budget or, on the basis of a unanimous decision, be charged to the member states in accordance with a scale to be decided (Article J11).

Defining the CFSP

The Council is the primary decision-making organ. Building on experience in EPC and especially under the SEA, its role is expanded by the TEU. The consultation and information exchange among the member states within the Council is designed to facilitate the most effective exertion of their combined influence by means of concerted and convergent action. This latitude permits deviations and does not require a uniform or harmonized policy. The Council is not required to define a common position. Instead, it retains discretion in deciding when a common position is necessary. Then, the member states are obliged to ensure that their national policies conform to the common position which they are obliged to uphold, by means of coordinated action, in international fora.

The Council assumes an equally strong position in determining whether, on the basis of European Council guidelines, an issue should be subject to joint action. While this could be a source of discrepancy and disagreement, the Council lays down the specific scope, the Union's general and specific objectives in carrying out joint action, its duration, means, procedures and conditions for its implementation. This is normally to be done by unanimity. Since this is a severe constraint, the result is likely to be either a weak CFSP, or a lowest common denominator approach to joint actions which might deter a bold approach and the adoption of joint action in the first place. This possibility is strengthened by the fact that only if a change in circumstances has a substantial effect in a question subject to joint action will the Council review it and take the necessary decisions. As long as the Council does not act, the joint action stands. Therefore, for procedural and political reasons states have to be very sure indeed that they want a joint action to start with because once it is adopted they are committed by it (Article J3 (3 and 4). Moreover, except for transposition measures, any plan to adopt a national position or to take national action pursuant to a joint action has to be notified to the Council with sufficient time for prior consultation within the Council. This obligation is weakened by the proviso that states may invoke 'imperative need' in cases of urgency providing that they inform the Council immediately. It is weakened further by another escape clause on the implementation of joint action. In case of major difficulty, states may refer them to the Council for discussion and solution. Such solutions may not run counter to the joint action's goals or impair its effectiveness, but they could be tantamount to a derogation.

Democratic control over the CFSP is as weak as is the case in national polities even though the European Parliament has somewhat greater powers of oversight in respect of the EPC than do national parliaments over national foreign policies.[31] In the CFSP, the EP has but a limited role. The Presidency is obliged to consult it on the main aspects and basic choices of the CFSP and is to ensure that its views are taken into account. This gives each Presidency a great deal of discretion to set positive precedents or to evade MEPs. Some Presidencies may interpret consultation in the limited terms of keeping the EP regularly informed about the development of the CFSP. The Commission is also obliged to do this and it is conceivable that it, too, would interpret the obligation restrictively. On the other hand, it may find it desirable to cultivate links with the EP in this area and so provide MEPs with useful information that they could turn to good account. The EP retains the right to question the Council and acquires the right to make recommendations to it. It may also hold an annual debate on progress in implementing the CFSP. These powers will no doubt be used in conjunction with its other powers of intervention, own initiative and urgency procedures which often involve foreign policy issues.

However, it must be remembered that since the EP sets its own agenda, it may deliberate on foreign policy issues that fall outside the scope of the CFSP. Where rapid decisions are required, moreover, there will be no chance for prior consultation with the EP. The Presidency will act on its own initiative, or at the request of the Commission or a member state, to convene an extraordinary Council meeting within 48 hours or, in an emergency, within a shorter period still. This conforms to current practice and means that consultation with the EP is likely to be post hoc and sporadic, or of limited usefulness if compressed into regular meetings with Foreign Ministers as before. Moreover, in times of crisis, member states do not always honour their commitment to consult each other in advance of taking action. Two examples of this norm being flouted recently include British support for US action against Libya in 1986 and French diplomacy on the eve of the Gulf war in 1991. Similar consultation deficits emerged during the escalation of the Yugoslav crisis in late 1990/91. The new TEU does not prevent or significantly discourage unilateral action by member states. As a result the credibility of the CFSP could be hard to establish. This is more likely to happen if states are unclear as to which issues are subject to CFSP and which are not. Differences of nuance and political sensitivity could easily be missed by third countries who expect, rightly or wrongly, the CFSP to exist in all areas of the EC's international activity. The practice of political cooperation and the activity of the Twelve within international organiz- ations, including the UN, suggests a move away from the '*domaines resérvés*' approach which tries to separate national interests sharply from the EC's general interest. While this approach is retained in the TEU, it may prove difficult to apply credibly as external pressure for a genuine CFSP continues to grow. Equally, it would be unhelpful to exaggerate the extent of solidarity among the Twelve simply by alluding to statistics which, as in the UN, show the Twelve voting together a little over half the time and mitigating differences the rest of the time. The relative importance of issues may account for sharp disagreement at times. Nevertheless, the trend towards a common voice persists.

The EP's foreign affairs role itself tends to suggest that the EC has far more coherent interests and a cohesive voice in international affairs than is in fact the case. It will therefore be important for the Presidency and the Commission to take their obligations vis-à-vis the EP seriously. What militates against the Council and the Presidency being too cavalier towards the EP are the EP's powers in respect of enlargement, associ- ation and treaties with financial implications. The SEA stressed the need for consistency between the economic and political aspects of external relations, and there are grounds for believing that the EC sometimes achieves greater consistency where it has a degree of economic influence. It would, therefore, be sensible for procedures to be developed to allow for genuine consultation, always bearing in mind the need for secrecy in many diplomatic activities and the impossibility of advance public parliamentary debate on sensitive measures, especially in security and defence areas. Similarly, the Commission's reallocation of portfolios at the end of 1992 was designed to instill greater coherence into its activities bearing on external affairs.

The sophistication of procedural and institutional devices will not mask policy failure. Given the impossibility, at this stage, of turning the EC into a federal state with a single foreign policy, a balance has to be struck between enabling it to act efficiently, credibly and coherently in accordance with its self-proclaimed norms and values, financial and logistical resources, and allowing member states to retain freedom of action in areas of particular national interest. Tensions will persist given the diverse backgrounds of the member states' histories and overseas obligations and interests. But the TEU is a step towards engendering a belief and genuine commitment among them to advancing a capability to speak increasingly with a common if not a single voice.

It is logical that this should be tested in the geopolitical arena of immediate interest to them. It does not mean that this will negate their involvement elsewhere although it may inevitably result in a reordering of priorities. Without the means to match its goals, the EC/Union will prove disappointing. Without the institutions and procedures to lend continuity and stability to the venture, little may be achieved. Without a commitment to continuing review of experience in this most sensitive of fields and without an albeit crude but necessary attempt to try and define what it stands for, the EU's endeavour to advance a CFSP could falter in the wake of competing external pressures and unrealistic demands and expectations. Consequently, the immediate and future challenge to the EU in this area is to develop both the ways and means of developing a CFSP that will enable it to respond effectively, coherently and credibly to international events. In the longer term, it may well augment its very weak capacity to take foreign policy initiatives. In the meantime, the big and sensitive matters of security and defence will inevitably remain tied to Atlantic considerations. Logistical and operational capabilities of an independent European sort are on the cards and being slowly developed but, for the foreseeable future, they are unlikely to function in isolation from arrangements that have served the member states well in the past.

The Union's role in the international arena in the light of enlarge-ment presents further challenges to the EU. There is a danger that the new Union will not be in a position to deal with the rising third state 'expectation overload' of it unless and until it resolves numerous issues associated with resourcing and with internal and external security. Unless institutional and political preconditions of effective action are dealt with and the Union is empowered to act, unless internal weaknesses are addressed, the EC/Union will fail to influence significantly the develop-ment of any new European security system. Its members must accept that if different historical traditions are used to dissipate attempts to foster the CFSP and to achieve common action for the common good, then the Union's credibility as an international and regional actor will be seriously eroded with severe consequences for the new Europe.

THE EU: BEYOND A REGIONAL CIVILIAN POWER?

The absence of a centre of political authority in the EU and the consequent reliance on a system of intergovernmental bargaining in the field of foreign affairs was severely tested during the Yugoslav crisis. Regional imperatives, US reticence to become involved, the effects of the USSR's disintegration and the clamour for independence and interna-tional statehood among the COMECON group created the impression that in the European sea of turbulence the EC was an island of stability. Against its wishes, the EC came to be drawn into the Yugoslav crisis. International expectations of it playing a determinant role in mediating in and solving the crisis helped to create a situation in which the normal EPC reactions to international crises were to be supplanted by direct intervention. At the time when the EC became involved, not only had the Maastricht treaty not been ratified but the EC was engaged in the IGC process itself. The EC's unfurling response to Yugoslav developments coloured the deliberations on the CFSP. It is easy to criticize the EC's response as inadequate. But, measured against its actual legal competence to do anything beyond making condemnatory rhetorical statements backed by the withdrawal of economic assistance, it did edge towards a common coherent position in the face of internal divisions that observers may well have seen as insuperable before. In addition, it must be recalled that the EC lacked the financial resources, budget line, military resources, personnel and political capacity to react as a government might have. It had not engaged in contingency planning. It could not direct personnel (including military personnel and the logistical resources to back up operational operations). It lacked technical expertise. EPC, itself, was subject to the six-month rotation of the EC Presidency (with all that implied for continuity) and the member governments were divided over whether to intervene and, if so, what form any intervention should take. There was also a strong sense that any intervention (even humanitarian intervention) needed the prior approval and legitimation of the UN.

While the Yugoslav saga did not confirm the EC's capacity to deliver a CFSP, it did condition its development. It also confronted the member states with the reality of their rhetoric in favour of a CFSP when they still proclaimed that the EU was a civilian power. The incongruities between rhetoric and reality had to be resolved. This, too, affected the IGC deliberations and helped member states to accept a defence dimension through the WEU and NATO that would have been unthinkable months before. The EU wishes to retain its civilian power image and objectives but now recognizes that they cannot be upheld and defended nor effectively and credibly advocated, promoted or implemented unless their sense of common identity, purpose and security is safeguarded by military mechanisms through NATO and the WEU. A separate EU military capability is neither sought nor wanted. A credible CFSP and international role is. The former makes the latter possible.

NOTES

1. High-level Group of Experts European, *Security Towards 2000: Ways and Means to Establish Genuine Credibility*, Brussels, 19 Dec 1994.
2. J. Santer, 'The European Union's Security and Defence Policy,' *NATO Review*, November 1995, p.6.
3. *Commission Report for the Reflection Group Intergovernmental Conference 1996*, 1995, p.66.
4. P. Ludlow with N. Ersboll, *Towards 1996: The Agenda of the Inter-Governmental Conference*, CEPS, Brussels, 1995, p.30.
5. P.Tsakaloyannis, 'From Civilian Power to Military Integration,' in J. Lodge (ed.), *The EC and the Challenge of the Future*, Pinter, London, 1989.
6. F. Duchene, 'The European Community and the Uncertainties of Interdependence,' in M. Kohnstamm and W. Hager (eds), *A Nation Writ Large?*, Macmillan, London, 1973.
7. Cf. J. Galtung, *Europe in the Making*, Crane Russak, New York, 1990.
8. H. Bull, 'Civilian Power Europe: A Contradiction in Terms?,' *Journal of Common Market Studies*, Vol.21, 1982.
9. J. Delors, 'The Role of the EC in the Future World System,' in A. Clesse and R. Vernon (eds), *The European Community after 1992*, Nomos, Baden-Baden, 1991; J. Delors 'European Integration and Security,' *Survival*, Vol.33, 1991. Statement to the European Parliament, *EC Bulletin*, Suppl.1/90, 36.

10. P. Taylor, 'Supranationalism: The Power and Authority of International Institutions,' in A.J.R. Groom and P. Taylor (eds.), *Frameworks for International Cooperation*, Pinter, London, 1991, p.120.

11. *Ibid*, p.114.

12. B. Buzan, *et. al.*, *The European Security Order Recast*, Macmillan, London, 1990; W. Wallace (ed.), *The Dynamics of European Integration*, Macmillan, London, 1991.

13. G. Sjostedt, *The External Role of the European Community*, Saxon House, Farnborough, 1977.

14. I. Damgaard Petersen, 'The Role of the EC in an Emerging New World Order,' in M. Kelstrup (ed.), *European Integration and Denmark's Participation*, Institute of Political Science, Copenhagen, 1992, p.89.

15. *Ibid.*, p.95.

16. Galtung, *op. cit.*, 26ff.

17. Santer, *op. cit*, p.1.

18. M. Weller, 'The International Response to the Dissolution of the Socialist Republic of Yugoslavia,' *The American Journal of International Law*, Vol.86, 1992, pp.569-607.

19. *Europe*, 14-16 February 1993.

20. Commission of the EC, *The Community and German Unification*, COM(90) 400 final. Vols I and II SYN 297-302, Brussels.

21. M. Telo (ed.), *Vers une nouvelle Europe?*, Universite Libre, Brussels, 1992.

22. J. Lodge, 'Plurilateralism and the Single European Act,' in W. Zartmann (ed.), *Multilateral Diplomacy*, (forthcoming).

23. European Commission, *From the Single Act to Maastricht and Beyond: The Means to Match our Ambitions*, Brussels, 11 February 1992.

24. R. Ruffieux, *La Suisse et son Avenir Européen*, Payot, Lausanne, 1989.

25. K. Ewig, 'The Development of Relations Between the European Community and EFTA in the Perspective of post-1992,' in Clesse and Vernon, *op. cit.*

26. *Target 92*, 8-1992.

27. T. Pedersen, 'EC-EFTA Relations: Neighbours in Search of a New Partnership,' in G. Edwards and E. Regelsberger (eds.), *Europe's Global Links*, Pinter, London, 1990.

28. E. Regelsberger, 'The Dialogue of the EC/Twelve with Other Regional Groups: a New European Identity in the International System?' in Edwards and Regelsberger, *ibid.*, p.12.

29. S. Nuttall, *European Political Cooperation*, Clarendon, Oxford, 1992, p.239.

30. Regelsberger, *op. cit.*, p.32.

31. J. Lodge, 'The European Parliament and Foreign Policy,' in M. Sondhi (ed.), *Foreign Policy and Legislatures*, Abhinav, New Delhi, 1988; F. Jacobs & R. Corbett, *The European Parliament*, Longman, London, 1990.

5 Manifest Destiny and the Pacific Century: Europe as No.3?

Robert O'Brien

Reflecting upon the changes of the early post-Cold War era, the Director of the Washington based think-tank Institute for International Economics argued that future US foreign policy would be characterized by the 'primacy of economics.'[1] With the end of the bipolar nuclear standoff, attention would move to economic relations between the triad powers in Europe, the Americas and East Asia. Security concerns would still exist, but they would not be the primary focus of US foreign policy as they had been in the Cold War environment. Although such an argument might be expected from the head of an economics institute, there is substantial support both for the view that economic issues are increasingly salient and that the rise of the Asia-Pacific region is a major challenge to US policy.

Any review of transatlantic relations, such as the collection of work in this book, can benefit from an examination of the increasing importance of economic issues and the shift in the global context in which those relations take place. This chapter considers one aspect of the global context – the movement to regional integration in the Americas and Asia-Pacific and its implications for the United States and the transatlantic relationship. It seeks to demonstrate that US priorities have shifted and will continue to shift in response to global competitive pressures. The late 1980s and early 1990s have seen increasing energy being devoted to a North/South axis as economic integration has highlighted US continental and hemispheric concerns. An even greater challenge to the post-1945 role of a Eurocentric US foreign policy comes from the East in the form of intensifying Asia-Pacific relations. Recent developments in the United States' political economy relations in the Americas and the Pacific Rim will be reviewed to gauge the significance for Euro-American relations. The subtitle 'Europe as No.3' is not meant to suggest that Europe's place in the world is behind that of the Americas and the

Asia-Pacific region, but that in many issue areas it has lost ground in US public policy to evolving and long term inter-American and trans-Pacific developments. European policy-makers will increasingly face competition for US attention and efforts will need to be made both to maintain a place on the US agenda and to convince Americans at all levels of the continued importance of transatlantic relationships.

Writing several decades from now commentators may well view the Cold War era and the intricate transatlantic Alliance as an aberration in US foreign relations. The end of the Cold War may mark the return of US policy to a respectful distance from European affairs, active engagement in the Americas and an ongoing attempt to tap the wealth of the Asian market. Increasing economic integration in the Americas and across the Pacific Ocean is raising the relative importance of these areas in US policy. It is accelerating domestic restructuring of work and employment which feeds into the foreign policy process. This changing environment presents new challenges for the transatlantic relationship. Prediction of future US policy is a risky business as numerous groups fight to influence the content of 'national interest.' The outcome of a struggle between the President, Congress, financial contributors to political machines, transnational corporations and social movements cannot be known in advance, but structural trends guiding the debate can be discerned. It is these trends which this chapter seeks to highlight. They include the regionalization of economic activity in a global context, pressures of increased competitiveness (for corporations and individuals) and new military concerns.

The argument is developed in three major sections. Section one examines the increasing role played by continental and hemispheric development in US policy. Key elements include the Canada-United States Free Trade Agreement (CUFTA), the North American Free Trade Agreement (NAFTA) and hemispheric relations. Section two moves on to consider the evolving Asia-Pacific relationship. After interrogating the notions of a Pacific Century and Asia-Pacific integration, the two most important bilateral relationships (US-Japan, US-China) are briefly reviewed. The competitiveness debate, which formerly kept Asian relations prominent in some sections of US foreign economic policy, is now being joined by a renewed security dimension. Section three focuses more directly on the implications of this evolving trend in US interests for European policy-makers intent on nurturing the transatlantic relationship. Prior to examining these areas it is helpful to consider a few thoughts about the global context in which the changes are taking place.

THE GLOBAL CONTEXT

The US move to strengthen its economic ties with regional partners is an aspect of a global trend. Recent years have witnessed an intensification of global competition and an accompanying trend towards regional integration. Within regional areas, business and state elites can cooperate for mutual benefit. Transnational corporations (TNCs) can secure increased mobility, diversity of cheap inputs (including labour), and large markets while states hope to create wealth by enticing global firms to locate production in their territory.[2] This key struggle for investment and profit binds state and economic elites together in the regional building project.

Increasing globalization of production and finance has also resulted in tighter structural constraints which have narrowed policy options for government decision-makers.[3] It should not be surprising that we see similar policies, including regional integration, being undertaken in numerous states. The elites of smaller states have sought protection in regional arrangements so that they can continue to attract investment. In the Asia-Pacific region the increased density of economic interaction has resulted in the need for institutions to manage conflict arising from increased competition and to provide rules for this activity.

The effort to accommodate increased globalization and regionalization intensifies old conflicts and creates new ones. Within states, class based conflict increases as social divisions widen between those that benefit from economic trends and those that are disadvantaged.[4] Conflict between states can erupt either as a result of changing economic fortunes or from pressure exerted because of their inability to compensate those sectors losing out in the new environment. The US restructuring of its relationship with the Americas and the Asia-Pacific region moves these issues higher up the political agenda and will have serious implications for Europeans and the transatlantic relationship.

MANIFEST DESTINY

Manifest Destiny refers to an ideology prominent in United States political affairs in the 1840s, used to justify its expansionism on the North American continent and the seizure of land from Mexico and aboriginal inhabitants. It was claimed that the United States had a mission, sanctioned by natural law, to expand into areas of Mexico, California, Oregon and even Central America and Cuba. A New York newspaper of September 1845 took the logic of expansionism a step further by arguing that the 'arms of the republic, it is clear to all men of sober discernment, must soon embrace the whole hemisphere, from the icy wilderness of the North to the most prolific regions of the smiling and prolific South.'[5]

Dreams of annexation have long since disappeared in the United States, but the parallel desire for hemispheric markets open to US commercial activity seemed to be on the verge of realization in the early 1990s. A free trade agreement with Canada in 1988 was trilateralized to include Mexico in 1992. Simultaneously, the United States government announced its intention to enter into framework discussions for free trade with all other Latin American and Caribbean governments except Cuba. In 1994, the US government reached out to other hemispheric governments through a symbolic Summit of the Americas and became more committed to the survival of the Mexican liberalization initiative with emergency financial aid in 1995. Although efforts at maintaining the newly cooperative relationship with the Americas continue, the potential collapse of the Mexican polity raises doubts about the ambitious US hemispheric vision.

The Canada-US FTA

The 1988 CUFTA was primarily the result of changing Canadian policies in the face of global economic forces. The election of a Conservative government in Canada in 1984 sealed the shift away from a nationalist economic strategy to a more liberal approach. The new government was eager to rebuild relations with the United States which had been damaged by such Canadian policies as the National Energy Program, Foreign Investment Review Agency and protection of cultural industries.[6] The pursuit of a comprehensive free trade agreement gradually became the cornerstone of Canadian economic and foreign policy as it tried to find shelter from US protectionism and to increase the competitiveness of domestic industries.[7]

The United States government saw the Canadian initiative for a free trade agreement as an opportunity to make some sharp points in the multilateral arena and to resolve long standing bilateral issues.[8] Canada represented only approximately 20% of US exports; thus any deal would have to be undertaken with an eye to its effect on the other 80% of US trade. The FTA offered the United States Administration an opportunity to send two signals to its other trading partners. Multilateral negotiations at the GATT had been stalled for a number of years, primarily because of disputes between the United States and its European trading partners. A deal with Canada would serve as a warning that the United States could pursue bilateral options if the multilateral level proved unsatisfactory. Perhaps more important than a warning to other states, the FTA could serve as a precedent for the multilateral round. The United States was eager to expand the GATT to cover new issues such as services, investment and intellectual property rights. A deal with Canada would demonstrate that agreement was possible and might encourage progress in the GATT.

For the US Congress and various industries the bilateral negotiations were an opportunity to resolve issues which had been fermenting for a number of years. Various trade disputes over fish, hogs, pork, softwood lumber, resource pricing and cultural industries had been a source of irritation. In most cases it was alleged that Canadians traded unfairly by subsidizing their exports in a variety of crafty methods. When Canadians complained about the use of US trade law to harass their exports, the Americans countered that if the Canadians ceased subsidizing, trade conflict would disappear.

The subsidy issue almost proved to be intractable. Canadians feared that the changes that the United States was seeking to their domestic political economy threatened basic values and institutions.[9] American trade negotiators were clear that the Congress would not approve any deal which would restrict their ability to enact legislation and target unfair trade practices. As the deadline for agreement approached the Canadian team suspended negotiations pending progress on the US countervailing duty law. A last minute deal produced a binational dispute settlement mechanism through which the Canadians had secured a means to review US cases while the Americans had ensured that their anti-protectionism laws remained in place.

With the acceptance of the FTA, a new economic constitution had been created to regulate the increasingly integrated economies of the world's largest bilateral trading relationship. Tariffs would be eliminated over the course of a decade, investment would flow more freely, a continental energy market was established and a new bilateral dispute settlement mechanism was created. A liberal, continental economy was finally institutionalized following two hundred years of economic relations that had oscillated between free trade and national economy building. United States government officials were satisfied that this institutionalization cemented Canadian policy and resolved a number of bilateral concerns.

Mexico Joins In

The inability of the Mexican government to service its debt burden in 1982 led to the official outbreak of the debt crisis and initiated a transformation in Mexican economic policies. Desperate to secure new sources of capital, the Mexican elite began a wide ranging liberalization programme which eventually led them to petition the United States for a North American Free Trade Agreement. [10] From 1982 to 1992 the Mexican government engaged in a liberal restructuring programme which included large scale privatizations, cuts in government subsidies, the reduction of tariffs and the easing of restrictions on foreign investment. In addition to making the Mexican economy more competitive, the goal of the restructuring was to attract investment. This included large sums of money that Mexicans had moved to the United States and foreign investment from the United States, Japan and Europe.

The initial response of the US to the Mexican calls for negotiations was slow, but the advantages of such a deal soon become apparent. The primary economic advantages would be the ability of US companies to use cheaper Mexican labour and the possibility of exporting to a growing Mexican market. Of these, the most important was the ability of North American firms to compete more effectively against foreign, especially Asian, producers because of low Mexican labour costs. Advocates of the pro-NAFTA strategy raised the possibility that North America could become a low cost producer of automobiles surpassing the Japanese and South Koreans. [11]

Paraphrasing President Clinton's successful election slogan, economist Paul Krugman argued that the NAFTA's economic effect was relatively unimportant and that 'It's Foreign Policy, Stupid.' [12] The US had two strategic objectives in the NAFTA. The first concerned the rewarding and supporting of a key friendly state in Latin America. The traditionally wary policy of the Mexican state to the United States had been replaced by a government for which good relations with the US was of the utmost importance. A NAFTA might support that government by ensuring that investors continued to put money into the economy. A prosperous Mexico would be a stable Mexico. The NAFTA also had the advantage of committing future Mexican governments to maintaining similar liberal policies. In theory, Mexican governments could withdraw from NAFTA, but in practice such a step would spark massive capital flight, effectively making such an option too costly to pursue. It had been over eighty years, during Mexico's pre-revolutionary days, since the US government had the possibility to cement relations with a government so amenable to US corporate interests.

A second strategic issue concerned the flow of Mexican immigrants to the United States. Mexican migration, legal and illegal, to the United States is a complicated issue because some flows are desired, but unrestricted flows are not. Numerous areas of the US economy rely on legal and illegal immigrants to provide cheap labour. Large sectors of the agricultural industry depend upon migrant and illegal labour to harvest crops cheaply. Mexican migrant labour is used for those tasks difficult to move south of the border.

Despite its abundant uses, too large an inflow of immigrants could upset social balances in a way that would undermine economic activity and political stability. A more liberal economic relationship with Mexico might result in the creation of employment within Mexico and slow the movement of immigrants into the United States. With jobs south of the Rio Grande, there would be less incentive to make the difficult, expensive and sometimes dangerous journey to the United States. The movement of people would not be stopped, but might be slowed.

A third possible advantage of responding favourably to the Mexican approach was that the Mexican government might be more open to initiatives in policy areas of concern to the US government.[13] A key issue was drugs. Mexico had become an important country for the trans-shipment of drugs from South America to the United States. A sounder bilateral relationship might allow the US government to press the Mexicans to do more about cracking down on the smuggling of illegal drugs into the United States.

The NAFTA implementing legislation struggled in the US House of Representatives, but was eventually passed in November 1993. A year later the US government was forced to rush to the aid of the Mexican economy in the wake of capital flight. Firmly committed to the Mexican liberalization process, the United States provided the Mexican government with an emergency credit line and pressured its European Allies to agree that the IMF and World Bank should make similar credits available. The Mexican bailout was the largest US nonmilitary international financial commitment since the Marshall Plan. Rather than shake the US commitment to Mexico, the late 1994–early 1995 financial crisis brought the two countries even closer together politically and economically. The US President's action in providing money against Congressional opposition highlighted the degree to which the Administration valued the bilateral relationship. The Mexican government owed its ability to continue with a liberal economic strategy directly to the willingness of the US Administration to bail them out of the financial crisis. On the financial side, the bailout provided for US control of Mexican oil profits in the event of default or difficulties repaying the US government. A traditionally sensitive area of the Mexican economy which had been protected in the NAFTA agreement now stood as collateral to the US government.

From the Arctic Circle to Tierra Del Fuego

As the United States was deepening its relationship with Canada and Mexico, it was also taking steps to bring in other areas of the Americas. The Enterprise for the Americas Initiative (EAI) was announced by President George Bush in June 1990 only two weeks after the United States had accepted NAFTA negotiations with Mexico.[14] Its long term goal was the establishment of a free trade zone from Anchorage to Tierra del Fuego. In the short term it proposed two major steps. The first was to initiate a series of framework agreements which would clear the negotiating ground for detailed consideration of free trade arrangements. Within two years virtually all Latin American and Caribbean countries were involved in this process with the exception of Cuba, Haiti and Surinam. The second objective was to solicit support for the US proposals in the Uruguay round in return for more favourable treatment of Latin American products in the US market. The EAI also contained some provisions on debt and on increasing the role of the Inter-American Development Bank, but these were of secondary importance.

The effect of the EAI was to shift US policy to hemispheric plans rather than to particular countries or subregions. Within the hemisphere, member states lined up to engage in negotiations. The Caribbean states, in particular, had to consider seriously extending integration arrangements with the US economy to keep up with the special deal which Mexico had achieved.[15] Alternatives to joining the US bandwagon seemed infeasible in an environment of increasing competition for investment and access to the US market. From a US perspective, a stable and more prosperous Latin America open to US business interests might go some way to reviving the health of the American economy.[16] US exporters had suffered from the collapse in Latin American markets during the debt crisis of the 1980s.

Renewed US interest in the Americas became evident on 1 December 1993 when US Vice-President Al Gore announced that the President was inviting leaders of democratically elected governments in the western hemisphere to a summit in Miami.[17] Such a meeting had last taken place in April 1967 and marked the end of the Alliance for Progress and a lessening of US involvement on a hemispheric basis. While the United States remained engaged in Latin America and the Caribbean in the 1970s and 1980s, its actions tended to focus on the anticommunist crusade and on assisting its financial institutions in coping with the debt crisis.

The leaders of the governments of the Americas (except Cuba) met in Miami in December 1994. They agreed to work towards a Free Trade Area of the Americas by the year 2005.[18] Chile received a separate invitation to apply to join NAFTA. The Organization of American States was given the task of coordinating arrangements between hemispheric regional integration projects. The practical difficulties of moving from a declaration of interest in creating an FTAA and actually achieving one were obscured by the Summit bravado. The primary obstacle lies in the United States where the fast-track negotiating authority needed from Congress could be difficult to secure. Many Republicans favour freer trade, but oppose any side deals. Most Democrats will insist on labour and environmental side deals, as may the Canadian and Mexican governments. Following the Mexican financial crisis and US bailout Congress may be sceptical of further special economic arrangements.

The past decade has seen a tremendous shift in interamerican relations. The three North American states are now bound together through the NAFTA and TNCs are moving to bring a single North American market closer through their investment decisions. One can also see the beginning of a continental community at non-elite levels as social movements in the labour, environment, women and aboriginal areas are increasingly organizing on a transnational basis. Although the institutional structure created to oversee these developments is weak and is likely to remain so, an emerging North American political community is visible. Beyond North America, the United States has reached out to Latin American and Caribbean states through proposals for freer trade. The goal is to stitch together the economies of the western hemisphere through regional liberalization.

THE PACIFIC CENTURY

At the same time that US interest in the Americas is being renewed, the pull of the Asia-Pacific region on the United States is growing. Similar to Manifest Destiny, the notion of a Pacific Century can be traced to the nineteenth century. The view that the motor of history was moving from the Atlantic to the Pacific mirrored US expansion across the continent to the west coast. In recent years the US navy and Californian business interests have both advanced the cause of the Pacific Century to further their own particular concerns. Yet the repeated false dawns of a Pacific Century as optimism encountered Japanese militarism, the Chinese Revolution and the Cold War raised doubts about its arrival.[19] While talk of a Pacific Century has been both fanciful and imprecise, it does capture the sense that this area of the world is becoming more crucial to global economic and security affairs. This movement can be seen in economic trends and the various responses to these. The economic trends of note have been the staggering growth rates in East Asia and the increase in Asia-Pacific trade and investment, while key responses have been the creation of new institutions, the US competitiveness debate, and security concerns. All of these elements indicate that an increasing amount of attention may be paid to the Asia-Pacific region in Washington.

At the most basic level the Asia-Pacific region is important because it contains the three largest economies in the world. Recent reinterpretation of economic data suggests that the United States leads with a 22% share of global GDP, Japan comes second with 7.6%, followed by a growing China with 6%.[20] The policies of these three states influences 35% of world GDP.[21]

Perhaps more important than size is the rate of economic growth. The economic dynamism of the East Asian region is most clearly seen in higher than average rates of growth in comparison to North America and Western Europe. Between 1960 and 1970 the Four Tigers (South Korea, Taiwan, Hong Kong and Singapore) and Japan grew at rates of between 8 and 10% per year while growth in the United States averaged only 3.8%.[22] Between 1970 and 1980 the Tigers continued to grow at similar rates. Japanese growth levelled off at 4.7% and US growth declined to an average of 2.8%. In the 1980s, US and Japanese growth rates narrowed with the former edging up into the 3% area and the latter maintaining an average of 4%. Korea, Taiwan and Singapore maintained growth rates twice as high. In addition, Chinese growth rates began to increase from around 5% in the 1970s to 9-10% in the 1980s. It has been estimated that East Asian growth rates from 1986 to 1990 averaged 5.4% compared to 2.8% of the NAFTA countries and 3.1% of the European Community.

This rapid growth in East, and more recently Southeast Asia accounts for this region's increasing importance to the United States' economy. Steve Chan points to a number of statistics in US-Asia trade relations to bolster his case for the dawning of a Pacific Century. These include such factors as US-Asia Pacific trade being one-third higher than transatlantic commerce in 1991, US exports to Thailand exceeding exports to the former Soviet Union, Indonesia being a larger US trading partner than all of Eastern Europe, and a country such as Singapore with a population of under 3 million being a larger market for the US than Italy which has a population of 57 million.[23] It has been estimated that by the year 2000 Pacific trade will be double the volume of Atlantic trade.[24]

Regional integration in the Asia-Pacific has been dominated by the activity of private corporations, with governments only recently agreeing to create institutions to manage the economic relationships. Before considering these institutions in the following section it is helpful to outline the nature of this regional integration. The states of the region can be broken down into a number of categories. Japan stands alone as the single advanced capitalist liberal democracy in the region. Economically it is followed by the Four Tigers of South Korea, Taiwan, Hong Kong and Singapore. A third group of states has been trying to mimic the Four Tigers' rapid industrialisation. These are Malaysia and Thailand followed by Indonesia and, lagging substantially behind, the Philippines. China occupies a unique place as its coastal areas are rapidly becoming industrialized, but its vast interior remains largely rural and underdeveloped. China, Taiwan and Hong Kong are often grouped together and referred to as Greater China due to their rapid economic integration, cultural affinity and shared history.

Japanese activity has bound the economies of this region together.[25] Japan accounts for approximately 70% of the region's GDP and serves as the region's single largest importer. Approximately 30% of the region's net foreign direct investment (FDI) came from Japan in comparison to 10% from the United States in 1990. Another area where Japan has taken the lead is in development aid. In 1992 it was estimated that Japan provided over half the official development assistance for the region compared to only 6% contributed by the United States.

A significant aspect of Japanese FDI in the region is that receiving countries run large trade deficits with Japan. Other Asian economies rely heavily on Japan for capital goods, material and parts for their domestic production. In addition, Japanese corporations operating in East Asia tend to import goods from Japan. It is hard to avoid the conclusion that 'the persistent trade deficit with Japan is due intrinsically to the structural dependence of the region on Japan ... established by Japanese multinational corporations.'[26] More mercantilist views describe Japanese dominance of investment and trade flows in East Asia as a form of hegemony.[27] The result of this structural imbalance is that most East

Asian countries are import and investment dependent on Japan and export dependent on the United States. In order to support imports and investment from Japan they must export to the United States and other areas of the world.

Although East Asian integration has grown, the degree to which countries are tied into the North American and global economy is significant. Although Japanese investment in East Asia has been substantial, it has declined relative to its activity in North America and Europe. In 1982 Japanese investors split their investment roughly equally between North America and East Asia excluding China (about $15 billion each). By 1988 the North American figure had grown to $475 billion while the East Asian had grown only to $30 billion.[28] A cumulative total of Japanese FDI from 1951 to 1991 shows that 44% has gone to North America, 15% to Asia, 19% to Europe and 21% to the rest of the world.[29]

Trade figures for the East Asian region tell a similar story. Japanese trade has increased both with East Asia and the United States. Trade with East Asian countries increased from 20.5% to 26.5% from 1980 to 1991 and increased from 20.6% to 26.6% with the United States during the same period.[30] This seems to indicate that the growth in East Asian regional integration is part of a broad internationalization, or globalization, of the region's economies. Although East Asian intra-regional trade may have expanded from 31% in 1970 to 39% in 1990, the single largest destination remains the United States.[31] In 1991, Hong Kong, Korea, Singapore, Taiwan, China, Malaysia, Philippines, Thailand and Singapore exported more to the United States than Japan. Individually these countries remain susceptible to US pressure. Both South Korea and China export a quarter of their products to the United States. However, these countries exported more to each other as a group than to the United States.

A recent activity that has contributed to closer ties between states in the region has been the growth of foreign investment from the second tier states. In the late 1980s and early 1990s the newly industrializing countries (NICs) began to invest in other East Asian economies. Feeling similar pressures of rising wages, currency appreciation and resource requirements, they sought out neighbouring states to increase their competitiveness. For example, NIC investment in the Philippines now exceeds Japanese investment and is equivalent to two-thirds of Japanese investment in other East Asian countries such as Thailand.[32]

Due to the strong links between the East Asian and North American economies the immediate prospects of an exclusive East Asian regional integration framework are poor. The primary, although declining, trade and/or investment relationship for many East Asian states is with the United States. They are reluctant to take any steps that might alienate US interests. The US can threaten to cut off particular markets for East Asian states or it can offer individual preferential access through accession to NAFTA, for example. As a result, there has been a move towards broader Asia-Pacific institutions to oversee the dynamic growth around many areas of the Pacific basin.

Institutional Developments

There have been a number of attempts to build regional institutions in the Asia-Pacific region, but most have been limited in scope and success. Two key features of institutional development in the region have been the focus on economic issues and the influence of business, academic, and government elites.[33] In 1967 the Pacific Basin Economic Council (PBEC) was formed, bringing together groups of business managers to discuss common problems. The same year saw the founding of the Association of South-East Asian Nations (ASEAN) which included Indonesia, Malaysia, the Philippines and Singapore.[34] In 1968, the Pacific Trade and Development Conference (PAFTAD) was formed as a forum for economists with an interest in the region. The Pacific Economic Cooperation Conference (PECC) was founded in Canberra in September 1980 and was attended by representatives from the US, Japan, Canada, Australia, New Zealand, South Korea and ASEAN. PECC has a tripartite structure which includes representatives from government, business and academia.

The increasing integration of Asia-Pacific economies, concern about the future of multilateralism and the deepening integration of economies in Western Europe and North America contributed to the creation of an intergovernmental body in the Asia-Pacific in 1989. The process began in the late 1980s, when the Australian government launched an initiative to create an intergovernmental organization that would give greater substance to the non-governmental cooperation that had been building over the previous decade. The first meeting of the new forum for Asia-Pacific Economic Cooperation (APEC) took place in Canberra in November 1989. Government officials from the US, Canada, Japan, South Korea, New Zealand and ASEAN joined the Australians.

A number of factors prompted such a meeting.[35] The level of regional economic activity had increased. A number of countries such as Malaysia, Indonesia, Thailand and Australia were increasingly following liberal policies which allowed for some degree of policy convergence. Many Asian countries were concerned about the US-Japanese trade conflicts and bilaterally negotiated solutions which might harm their interests. A regional forum might allow for some input from other countries. The Australians in particular were worried about being excluded from regional groupings with the developments in North America (FTA) and Western Europe (Single Market project). East Asian leaders were also worried by the possibility of Fortresses in Europe and North America, as well as the possible diversion of investment flows to Eastern Europe.

The United States previously had not been encouraging of Asia-Pacific groupings. US policy had favoured multilateral organizations such as GATT, combined with the possibility of dealing with Asian countries bilaterally. Broad liberal principles were supported at GATT, but the US could exercise its power by pressuring individual countries such as Taiwan or South Korea to increase their exchange rate or to reduce trade surpluses. Policy began to change as the US feared that it might be excluded from regional developments. The original APEC proposal put forward by Australian Prime Minister Bob Hawke excluded the North American countries. His idea was that a Pacific organization could serve as a counterweight to the United States. US decision-makers decided to join the organization to have an influence on its agenda. The exclusion of the United States was also not popular with ASEAN states which were concerned by an organization that would be dominated by Japan and which feared the loss of vital US export markets.

In December 1990, the Malaysian Prime Minister proposed the formation of an East Asian Economic Grouping which would bring together Asian states from ASEAN to Japan including South Korea, Japan, Hong Kong, Taiwan and China, but excluding the non-Asian states of Australia, New Zealand, Canada and the United States. Such a grouping was seen as detrimental by the US, which was already concerned about the export led growth of Asian countries. The US government exerted pressure on Japan and a number of ASEAN states to reject the proposal.[36] The United States raised concerns that the Malaysian proposal would divide the region in half rather than bring it together as in the APEC initiative. The Malaysian proposal has since evolved into an East Asian Economic Caucus which serves as a subgroup within APEC. Its potential as a forum for East Asian views to counter Western positions, such as on human rights or protectionism, remains.

An important step in the evolution of APEC was President Clinton's initiative to upgrade the November 1993 APEC meeting in Seattle by tagging on an informal leadership meeting. APEC finished with a gathering where leaders of countries in the most economic dynamic region of the world could discuss trade, military or human rights issues. APEC had moved from a low profile organization to a form of regional summit. This Asia-Pacific summit excluded the Europeans as the EU was denied observer status. In contrast to the G7 meetings of advanced industrialized states which has only one Asian member (Japan) and four European states (UK, France, Germany, Italy), APEC has a majority of Asian members and no Europeans.

The sense of exclusion in Europe was heightened by the coincidence of the APEC summit coming less than a week after NAFTA was approved by the US House of Representatives. It appeared that the US was moving quickly to create regional groupings in the Americas and Asia which would work to the disadvantage of Europe. European nervousness had been evident a month earlier when the US Secretary of State commented that 'Western Europe is no longer the dominant area of the world' and that this was something that both US and European policy-makers should keep in mind.[37] Rifts over Bosnia and US attention to the Americas and Asia made European policy-makers reassess their relationship with the United States. The sense of falling behind was illustrated in the lead editorial of the British newspaper *The Independent*, which debated 'How Europe Can Arrest Its Decline.'[38]

The future of APEC is not yet settled. It could evolve into a large free trade area, similar to NAFTA. A link could be created between APEC states and the existing NAFTA. It is possible that APEC could become a Pacific OECD whose main function would be to monitor and advise governments rather than act as an institution overseeing liberalization. This monitoring may not be welcome to East Asian states as it could provide an avenue for increased conflict with the United States. In 1993 an Eminent Persons Group report to APEC advocated the creation of an Asian Pacific Economic Community that would pursue free trade consistent with GATT, which would bolster multilateral liberalization.[39] The November 1994 meeting in Indonesia agreed that a free trade area be created between member states by the year 2020.[40] Developed countries would participate by 2010 while developing countries would have an additional decade to adjust. Similar to the agreement for western hemispheric trade, the specifics were unclear. The reluctant Malaysian government secured an opt-out while the United States' and Australians' desire for rapid tariff removal clashed with the Japanese and Thais who favoured a slower approach in concert with the World Trade Organization. The road from principle to practice will be difficult. Although

APEC's precise fate is unclear, it appears that the organization will have an increasingly important role in the management of transpacific relations.

A crucial aspect of Asia-Pacific relations is the shallowness of the institutions and dominance of elite driven projects. The primary actors have been transnational firms and government representatives operating in a narrow consensus about policy in Asia-Pacific states. Because of their narrow base, they may not be able to deal adequately with popular resentment or hostility that can arise as a result of increased liberalization and skewed economic growth. There is evidence of growing transnational civil society at the non-elite level, but this has little overlap with the grand regional project. For example, peace groups have been active in creating nuclear free zones and lobbying against the presence of nuclear weapons in the Pacific, environmental groups have been attempting to stop the destruction of rainforests in Thailand, Malaysia and the Philippines, and a decolonization movement has been highlighting the plight of the peoples of Micronesia, New Caledonia, French Polynesia and East Timor. These movements, which might be able to bolster the legitimacy of evolving regional agreements, have no role in the elite agreements. [41]

CHALLENGES TO THE TRANSATLANTIC RELATIONSHIP

The developments described in the first two sections of this chapter raise a number of issues for the transatlantic Alliance. Is there a possibility that the regionalization of economic activity is leading to competitive, hostile trading blocs? What are the implications for Europe of the US drive for increased competitiveness? Does US social conflict in response to economic restructuring have any impact on the transatlantic relationship? Does this increased economic activity create new military security concerns that will overshadow the importance of the Atlantic Alliance?

Who's Afraid of Blocs?

Some analysis of regional integration in the late 1980s and early 1990s seems to be scarred by a false historical parallel with the 1930s. Fears have been raised about a breakdown of the trading system and a slide to economic and perhaps political or military conflict. [42] Such fears are misplaced for a number of reasons.

First, only the European Union comes close to anything resembling a 'bloc.' The NAFTA lacks common rules over matters such as competition policy, labour and environmental rules. Each government has resisted attempts to create supranational institutions. Activity is limited to overseeing the free flow of investment, goods and services. APEC is an even looser grouping, comprising numerous economic, political and cultural systems. Their watch word is open regionalism which entails integration in a global framework. There is little possibility of an exclusive grouping. In addition, it should be remembered that the 'blocs' often identified with interwar economic chaos were actually monetary areas such as the sterling area. The combination of a monetary area and privileged trading relations seems remote. The European Union continues its struggle to create a common currency, but NAFTA countries shy away from the idea and it is not on the agenda for APEC.

Second, some attention needs to be given to the political forces at work in the regionalization process. As mentioned earlier, the prime movers in the 1980s have been transnational business and state elites. TNCs are interested in creating an open global market, not closing it off. They have supported regional integration as a step in breaking down national obstacles. With the high cost of production, TNCs need to sell in all three major economic areas and work to resist political measures restricting such access. Helen Milner has demonstrated the crucial role that TNCs have played in keeping the global economy open in the face of economic problems.[43] If TNCs are the major force behind regional integration it seems unlikely that such integration will lead to exclusionary blocs.

The role of transnational business is a complex one. TNCs press governments to take hard positions in international negotiations to secure particular commercial advantages, but also work to keep the system open. For instance, the US entertainment business has strongly opposed French cultural policies, but they cannot, nor do they want to, force a closure of markets. It is a similar story with the Boeing-Airbus disputes. Boeing may urge the US to get tough with Airbus, but they oppose any action which might cut off their access to the lucrative European market.

Competition and Cohesion

Having declared that there is little possibility of hostile regional blocs being created, it is also necessary to point out that regional integration and the United States' deeper involvement with the Americas and Asia will probably complicate transatlantic relations and have implications for EU policy. Regional integration and liberalization can be expected to accelerate the economic restructuring process which has proved to be so difficult since the early 1970s. The social and political response to this restructuring could make transatlantic relations more conflictual. The NAFTA experience offers evidence of such a trend while competition from the East can be expected to intensify.

Increasingly, the flow of goods and capital between the United States, Mexico and Canada, facilitated by NAFTA, should result in an acceleration of economic restructuring. Although econometric predictions of NAFTA have tended to give a sanguine picture of the adjustment process there are reasons to expect a more wrenching dislocation.[44] Canadian and US high value-added producers should prosper, and Mexican labour-intensive producers should also benefit from being able to take advantage of their labour surplus. Thus, one could expect Canadian service and high technology industries such as Northern Telecom to increase business in the Mexican market while Ford or GM are likely to shift production to Mexico. Textile workers in Canada and the United States could suffer from Mexican competition. This mainly female workforce either will have to reduce their already low wages or give up this form of employment.

An area of great concern is Mexican subsistence agriculture which will wilt under competition from US and Canadian agribusiness. The implications for social stability as thousands and perhaps millions more Mexicans flow into urban areas may be profound. Indeed, the strains from the Mexican liberalization process became all too clear at the end of 1994. The ongoing rebellion in southern Mexico, widespread political discontent combined with a questionable overvaluation of the Mexican currency, and a heavy dependence on short term foreign capital came together in a currency crisis as international investors panicked and lost confidence in the Mexican project. The uprising in the south of Mexico began on the day NAFTA came into force. Peasants in the area made the point that they objected to changes in landholding rights which had been introduced to facilitate the concentration of Mexican agriculture for export purposes.[45]

The social tensions created by such restructuring in the US were highlighted by the NAFTA debate. Opposition to the agreement was fierce as it aligned US big business and liberal (in the economic sense) politicians against labour unions and environmentalists. Drawing upon the support of corporate America and liberal economist opinion, President Clinton was able to squeeze the agreement through the House of Representatives. Resistance was so strong in the Democratic Party that the President needed the support of otherwise hostile conservative

Republicans to ensure the NAFTA's successful ratification. In the November 1993 vote, 132 Republican votes had to be added to 102 Democrat votes to defeat 156 Democrats and 43 Republicans. The House whips switched positions with the Democrats working against the President and the Republicans for him. Equally telling about the divisions over NAFTA was a study which showed that the wealthier, more educated, more white collar a district was, the more likely it was that the Representative voted in favour of NAFTA.[46]

The NAFTA debate in North America has initiated two political changes in the continent. The first was at the non-elite level with the forging of alliances between various groups in society that had formerly operated independently or in competition with one another. These social groups expanded the trade debate to include numerous other subjects such as social standards, labour protection, environmental consequences and other agreements such as GATT. The second change was a delimitation of the extent to which US political institutions would be bound by a regional agreement. The US Congress ensured that continental institutions would not greatly infringe upon their power. Each of these developments will leave a lasting impression on US foreign relations.

The FTA and NAFTA liberalization projects were elite-driven, reflecting a consensus among business leaders, liberal economists and governing parties. Opposition came from a wide variety of groups seeking to dilute the liberal nature of the agreements. In Canada, the coalition consisted of organized labour, women's, church, cultural and nationalist groups. In the United States, opposition was led by organized labour and environmental groups, but was joined by nationalist/isolationist forces inspired by Ross Perot. These coalitions had two important characteristics. The first was that they united a broad based opposition to elite initiatives amongst formerly diverse groups. Particularly significant was the cooperation between labour and environmental groups. In other circumstances environmental initiatives can be resisted by labour because they fear job losses. In the NAFTA case, both groups shared an interest in the creation of rules and institutions which would restrict the activities of TNCs. Environmentalists and labour shared the concern that transnational capital would force down environmental standards and wages by taking advantage of diverse regulation in the three states.

Another significant aspect of these alliances is that they became transnationalized. Their political opponents, whether they were transnational business, liberal technocrats or politicians were already operating on a trilateral basis. It soon became apparent that a counter strategy would have to include similar elements of transnational organization. This is especially significant in the case of organized labour.[47] Whereas Canadian and US workers formerly regarded workers in developing countries, such as Mexico, as directly threatening their livelihood, the NAFTA debate showed that they were allies with a common adversary. Labour in the US and Canada cannot block increased competition with Mexico so it is increasingly trying to help Mexican labour to improve its working conditions. Part of the threat of low Mexican wages arises from the suppression of independent trade unions and the dominance of corporatist unions more concerned with government desires than representing their members' rights. Another example of transnational organizing has been the activity of Canadian and Mexican women's groups struggling to cooperate in taming the neoliberal project while acknowledging differences in perspectives and interests between groups of women.[48]

A second key aspect of this transformation of non-elite politics in North American is that attention is not limited to North American issues. After suffering defeat at the hands of the pro-NAFTA forces attention immediately turned to influencing the ratification of the multilateral Uruguay round. Environmentalists lobbied against the power of GATT to undermine environmental protections while labour pressed for labour rights to be protected under the new World Trade Organization. These groups recognized that the liberalization, which they saw as threatening important values and practices, was not confined to domestic or regional politics, but also had an important global dimension. Greenpeace President Barbara Dudley dismissed the temporary defeat in the NAFTA struggle by predicting that the coalition built around environmentalists, family farmers and working people would survive to build a sustainable economy for workers and the environment while the Public Citizen President claimed that 'This is a grass roots movement that is not going to stop. This is really just the beginning. And the whole issue of trade will never, never be the same again.'[49] If the prediction is fulfilled, trade relations with Europe and other partners could similarly be changed.

A disturbing aspect of the NAFTA debate was the role played by the populist Ross Perot. His campaign against NAFTA was fought along traditional nationalist lines. Declaring that he could hear the sucking sounds as jobs were being lost to Mexico, Perot played upon the fears of new economic insecurity. In contrast to labour and environmental groups trying to build bridges to Mexicans, the Perot attack contained elements of racism and xenophobia. It has fed into a broader reconsideration of immigration in the US and the relationship between the US and developing countries.[50] His nationalist rhetoric foreshadowed the rise of the Republican isolationist right in the 1994 elections.

The outcome of these trends in North American trade politics is to greatly complicate and marginally democratize aspects of the United States' foreign economic policy. Attempts to depoliticize economic issues through liberalizing the market were not successful because they inspired mobilization around the trade agreements by large sectors of US society. Increased attention was focused on NAFTA, the activity of TNCs, labour and environmental standards and the GATT. Whereas the drafters of NAFTA wanted an agreement restricted to liberalizing trade and investment, they were forced to make some concession to opponents by adding side accords in labour and the environment. This renewed politicization goes much further than the usual concerns about commercial interest group lobbies raised by public choice theorists. It represents a fundamental conflict of values and interests which could continue to pose challenges both to the US government and to its trading partners.

At the same time as the American polity is dealing with the changes surrounding NAFTA, the United States continues to deal with increased economic competition from Asian countries. The term Nibichei Economy is used by some commentators as a label for the increasing integration of the world's two largest economies, the United States and Japan. It refers to the heavy reliance of the Japanese economy on the US market for exports and the heavy reliance of the US economy on the Japanese for capital, especially since the mid-1980s. The US consumption binge of the last decade has been financed by personal and government debt and Japanese capital surpluses have played a prominent role in bankrolling this debt. In addition, Japanese foreign direct investment poured into the United States to take advantage of a declining dollar (therefore cheaper asset prices) and to get around US protectionism.

In the 1980s some sectors of US opinion became worried by the inflow of Japanese investment and consistent trade deficits. Because of the 1985 revaluation of the Japanese yen in the wake of the Plaza Accord and fears of increased protectionism in developed countries, large Japanese surpluses began to be invested broad. Japanese FDI in the US rose from $5.8 billion in 1985 to $45.2 billion in 1989. The flow of Japanese money into the United States created wide-spread concern as Americans saw the Japanese buy prime real estate, baseball teams and movie picture studios. However, the flow of capital has decreased dramatically as the total of Japanese FDI plummeted to $14.5 billion in 1992 following its real estate and stock market crashes.[51]

The US trade deficit became a concern in the 1980s as a number of industries were unable to compete with foreign competition. Damage to the US car, electronics, steel, and textile industries created problems on the employment side. Japanese success in the high technology sectors such as computers and semiconductors raised fears that the United States security machine might become dependent on foreign technologies. US trade law was used as a weapon to reduce the bilateral deficit even though US macroeconomic policies such as the budget deficit, low savings, high consumption and high interest rates were the primary culprits.[52] The Japanese and other East Asians were the source of a large share of the trade deficit and were seen to be engaging in unfair trade practices. Concern about the rise of the Japanese economy became so great that trade analyst Clyde Prestowitz's 1988 book tried to explain how the Japanese had overtaken the Americans in the most crucial and dynamic industries of the late twentieth Century.[53]

The United States and Japan engaged in numerous bilateral negotiations in an attempt to resolve the trade deficit problem and to reduce tension. In 1985, the Reagan Administration initiated the Market Oriented Sector Specific (MOSS) talks to pry open the Japanese telecommunications, pharmaceuticals, microelectronics and wood product markets. Bilateral deals on automobiles and semiconductors were also conducted. In 1989 the wide ranging Structural Impediments Initiative (SII) began in an effort to restructure each country's domestic political economy so that trade would be facilitated. Discussions focused on structural economic arrangements such as retail and distribution systems, investment and savings patterns and government-business relations. However, the Americans were not prepared to reduce consumption and the Japanese were paralysed by a domestic political process which prevented sweeping internal changes.

The Japanese trade surpluses with the United States continue despite the yen reaching record highs against the dollar in 1995. As this chapter was being prepared, the US and Japanese were engaged in a struggle over luxury automobile exports. Although the trade imbalance should decrease as US exports become more competitive at the new currency levels, conflict will continue as the United States continues to demand Japanese restructuring and the Japanese become less willing or able to accommodate such demands.

In forty years Japan has grown from having an economy that was devastated by war to one that is 60% the size of the United States'. It has become the world's largest creditor (as the United States became the largest debtor), the third largest exporter of manufactured goods, the second largest contributor to the United Nations and the world's largest donor of foreign aid.[54] The increasing economic success of Japan fed a debate about the decline of US hegemony. The sense of US decline was probably best captured by Paul Kennedy's 1987 surprise bestseller, *The Rise and Fall of the Great Powers.*[55] In the mid-1990s the sense of Japanese threat may be diminishing as the invincibility of the Japanese miracle comes increasingly into question. The early 1990s saw Japan weather a difficult recession, struggle with a political system riddled by corruption and inertia and, more recently, revealed the stress of dealing with the Kobe earthquake and poison gas attacks upon public transport systems. In the United States, Japanese investment in the entertainment industry and New York real estate market that caused concern in the late 1980s now seem to have been serious commercial mistakes. The fears of earlier years appear exaggerated.

The relationship with Japan will continue to be both important and difficult for the United States. Economic tensions could persist as the US economy continues to adjust and the Japanese increasingly resist US demands. In addition to domestic and bilateral developments posing challenges, the relationship will also be influenced by the re-emergence of China as a regional economic and military power.

Just as Japan seemed to dominate the thoughts of some US foreign economic policy-makers and politicians in the late 1990s, China is now beginning to take on increased importance in US eyes. Its rapid transition to capitalism in the coastal areas and high growth rates has attracted attention. Former Beijing Bureau Chief for *The New York Times*, Nicolas Kristof, captured this spirit when he argued that 'This Time it is Real.'[56] Kristof confidently predicted that based upon present trends the Chinese economy would come close to being the world's largest early in the next century and that it would also become the world's greatest producer of acid rain.

Recent relations between China and the United States have been difficult. Following the Chinese suppression of pro-democracy demonstrators in Tienanmen Square in June 1989, the issue of human rights has been a source of bilateral conflict. After some debate the Clinton Administration severed the link between human rights and trade relations in May 1994 as he renewed China's most-favoured-nation trading status. Despite taking the human rights 'irritant' away from trade relations, disputes continue to emerge. In 1994-95, the major issue was the infringement of US intellectual property rights and large scale copying of US products in China. In February 1995, in response to an estimated loss of $1.1 billion in sales, the US imposed 100% tariffs on $1.08 billion of Chinese exports to the US.[57] These were the largest sanctions in US history and covered Chinese products from bicycles and running shoes to cellular phones and silk.

The tough US position eventually brought a Chinese commitment in March 1995 to enforce intellectual property rights and to close offending plants. At the same time, however, the Chinese government reasserted its right to export nuclear technology world-wide and reaffirmed that it would continue nuclear weapons testing.[58] It appears that the Chinese government feels that concessions in the economic sphere need to be matched by a reassertion of sovereignty in the military and security spheres. This could prove to be a difficult issue in future. Another could concern Chinese prison labour and the artificial suppression of wages in the export sector.

Both Japan and China compete with the United States, but from different angles. The Japanese challenge has been in consumer products such as electronics and more recently in high technology. Chinese competition comes in at the low wage end of the economy and is beginning to pick up in areas formerly dominated by the Japanese. Similar to European producers, the US must meet a challenge in both the high and low value product sectors. Unlike Europe, the US has the flexibility both domestically and through NAFTA to compete both in wages and technology.

While increased Asian economic competition might be a threat to some US corporations it could be seen as a greater threat to US workers and social stability. Many US corporations have met and continue to meet the Asian challenge by adopting new production methods, greater innovation, or offshore production. Indeed, the creation of NAFTA may allow some US corporations to use continental cheap labour in their competition with Asian production zones. The likely result is an increase in social polarization. The competitiveness challenges faced by the United States are not unique; they are common to all advanced industrialized economies. All developed countries must meet the threat of low wage, high quality products coming from NICs and engage in a race to produce high value added products. The significant aspect is that the United States' perception is that this threat comes primarily from the East. As a result, domestic reform measures are accompanied by foreign policy initiatives aimed at finding a solution to the Pacific challenge. While European activity in some sectors, particularly agriculture, aerospace, and entertainment, annoy the US, the Europeans are largely peripheral to the competitiveness issue because Asian societies are seen to pose a broad challenge to the US. This means that US attention is more focused across the Pacific than across the Atlantic. For Europeans, the diversion of US wrath may be welcome. However, a perceived diversion of attention is less so.

Military Security Concerns

Although the Cold War rivalry focused attention on the Soviet-US nuclear relationship, the United States' intense military activity in the Asia-Pacific region should not be forgotten. It was the Japanese attack on Pearl Harbor which brought the United States directly into the Second World War and the Japanese suffered from the first and only use of atomic weapons. In addition to setting up military alliances and bolstering the economies of Asian allies the United States fought land wars in Korea and Vietnam in the thirty years following the Second World War. In contrast to the withdrawal of US troops from Western Europe and the downgrading of the US military role there, the Pacific theatre remains a bastion of American military and naval power. The US Pacific Command controls roughly half of US warships, two-thirds of the Marine Corps, two Army Divisions, a wing of the US Strategic Air Command and several tactical fighter wings of the Air Force.[59]

The immediate security issue in the Asia-Pacific region centres around the division of the Korean peninsula and possible conflict between the US and North Korea over the issue of nuclear weapons development. With the end of the Cold War and China's transition to capitalism, the North Korean government looks more and more like an anachronism on the verge of dissolution. The death of North Korea's dictator Kim Il Sung in 1994 and his son's precarious hold on power makes the future of the state even more problematic. While there is a possibility of renewed conflict in a time of internal insecurity or transition in North Korea, the long term security challenges lie elsewhere.

Similar to the economic field, the key relationships to be concerned with is the Japan-China-United States triangle. If the optimistic growth rates predicted for China are sustained the size of the Chinese economy as well as military expenditures and trade surpluses in absolute terms will surpass that of Japan before Japan is able to surpass the United States. As Robert Gilpin has suggested, the accommodation of a rising power by status quo powers is an exercise that can lead to violent conflict if not handled with extreme care.[60] The accommodation of China by the US and Japan will pose a formidable challenge.

There are a number of areas of potential conflict between Japan and China.[61] China's claim to territory in the Senkaku Islands and in the

South China Sea raise fears of Chinese expansionism in Japan. Chinese weapons policy, particularly the purchase of former Soviet long range naval and air forces and the continued development of its nuclear arsenal, increase insecurity.

Interstate rivalry is not the only security concern around China's rapid incorporation into the global economy. China risks self-destruction through regionalism. China's accelerating integration into the Asia-Pacific economy has been taking place on a subregional basis. Four distinctive zones can be identified: the Greater South China Economic Zone which includes South China (Guangdon and Fujian provinces), Hong Kong and Taiwan; the Yellow Sea Economic Zone which brings together Chinese (Liaoning and Shandong) provinces, Japanese and South Korean regions around the Yellow Sea; Shanghai-Pudon Economic Zone which links the port of Shanghai and its hinterland with the global economy; and the Sino-Russia border areas.[62]

Such a pattern of integration poses three problems. The first is there may be conflicting interests between these growth regions which may not be adequately reconciled by macro institutions such as APEC. Smaller, transnational subregional institutions may be required to deal with local issues. A second problem is the growing disparity between capitalist coastal growth regions and inland areas of China. Conflicts of interest and antagonism between the inland and coastal regions may not be adequately resolved by the lumbering Chinese state. The majority of China's population continues to live in poverty in rural areas and may increasingly resent the conspicuous consumption of other areas. In addition to tensions between different regions, class conflict may erupt between the masses of peasants moving into the coastal areas and the Chinese entrepreneurs rapidly amassing capital. Rapid economic growth may create explosive social tensions which could spill over into external security relations.

The increased possibility for conflict in the region will necessitate an active US role. A US presence in Japan can provide a stabilizing influence by reassuring the Japanese government that it need not engage in rapid rearmament to deal with possible security threats. Similarly, a secure Japan may lessen China's need to increase its military expenditures to deal with a technologically advanced and increasingly more confident Japanese government. Other Asian states are also interested in a continued US military presence. For example, in April 1995 the commander of the Indonesian armed forces asked for, and received, assurances that the US would maintain 100,000 troops in Asia.[63] His particular concern was with Chinese expansion in the South China Sea.

Another source of worry to the dominant Western powers, especially the United States, is China's policy of weapons sales. Sales of missiles to Pakistan and possible cooperation with Iranian nuclear and chemical weapons projects has raised concern in Washington. China is outside the Western consensus concerning which countries should be denied the capacity for offensive weapons of mass destruction. As indicated earlier, the Chinese government is anxious to maintain its security policy independence as it is forced into concessions on the economic front. At the moment the Asia-Pacific region lacks a strong institutional mechanism to deal with such disagreements. Regional security issues are explored in the ASEAN Post-Ministerial conference which is an annual meeting which now includes Japan, South Korea, Australia, Canada, New Zealand, the US, China, Russia and Vietnam.

Increasing attention to Asian problems in the security field may raise some concern in European capitals. Following the collapse of the Soviet Union and its military power it is difficult to see how vital US interests could seriously be challenged in Europe. Civil wars and communal conflict such as in the former Yugoslavia are a far greater problem for Europeans than for the United States. Surveying the new strategic environment from Washington, some interests remain the same. As the Gulf war demonstrated, control over oil remains a US priority. Following the change in economic gravity, the Asia-Pacific region assumes an increasing importance with a majority of US trade and vital investment flows in that area. The potential for major conflict also appears great in the region as China improves its military capability. Of course, Europe will retain a distinctive place in US policy. France and Britain remain nuclear powers and are among the few states willing to contribute combat forces to military missions. Though the NATO Alliance will persist in Europe, European security matters could take second or even third place to US interests in other parts of the world.

CONCLUSION

The late 1980s and early 1990s have seen a shift in emphasis in US foreign relations with more attention being paid to the economic challenges and possibilities of the American hemisphere and the Asia-Pacific region. In a world characterized by three large political economic regions, the US has been busy securing its interests in the two largest. A series of developments on the competitiveness front could serve to loosen ties with the European Union relative to other areas of the world.

NAFTA does not threaten to become an exclusionary trading bloc, but it does pose serious challenges for Europeans. The first is an increasingly competitive US corporate sector. NAFTA secures vital resources for North American-based TNCs. Canada will continue to provide a secure stream of natural resources and increased access to a developed market for US goods and investment. Mexico provides some natural resources, but more importantly, low cost labour. Mexican labour should allow North American-based TNCs to compete on a renewed basis with Asian producers that have been transferring production to Southeast Asia and China. This increased competitiveness will create difficulties for Europeans and European corporations. Europeans will be forced to address the ability of North American TNCs to lower costs by tapping sources of cheap labour. One should expect this to feed into Europe's own competitiveness debates in calls to reduce European social programmes and reduce the rigidity of the European labour market. Increased pressure can be expected on the European welfare system as European-based TNCs shift production to North America to capitalize on the continental, and eventual hemispheric, markets.

Another area that might be influenced by US policy is the status of Central and Eastern European countries in the EU. An ideal arrangement, from the European TNCs' perspective, would be a captive cheap labour pool similar to Mexico. This might be accomplished by providing Central and Eastern European states, and the West European industries producing there, with relatively free access to the EU market, but without integrating these states completely into the EU structure. Partially excluding the Eastern states would prevent them from raising wages through Western type social programmes.

Increasing US engagement with the Asia Pacific region may similarly lead to an increase in the competitiveness of US firms. Firms that are successful in this arena should have an edge over European rivals which are sheltered from Asian competition to a greater degree. European firms could lose ground in their domestic markets as well as third country markets if US and Asian producers continue to increase competitiveness through fierce bilateral competition.

The other side of the increased competitiveness of corporate America may be increased social tensions within the United States. Sectors of the US economy will be able to thrive in the renewed competition with the Americas and Asia. Skilled workers will benefit from increased access to growing foreign markets and will be able to prosper. However, many semi or unskilled workers will see their wages come under increasing pressure as they compete directly with Mexican and Asian workers. An inability to smooth over increasing divisions of wealth and power in US society may lead to increased social conflict and scapegoating of foreigners as the cause of US ills. Such an approach will lead to much more difficult relations between the United States and its trading partners. One can expect external targets, such as migrant workers and foreigners who 'cheat' in trade, to attract more attention. This may be accompanied by a general reluctance to bear the cost of an interventionist foreign policy seen to benefit others primarily. The rise of right wing populism in the US can be attributed partially to an unease about the loss of control in a globalized environment.

Another problem with US attention to the hemisphere and, more particularly, East Asia is that economic arrangements may be constructed which will work to the detriment of European interests. US bilateral negotiation with Japan over trade issues is a good example. Japanese measures to open its market might apply primarily to US firms, to the exclusion of European products. Decisions made in APEC could be taken without reference to Europe and could similarly work to the EU's disadvantage.

Institutionally, the movement in US policy and the rise of the Pacific region needs to be accommodated. A stronger security institution is needed in the Pacific, but Europe's participation is questionable. Reform of the UN Security Council is on the agenda to include Japan, but the position of the European seats and status of new members has yet to be agreed. China's role in international economic institutions is still restricted and there are questions about some of the NICs graduating to developed country status for trade purposes. Japan has recently increased its power in multilateral lending agencies such as the IMF and other Asian countries can be expected to play more prominent roles. Both the United States and Western European states must adapt to such changes, but it will be more difficult for the Europeans who are less integrated into the Pacific economy.

The centre of gravity for US foreign policy is shifting back to its pre-Cold War roots. More emphasis has been placed on its own backyard in the Americas and the commercial possibilities of the Pacific. Distinctly European concerns, such as the Bosnian conflict, attract less attention and little concern in mainstream US politics. Intensifying regional economies combined with the end of the Cold War point to a continuation of this trend. Despite muted proposals for a Transatlantic Free Trade Area (TAFTA) to rebuild the transatlantic links it is likely that the relationship will be one of continuing, but lessening, importance. Some may mourn the loss of a transatlantic Alliance steering the capitalist world through the Cold War years. The new environment may be more complex, and power more diffuse, but there is no *a priori* reason to suggest that it is any less desirable.

NOTES

1. C. Fred Bergsten, 'The Primacy of Economics,' *Foreign Policy*, Vol.87, Summer 1992, pp.3-24.
2. For a general discussion of the possibility of overlapping interests in the state-firm relationship see John H. Dunning, 'Governments and Multinational Enterprises: From Confrontation to Co-operation?,' *Millennium: Journal of International Studies*, Vol.20, Summer 1991, pp.225-244. Strategies for the state in this environment can be found in Robert Reich, *The Work of Nations*, Vintage Books, New York, 1992; John Stopford and Susan Strange, *Rival States, Rival Firms*, Cambridge University Press, Cambridge, 1991; and Michael Porter, *The Competitive Advantage of Nations*, Free Press, New York, 1990.
3. On the structural power of capital see Stephen Gill and David Law, 'Global Hegemony and the Structural Power of Capital,' *International Studies Quarterly*, Vol.33, 1989, pp.475-499. Thomas J. Biersteker outlines the constraints on developing countries in 'The Triumph of Neoclassical Economics in the Developing World' James N. Rosenau and Ernst-Otto Czempiel, (eds.), *Governance Without Government: Order and Change in World Politics*, Cambridge University Press, Cambridge, 1992, pp.102-131.
4. Robert Reich charts the rise of the symbolic analyst and the demise of unskilled workers in *The Work of Nations, op. cit.*
5. *Herald*, 25 September, quoted in Norman A. Graebner (ed.), *Manifest Destiny*, Bobbs-Merril, New York, 1968, p.xxxvii.
6. For a review of disputes in the areas of the National Energy Policy, softwood lumber and culture in the early 1980s see David Leyton-Brown, *Weathering the Storm: Canadian-US Relations, 1980-1983*, Canadian American Committee, Toronto, 1985.
7. The Canada-United States Free Trade Agreement has generated a huge literature, partially because of its controversial nature. A pro-FTA collection of papers is contained in John Crispo (ed.), *Free Trade: The Real Story*, Gage, Toronto, 1988 while Linda McQuaig provides a critique of the government's neoliberal policies in *The Quick and the Dead*, Viking, Toronto, 1991. A balanced collection of short essays is Marc Gold and David Leyton-Brown (eds.), *Trade-offs on Free Trade*, Carswell, Toronto, 1988, while two useful books on the negotiations themselves are Bruce Doern and Brian Tomlin, *Faith and Fear*, Stoddart, Toronto, 1991, and Michael Hart, *Decision at Midnight*, UBC Press, Vancouver, 1994.
8   See C. Michael Aho, 'A U.S. Perspective,' in Crispo (ed.), *op. cit.*, pp.180-187, and with Marc Levinson, 'A Canadian Opportunity,' *Foreign Policy*, Vol.66, Spring 1986, pp.143-155.
9. Robert O'Brien, 'The Canada-US Subsidy Negotiations: Socioeconomic Harmonization as the Price for Market Access?,' *Global Restructuring: Canada in the 1990s*, Association for Canadian Studies, Montreal, 1992, pp.49-76.

10. For background material see Nora Lustig, *The Remaking of an Economy*, Brookings, Washington, 1992; Sidney Weintraub, *Transforming the Mexican Economy: The Salinas Sexino*, National Planning Association, Washington, 1990; and Miguel Ramirez, *Mexico's Economic Crisis: Its Origins and Consequences*, Praeger, New York, 1989.

11. Gary Clyde Hufbauer and Jeffrey J. Schott, 'Prescription for Growth,' *Foreign Policy*, Vol.93, Winter 1993-1994, p.109. Peter Morici also stresses the advantage of gaining competitiveness over Asian producers in 'Free Trade with Mexico,' *Foreign Policy*, Vol.87, Summer 1992, pp.88-104.

12. Paul Krugman, 'The Uncomfortable Truth About NAFTA,' *Foreign Affairs*, Vol.72, No.5, November/December 1993, p.13.

13. William D. Rogers tries to make the connection between issues such as improved economic relations, immigration concerns and reducing the flow of drugs from Mexico in 'Approaching Mexico,' *Foreign Policy*, Vol.72, 1988, pp.196-209.

14. Background leading up to the EAI is provided in Eduardo Gitli and Gunilla Ryd, 'Latin American Integration and the Enterprise for the Americas Initiative,' *Journal of World Trade*, Vol.26, No.5, August 1992, pp.25-45.

15. Anthony Payne considers the changing role of the Caribbean in 'US Hegemony and the Reconfiguration of the Caribbean,' *Review of International Studies*, Vol.20, No.2, April 1994, pp.149-168.

16. Robert Pastor, 'The Latin American Option,' *Foreign Policy*, Vol.88, Fall 1992, pp.107-125.

17. In anticipation of the upcoming summit the *Journal of Interamerican Studies* published a special summit issue outlining key topics. See Vol.36, No.3, Fall 1994.

18. *The Economist*, 17 December 1994.

19. A dated, but interesting, example of the cautionary approach from a European perspective is provided by Christopher Coker 'The Pacific Century: Myth or Reality,' in Cheng-Wen Tasi (ed.), *Impact of Pacific Century on Euro-Asian Relations*, National Taiwan University, Taipei, 1988, pp.3-16. Bruce Cumings takes a critical approach to the liberal view of a thriving Asia-Pacific Community in 'Rimspeak; or, The Discourse of the Pacific Rim,' in Arif Dirlik (ed.), *What is in a Rim?: Critical Perspectives on the Pacific Region Idea*, Westview Press, Boulder, 1993, pp.29-47.

20. Wendy Dobson and Lee Tsao, 'APEC co-operation Amidst Diversity,' *ASEAN Economic Bulletin*, Vol.10, No.3, March 1994, p.232.

21. More traditional estimates put the US-Japanese share of world GDP at close to 40%. Joseph S. Nye, Jr., 'Coping With Japan,' *Foreign Policy*, Vol.89, Winter 1992, p.97.

22. Statistics in this paragraph are taken from Ippei Yamazawa, 'On Pacific Economic Integration,' *The Economic Journal*, Vol.102, November 1992, pp.1519-1529.

23. *East Asian Dynamism*, Westview Press, Boulder, 1993, p.1.

24. Robert B. Oxnam, 'Asia/Pacific Challenges,' *Foreign Affairs*, Vol.72, No.1, 1992/1993, p.57.

25. Statistics in this paragraph are taken from Arvind Panagariya, 'East Asia in the New Regionalism in World Trade,' *The World Economy*, Vol.17, No.6, November 1994, pp.817-839.

26. Sheng-Yann Lii, 'Japanese Direct Foreign Investment and Trade Flows in the Asia-Pacific Region,' *Asian Economic Journal*, Vol.8, No.21, 1994, p.201.

27. William R. Nester, *Japan's Growing Power East Asia and the World Economy*, Macmillan, London, 1990.

28. Stephen Guisinger, 'Foreign Direct Investment Flows in East and South East Asia,' *ASEAN Economic Bulletin*, Vol.8, No.1, July 1991, p.30.

29. Sheng-Yann Lii, *op.cit.*, p.189.

30. S. Javed Maswood, 'Japan and East Asian Regionalism,' *ASEAN Economic Bulletin*, Vol.11, No.1, July 1994, p.74.

31. *Ibid.*, p.70.

32. Guisinger, *op.cit.*, p.36.

33. Stuart Harris provides a helpful overview of the elite nature of the project in 'Policy Networks and Economic Cooperation: Policy Coordination in the Asia-Pacific Region,' *The Pacific Review*, Vol.7, No.4, 1994, pp.381-395.

34. Brunei joined in 1984. ASEAN has had some success in serving as a forum for the member countries to discuss regional issues, but has had little economic impact. In January 1992, ASEAN announced that it planned to form an ASEAN Free Trade Area (AFTA) by the year 2007. Its prospects for success are limited by the same factors that have hindered ASEAN integration to date.

35. See Donald Crone, 'The Politics of Emerging Pacific Cooperation,' *Pacific Affairs*, Vol.65, No.1, Spring 1992, pp.50-83.

36. *Ibid.*, p.77.

37. *The Guardian*, 18 October 1993.

38. *The Independent*, 20 November 1993.

39. Eminent Person Group, 'A Vision for APEC,' Asia-Pacific Economic Cooperation, Singapore, 1993.

40. *The Economist*, 19 November 1994.

41. Walden Bello and Eric Blantz set out a number of ways in which such groups could influence Asia-Pacific relations in 'Perils and Possibilities: Carving Out Alternative Order in the Pacific,' *Alternatives*, Vol.17, 1992, p.2.

42. Economist Jagdish Bhagwati has expressed concerns about regionalism undercutting multilateralism in *The World Trading System at Risk*, Wheatsheaf, London, 1991, esp. pp.58-79.

43. Helen V. Milner, *Resisting Protections: Global Industries and the Politics of International Trade*, Princeton University Press, Princeton, NJ, 1988.

44. Economic predictions about the positive effects of the Canada-US FTA and the EC 1992 project tended to be on the optimistic side and were thrown off by other economic factors such as low inflation policies, currency instability or recession. Michael E. Conroy and Amy K. Glasmeier raise the possibility of heavy NAFTA adjustment costs in 'Unprecedented Disparities, Unparalleled Adjustment Needs: Winners and Losers on the NAFTA Fast Track,' *Journal of Interamerican Affairs*, Vol.34, No.4, Winter 1992-1993, pp.1-27.

45. Andrew Reding provides a useful overview of Mexico's recent political crisis in 'Chiapas Is Mexico,' *World Policy Journal*, Vol.XI, No.1, Spring 1994, pp.11-25.

46. See 'Clinton Forms New Coalition to Win NAFTA's Approval,' *Congressional Quarterly Weekly*, 20 November 1993, pp.3181-3185.

47. US labour gradually has been moving to a more internationalist perspective and NAFTA seems to have accelerated this movement. For an internationalist perspective see Jeremy Brecher and Tim Costello, *Global Village vs. Global Pillage: A One World Strategy for Labor*, ILREF, Washington, 1991.

48. Christina Gabriel and Laura Macdonald, 'NAFTA, Women and Organizing in Canada and Mexico: Forging a Feminist Internationality,' *Millennium*, Vol.23, No.3, pp.535-563.

49. *International Trade Reporter*, 24 November 1993.

50. See, for example, James C. Clad, 'Slowing the Wave,' and Jeffrey S. Passel and Michael Fix, 'Myths About Immigrants,' *Foreign Policy*, Vol.95, Summer 1994, pp.139-160.

51. Maswood, *op.cit.*, p.75.

52. For an in-depth analysis of the US system see I.M. Destler, *American Trade Politics*, 2nd.ed., Institute for International Economics, Washington, 1992.

53. *Trading Places: How We Allowed Japan to Take the Lead*, Basic Books, New York, 1988.

54. Nye, *op.cit.*, pp.97-98.

55. Paul Kennedy, *The Rise and Fall of the Great Powers*, Random House, New York, 1987.

56. 'The Rise of China,' *Foreign Affairs*, Vol.72, No.5, November-December 1993, pp.59-64.

57. *Far Eastern Economic Review*, 16 February 1995.

58. *Far Eastern Economic Review*, 9 March 1995.

59. Bello and Blantz, *op.cit.*, p.2.

60. *War and Change in World Politics*, Cambridge University Press, Cambridge, 1981.

61. George Segal, 'The Coming Confrontation between China and Japan?,' *World Policy Journal*, Vol.X, No.2, Summer 1993, pp.27-32.

62. For details see Xiangming Chen, 'China's Growing Integration with the Asia-Pacific Economy' in *What is a Rim, op. cit*, pp.89-119.

63. *The Economist*, 29 April 1995.

6 Transatlantic Trade: Economic Security, Agriculture, and the Politics of Technology

Jarrod Wiener[1]

The Uruguay round of multilateral trade negotiations (MTN), successfully completed, will drift into the history of post-war international commercial diplomacy. Along with it will go much of the sound and fury that characterized its arduous negotiations. During the course of the MTN, it seemed for a time that the General Agreement on Tariffs and Trade (GATT) no longer expressed a political-economic consensus between the United States and many European states, and that negotiations within the institution, as exemplified most markedly over the issue of agriculture, served only to highlight divergent national priorities. The issue of agriculture captured the attention of observers, understandably, since it appeared to impede progress in the MTN as a whole and to bring the United States and the European Union[2] to the brink of the largest trade war in the history of the post-war international trade system. With the benefit of hindsight, however, some important lessons of the Uruguay round become perceptible.

One important lesson could be to resist the temptation to overstate the importance of disagreements in the GATT, such as that over agriculture. This dispute was amplified by the structure of the negotiations – that is by virtue of cross-issue linkages in a large and complex agenda – rather than by the political capital actually invested in them. When, in 1988, Lester Thurow declared that 'the GATT is dead',[3] he was in the company of many distinguished observers who have been proved correct, not because of the failure of the Uruguay round, but by its success in replacing the GATT with the more comprehensive World Trade Organization (WTO). Prior to and during the Uruguay round, the US and the EU cooperated in a number of areas which, one hastens to add, were of far greater commercial importance than was agriculture.

128

Indeed, in areas where their interests were congruent, the US and the EU, acting in concert, demonstrated a capacity to set the agenda for the negotiations, notably for trade in services. Even in the area of agriculture, the US and the EU also had shared interests in curtailing spiralling agriculture support budgets and in constructing a more rational system for the production and trade in agricultural commodities.

Another important lesson of the Uruguay round could be that, irrespective of the political capital invested in an issue, the social concerns of a minority of people in politically sensitive industries *can* hold the world trade system to ransom. In addition to farmers, European film-makers, who are also of relatively minor commercial importance in Europe when compared with the overall gains from the Uruguay round, threatened to delay the conclusion of the negotiations. What is interesting about both the issues of agriculture and cinematographic films is the manner in which those resistant to liberalization in the EU framed their positions. Farming and film-making were portrayed as primarily social and cultural, rather than economic activities and their protection was justified for reasons of 'societal security.' It was as difficult for politicians to deny this in the domestic context as it was to reconcile such argumentation with the normal discourse of the international trade institution.

That some will resist liberalization is neither new to the GATT, nor to efforts at liberalization that predate that institution. One need only think of the circumstances in which the theory of Mercantilism was first expounded in a systematic way. It was for social concerns, after all, that the principle that liberalization should not present economic security threats was ingrained into the GATT. What is perhaps new is that the language in which the debates over agriculture and cinematographic films in the Uruguay round were termed was in a sense alien to the GATT. Liberalization and efficiency were juxtaposed not to the decimation of industry and unemployment, *per se*, but to preserving a 'rural way of life' in the case of farming, and of maintaining a 'distinct cultural identity' in the case of films.

If liberalization continues to spread to new areas as it did under the Uruguay round, future negotiations could similarly talk at cross-purposes. The issue of agriculture most likely will lose salience in the medium term, if for no other reason than that farm populations in Europe are ageing and declining in numbers. On the other hand, the development of new technologies in the audio-visual industry could raise even greater concerns for the preservation of 'identity' than was highlighted in the dispute in the Uruguay round over films. As the digital transmission of

signals and the spread of fibre-optic and satellite delivery systems shrinks
the global market-place for the 'culture industry,' there is a likelihood
that objections to 'cultural imperialism' and concerns for the preservation
of 'identity' could become accentuated, even if these are only excuses to
mask economic inefficiency, or to gain a greater share of a growing
market.

Perhaps the greatest lesson of the Uruguay round, however, lies in
the very fact that it was convened. This highlighted a disjuncture
between the macro-political and commercial interests that the US and the
EU shared, and the micro-social insecurities that this raised for certain
of their domestic constituencies.[4] The decision to convene the MTN was
due to political pressures to keep the GATT process moving, to restore
the faltering credibility of multilateralism, and to derive commercial
benefit from the negotiations. In the 'crisis' in the trade system of the
early 1980s states did not turn inwards, but sought further liberalization.
The main momentum driving the negotiations was at the macro-political
level. However, the effort to liberalize new areas of commercial activity
raised societal concerns at the micro-level, for instance in the farming
community. It seems that as liberalization rolls on and, seemingly of
necessity, encompasses new areas as it goes, it could continue to raise
voices of resistance, and such constituencies could continue to express
their concerns in a language that is difficult to reconcile within the
normal institutional discourse of the trade regime. The US and the EU
cooperated to launch the Uruguay round.

A 'PYRAMIDAL' STRUCTURE IN THE GATT

With a total bilateral annual merchandise trade of US$225 billion[5], the
United States and the European Union may not be the world's largest
trade partners[6], but these actors wield perhaps the greatest influence over
the international trade organization. Together they overcame opposition
from many contracting parties of the GATT to negotiate aspects of trade
in services, trade-related investment measures (TRIMS), and the
protection of trade-related intellectual property rights (TRIPS). Where
their interests diverged, these trade partners demonstrated the capacity to
set the pace for, and even to interrupt, multilateral negotiations. The
uncertain progress of the Uruguay round of the GATT as a result of a
difference of opinion about agricultural trade called into question the
credibility of the international organization without the support of these
two main players. The commitment of these partners to multilateralism

is therefore vital to the maintenance and progress of a liberal international trade order.

That the most powerful trading nations should exert such influence is nothing new to the international trade system. In 1950, John Condliffe observed that 'leadership in establishing the rule of law lay ... as it always lies, in the hands of great trading nations.'[7] Nor is this new to the GATT, or particular to the Uruguay round. Reflecting on the Tokyo round of the GATT, Gilbert Winham described a 'pyramidal' structure of negotiations where the main bargains were struck among the most powerful actors.[8] Following the Uruguay round negotiations in December 1993, *The Economist* echoed this by commenting that the United States and the European Union had 'turned multilateral talks into a two-way bargain.'[9]

The pyramidal structure that Winham observed perhaps was accentuated in the Uruguay round. This is due to many factors, including the increased number of states participating in the Uruguay round that gave the metaphorical pyramid a larger base, and hence the constituency which the US and EU influenced was physically larger. Another factor is that the agenda was more elaborate and complex than that of previous negotiations. The new issues of services, TRIPS, and TRIMS increased the facets of the 'pyramid' in which these central players could exert influence. Cross-issue linkages assured that they could also exert influence over the entire MTN from within any one issue-area.[10] Finally, the Uruguay round engaged seriously the difficult issue of agriculture for the first time.

One could identify two distinct ways in which the US and the EU exerted centrifugal forces upon the Uruguay round. These mirror Stephen Lukes' second and third 'faces' of political power. These are, respectively, the exercise of negative influence, and the use of structurally endowed normative coercion.[11]

The second 'face' of power relates to having the capacity to prevent decisions from being taken and to impede negotiations through non-decision. The failure of the US and EU to reach an agreement on agriculture within the allotted time-frame caused the entire Uruguay round to be postponed for a number of months until these main players could resolve that particular issue.[12] It was the EU's failure to reform its Common Agricultural Policy (CAP) sufficiently to enable it to present a negotiating proposal that would be acceptable to the US that caused the most delay. Some EU member states were unwilling or unable for domestic reasons to agree to certain reforms, which delayed the preparation of a negotiating mandate for at least nine months in 1992.

This caused a lacuna in the Uruguay round. By non-decision, therefore, the EU exercised power over the negotiations. One might argue that the EU was in a sense 'permitted' to exert such power by the US which, believing that no agreement was better than a poor agreement, did not engage in substantive negotiations until a CAP reform was concluded. Regardless of one's view, the fact remains that these two players influenced, if not controlled, the pace of progress of the GATT round.

The third 'face' of power relates to the ability to set the agenda, and to control from the outset which issues would be negotiated and which would not. As important, it involves the ability to determine in which international institution issues would be negotiated, thereby choosing the rules and norms to one's advantage. This third 'face' assumed an interesting dimension in the Uruguay round, in that it was the first time that trade in services and intellectual property rights were introduced into the GATT for consideration. It is important to point out that in these areas the interests of the US and EU were more or less congruent.

The US and the EU were able to determine in which international organization the issues of services and intellectual property rights would be raised, thus *a priori* influencing the manner in which they would be treated.[13] Developing countries questioned the jurisdiction of the GATT by arguing that the trade regime was not competent in any areas other than manufactured goods[14], and that better fora would be the World Intellectual Property Organization (WIPO) and the United Nations Conference on Trade and Development (UNCTAD), which already had experience in dealing with intellectual property, and services, respectively. For the US and the EU, the success of a round of negotiations with such a diverse agenda demanded that cross-issue linkages should be maintained. Whilst this was not achieved – the services negotiations were legally 'parallel but separate' from the rest of the Uruguay round – the issue was negotiated within the GATT, a regime whose explicit norms are those of liberalization and non-discrimination, rather than a forum which historically had been guided by essentially anti-liberal views, such as the UNCTAD.

The first 'face' of power, that of the purposive use of direct coercion, occurred as much between the US and the EU as it did between them and the other members of the trade regime. What is important to recognize, however, is that on many important issues the US and EU shared similar interests, and that the institutionally endowed normative power of the trade regime reinforced the influence that both exerted over the course of the negotiations. This is easily overlooked, since the overt use of coercion between them in the agricultural dispute seemed to capture attention.[15]

A DISPUTED RELATIONSHIP

Despite their broad agreement in a number of areas, the US-EU trade relationship has been characterized by a number of trade disputes since the early 1980s. This is perhaps not surprising, given such a large bilateral volume of trade, the fact that one partner has been engaged in the creation of a unified economic area that requires the regional harmonization of a number of policies, and that these potentially could prejudice the interests of the other on a massive scale.

Among the transatlantic trade disputes have been a number of subsidies for common European projects, such as for aircraft (Airbus), as well as for certain socially-sensitive industries in EU member-states (such as shipbuilding and coal mining); quotas and import licences, such as on bananas; a range of directives relating to technical, sanitary and safety standards, such as labelling and certification (the CE Mark); government procurement practices, such as the 'Utilities Directive' that discriminated against bids without a 50% European content and which accorded preference to European bids even if these were more highly priced by 3%; and disputes over telecommunications, which involved intellectual property rights protection and public procurement.

On the surface, it seems that the issues that were the most politically sensitive and publicized did not concern very large amounts of trade. The majority of trade disputes that had escalated most vociferously to the brink of 'trade war' concerned agriculture. Agriculture is certainly a large component of transatlantic trade. Yet each individual dispute concerned a relatively small amount of trade; for instance, $55 million of feedgrains as a result of the incorporation of Spain and Portugal into the Community in 1986, and $1 billion worth of soyabeans in 1992-3. On paper these issues pale into insignificance relative to the total value of bilateral trade. One would not have thought, given the bitter acrimony over agriculture in the concluding stages of the Uruguay round, that the EU was already the largest importer of US agricultural commodities.[16] While there were some real domestic pressures that drove this issue – as will be seen below – it seems not entirely unreasonable to suggest that the degree of acrimony in the GATT was in a sense 'created' by the process of negotiation; it was a feature of the GATT process, rather than of intrinsic importance.

Though the agricultural subsidies of the CAP have been the cause of long-standing differences between the US and the EU, disputes over agriculture escalated in the mid-1980s. Several GATT dispute panels were convened to consider both domestic support systems and export subsidies on such commodities as wheat, flour, sugar, poultry, pasta, citrus fruits, tinned fruits, and oilseeds.[17] A major dispute erupted concerning wine certification, oenological practices, and corn gluten feed, which became bundled into a 'Corn Gluten-Wine Equity Dispute.' Another concerned veterinary standards for slaughterhouses, and the Meat Directive which banned the use of the bovine hormone Somatotropin (BST). And, of course, the serious agricultural dispute over EU subsidies on oilseeds was linked to the reform of the CAP during the closing acts of the Uruguay round in 1992-3.

Throughout the Uruguay round it seemed that a handful of European farmers could destabilize a large bilateral trade relationship and imperil an international negotiation in which between $212 and $274 billion in annual world income gains were at stake.[18] Several factors were responsible for agriculture capturing the headlines. The first was that farmers were well organized, lobbied effectively, and were able to attract media attention by protesting visibly in the streets of European capitals, disrupting traffic and burning effigies. The US also kept agriculture in the limelight by blaming a lack of progress in all areas of the round – even those for which it was responsible – on the inability of the EU to compromise in this one area.[19]

Perhaps the greatest factor was that the prospect of liberalizing the international trade in agricultural commodities entailed changes to domestic support policies, which raised social defence mechanisms. While each agriculture dispute enumerated above seems small when taken in isolation, these were individual salvos by the US on the core principles of the CAP. Rioting farmers hit a chord of historical import-ance. Following the Second World War, European states were very sensitive to their farming constituencies, and a generation of Europeans still can remember being hungry after the war. This issue is not one that can be dismissed lightly. Thus, the language of resistance was not simply against the liberalization of particular commodities, but of preserving the 'economic security' of the whole farming population against the predatory practices of the US and its 'Rambo-style' diplomacy. European politicians sympathetic to the farmers' cause argued that agriculture was not simply another manufactured product that was amenable to being subjected to the liberal disciplines of the GATT. Rather, the agriculture community was intrinsic to safeguarding a rural 'way of life'; the programmes that were in place to shelter farmers from international competition were not protectionist in the strictest economic sense, but were social in design.

An area where similar concerns were raised was in the context of cinematographic films. It seemed, during December 1993, that the entrenched opposition of some member states to the liberalization of films and television would prevent the EU from endorsing a Uruguay round agreement. Certain member states, led by France, wished to maintain certain 'cultural' initiatives such as the 'Television Without Frontiers' directive that requires a quota of European content in television programming. Many Europeans argued that television and films are art, an expression of culture, and that they should not be liberalized in the same manner as manufactured products. They demanded a 'cultural exclusion' from the services agreement in cinematographic films as a barrier against the 'cultural imperialism' of the United States.

What agriculture and films have in common is that mainly non-economic arguments were used to justify a defence against liberalism. Commercial considerations unquestionably did underlie both of these issues, but the language of maintaining a 'distinct cultural identity' used by Europeans was difficult to refute within the confines of the sterile language of 'efficiency' and 'comparative advantage.' There are, of course, significant differences between agriculture and films. At least one major difference is as important to the argument developed below as are their similarities. Agriculture is a declining industry, whilst the film and television industry has a potential to expand rapidly. For this reason, the motives for negotiating agriculture differed significantly from those for negotiating services, of which films and television were part. Agriculture came to the fore as an issue due to structural surpluses and a depression in farming communities; the entertainment industry, on the other hand, promises to be a high-growth area. An elaboration of this structural difference is crucial, since the issue of films is likely to become amplified, whilst that of agriculture is likely to decrease in importance.

THE 'FORCED CHANGED MANDATE' OF THE GATT

Before examining these issues in detail, it is interesting to inquire why the US and the EU desired in the first place to launch a new round of trade negotiations with the issues of agriculture services on its agenda. The Uruguay round can be explained as the product of three factors: first, at the macro-political level, by a shared desire among the US and the EU for political stability in the trade system; second, to permit this, by the political necessity of courting new political constituencies to counteract protectionism at the domestic level; and third, by the sheer commercial advantages that would accrue from the liberalization of new, dynamic areas in which the US and EU had a competitive advantage.

A main political imperative shared by the US and the EU was to safeguard the GATT as a forum through which to combat their domestic protectionist forces. Although the GATT was created on the basis of a liberal ideal, its mechanisms reflected a pragmatic realization that this ideal is often difficult to 'sell' politically. A principal architect of the liberal post-war order, US Secretary of State Cordell Hull, expounded the classical liberal connection between free commerce, laissez-faire government, and peaceful international relations. Behind this rhetoric lay Hull's campaign since 1934 to destroy Britain's discriminatory Imperial Preference system that had excluded the US and which had caused US trade to decline dramatically. Following the war, while the United States wished to see an elimination of the Imperial system, Britain agreed in principle to liberalization, but in practice to only a process of negotiations towards more liberal policies. Furthermore, while the depression of the interwar years had imparted to liberal theory an enhanced credibility, it was difficult for the US to convince its partners, whose economies were ravaged by war, to place the ideal of liberalization above social concerns for employment and reconstruction. Thus, whereas pure liberal theory advocates that unilateral liberalization is a state's best policy, political imperatives caused the liberal goal to be achieved through mercantilistic means. The idea that liberalization should be progressive, and that it should take place according to the trading of 'concessions' implied that liberalization was not intrinsically beneficial but something that required 'safeguards' and 'compensation' though reciprocity.

As the system became operational, the GATT, which had been intended to protect the trade system by legally controlling the use of tariffs by governments, served to protect governments from their own protectionist forces. The United States, being the world's largest producer and trading nation immediately following the war did not have a large protectionist constituency. However, as it began to face competition in the 1970s, the rounds of the GATT enabled the executive to channel demands for protection into an expectation of negotiated market-access. The GATT also provided governments with the excuse that, as much as they would like to be sympathetic to domestic demands for protection, they were bound by an international treaty not to raise tariffs.[20]

However, by the early 1980s, a recession, slow growth, and declining annual volumes of international trade, compounded by competition from NICs contributed to a proliferation of extra-GATT arrangements, such as non-tariff barriers (NTBs) and orderly marketing arrangements. The 'law of constant protectionism' was offered to explain that there is a finite amount of protectionism within any economy, and that if one avenue for its expression is plugged, namely tariffs, it will manifest through other means.[21] Politically, it was feared that governments were no longer using the GATT as a tool in the management of domestic protectionism. The New Protectionism appeared to be eroding the basic consensus that had characterized the post-war period, and the authority of the GATT along with it. Two arguments, from very different theoretical traditions, hailed the apparent demise of the GATT.

The first was a neo-realist appraisal of the international trade system. This viewed the use of NTBs as an example that states would turn to whatever means available to protect their interests, and in the deteriorating economic climate they would continue to do so flagrantly.[22] The disputes on the floor of the GATT Council where Japan contended that French skis were unsafe on Japanese snow, and the French retorting that French roads were unsuitable for Japanese motorcycles indicated to some that states were no longer attempting to mask the fact that technical and safety standards had in some cases become blatant protectionist instruments. The underlying reason for this inability to police the rules, it was contended, was the decline of the United States from a position of hegemony. When the US was materially preponderant and able to offer incentives to its trade partners, they would cooperate and adhere to the rules of the regime. However, since the US had declined relative to its partners, and could not continue to offer greater concessions than it received, it was demanding equal reciprocity. Thus, the neo-realist view of cooperation was based upon a belief that states would adhere to the norms of the regime so long as a dominant state provided benefits and maintained the legitimacy to enforce the system.[23]

The second critique of the GATT was perhaps more devastating. Complementary positions from neo-classical and structural perspectives were intended to show how the neo-realist concern over growing grey-area mercantilism was misplaced, and in so doing criticized the very relevance of the GATT. It was argued that both the neo-realists and the GATT held to an outdated conception of international trade that was state-centric. That is, the definition of international trade as only the passage of goods between two customs points overlooked the fact that through foreign investment 'foreign' products could be purchased by consumers without these having passed a customs point in their finished form. Conversely, production, having become global, produced a situation where, for instance, American products, produced outside the United States by American corporations, were being counted as 'foreign' trade once these were shipped into the US market.[24] It was also argued that credit was the predominant force of the international economy, rather than trade. Without access to finance, international trade becomes difficult. Thus, the trade system was subordinate to the financial structure of the international economy. Given that credit was not only freely available, but was expanding in the 1980s, and that foreign investment was also growing at a rate faster than trade, it was suggested that it would not matter if the multilateral trade system of the GATT were to perish.[25] Since the importance of the GATT was minimal, by extension the concern about neo-mercantilism had been overstated.

While neo-realists did have a rather unsophisticated view of the relative importance of the structures of the international political economy, the arguments concerning the globalization of capital and investment, although academically correct, would not easily be made within a legislative framework. Congressmen in the US tend to be sympathetic to their constituents, and to their subjective perceptions of competition, even if the reality is that trade is of minor importance to the functioning of the international economy. The reality that was facing US legislators in the early 1980s was that the US trade deficit was growing every year, and demands for protection began to spill over the traditional channels that were designed to manage such pressure. Petitions to the International Trade Commission (ITC) for investigations into anti-dumping and countervailing duty actions had increased from an average of 50 per annum during the 1970s to 200 in 1982 alone. Many petitioners, dissatisfied with unfavourable findings, channelled their demands for trade remedies to Congress.[26] As Congressmen began to draft 'sectoral reciprocity' bills and threatened to require the US Trade Representative to retaliate against trade partners, fears grew over the future of the rules-based multilateral trade system.

Paradoxically, such concerns came at a time when the GATT had accomplished its mission remarkably well. Through successive negotiating rounds conducted under its auspices, the average tariff rate had fallen from over 40% in 1947 to approximately 6% which would pertain after the full implementation of the schedules from the Tokyo round. Taken together, the coincidence of these two factors created a situation where protectionist sentiments were increasing, but it was difficult for governments to maintain a momentum behind the liberalization project. Low average tariff levels meant that many tariffs were already very low, and many others were at the threshold of what was politically tolerable. It was exceptionally difficult, therefore, to cultivate a pro-export lobby behind the liberalization effort. The traditional trade constituency was more or less satisfied.

The institutional memory of the protectionism and discriminatory trade arrangements of the interwar years prompted governments to desire to rescue the faltering credibility of the GATT, but the international economic situation had made this exceptionally difficult to sustain politically. It was therefore necessary for governments to look to sectors of the economy that were not already being served by the GATT system from which to cultivate liberal interests. The GATT, which was intended originally to apply only to industrial, manufactured products, omitted many such sectors. Yet revenues from the international trade in services and from the exploitation of intellectual property rights grew by 256% and 132%, respectively, in the 1980s as compared with 95% for trade in goods.[27]

The US government 'realized' that service industries accounted for 57% of GNP. The US had a competitive advantage in telecommunications, information services, audio-visual entertainment, and in some aspects of consulting, such as legal services.[28] In fact, it has been argued that a coterie of service industries internationally, but mainly in the US, had opened the minds of governments to the possibility of enhancing market access opportunities for the international trade in services, as opposed to governments having to seek out these interests.[29]

In addition, many American firms were concerned about the flouting of copyrights and patents due to an ineffectual regime administered by WIPO. It was estimated that American firms lost $2 billion annually in potential trade due to infringements of intellectual property rights.[30] The US could gain the support of computer software firms, recording companies, and pharmaceutical companies which desired stronger protection of their trademarks and patents. The US therefore proposed to launch a new GATT round to negotiate these issues.

The member states of the EU initially were suspicious of the US agenda, though many accepted a new round in principle.[31] The EU reversed its initial scepticism when it realized that, as a whole, European states had a larger share of world trade in services than the US. In 1987, the US was the world's largest services exporter, with an 11.2% share, but was followed closely by France, with 10.6%, the UK with 8.6%, the Federal Republic of Germany with 8.2%, Italy with 6.5%, and Spain with 4.3%.[32] Similarly, income from intellectual property among the G7 in 1991 was $30 billion, of which the United States accounted for $18.5 billion, followed by France, which was the second largest national producer of patents and copyrights.[33]

Underpinning the launching of the Uruguay round, one can therefore identify common political and economic interests among the transatlantic partners at both the governmental and domestic levels. There was a realization that for political reasons, protectionist pressures needed to be managed. Prior to the ministerial meeting that launched the Uruguay round, European Commissioner Willy De Clerq agreed with the US that, 'failure at Punta del Este would mean the slow death of the GATT and bring with it the greatest possible disorder in international trade relations.'[34] There was also the sheer commercial realization on the part of both the US and the EU member states that they would benefit from market access opportunities in these new areas. Just as important was a need at the domestic level to cultivate these industries to counteract growing protectionism. The discussion will now move on to consider the issue of agriculture, where it will be argued, perhaps controversially, that although this issue dominated the media attention devoted to the Uruguay round, the US and the EU shared fundamental interests in this issue-area as well.

AGRICULTURE: STRUCTURAL CRISIS AND COMPROMISE

Both the US and the EU were motivated to discuss agriculture in the Uruguay round by shared social problems in their agriculture sectors, and by mounting financial burdens on public resources. A structural crisis, caused by a condition of international surplus capacity, caused farm prices to decline and many farmers in both the US and Europe to become bankrupt. The burden on public treasuries was due to the fact that the US and the EU had similar price-related domestic support mechanisms.

During the 1970s, a naturally-endowed comparative advantage in the production of agricultural commodities and an undervalued dollar enabled the US to increase its agricultural trade balance from a surplus of $1.3 billion in 1970 to $26.6 billion in 1980.[35] With confidence in the export market, on which 60% of US wheat production became dependent, farmers borrowed heavily to purchase more land and equipment. Total US farm debt stood at $127 billion in 1982, much of which was borrowed with land as collateral.[36] But a series of factors in the early 1980s very quickly caused a farming crisis in the US. Bumper crops in 1981 and 1982 caused prices to decline, whilst an appreciating dollar made US farm products relatively more expensive on world markets. At the same time, the debt crisis had given developing countries an incentive to stimulate production to conserve foreign exchange. President Carter's use of agricultural embargoes as a political weapon had earned the US a reputation as an unreliable supplier, which contributed to falling exports as well. Through a combination of these factors, the US had lost many traditional customers, and US agricultural exports halved over the period from $45 billion in 1981 to $28 billion in 1986. Farm income fell sharply from $35 billion in 1979 to $19 billion in 1982, and voluntary liquidations of farms rose from 100 in 1981 to 7,000 in 1982.[37] In 1984, US farmers were indebted to the tune of $251 billion, but earned only $33 billion.[38]

At the same time, the cost to the US government grew exponentially. Government programmes since the 1930s had established social safety-nets whereby the government would intervene to purchase supplies from farmers at a set price which was higher than the market price. However, this price was lower than what farmers had expected to be able to service their loans.[39] Thus, rather than respond to falling market prices by curtailing production, farmers sought to compensate for losses of income by stimulating production. The cost of government programmes consequently increased to $11.7 billion in 1982, compared with an annual average of $2.8 billion throughout the 1970s.[40] This burden increased to $18.8 billion in 1985, and $25.5 billion in 1986, the year that the Uruguay round was convened. This amounted to 15% of the federal budget deficit for that year, and with little relief in sight, the government began to prepare military bases for the storage of surplus commodities.[41]

Though the US implemented various counter-measures, such as set-aside schemes and export promotion programmes, it became evident that in the long term the US could not manage the crisis through unilateral measures. For, while setting aside farm land decreased the amount of crops that the government had to finance, it also decreased the potential of the US to export. The US government recognized that the US had a comparative advantage in the production of many crops, and that the EU, which on the whole did not enjoy such favourable growing conditions, had increased its exports by 154% from 1979 to 1982 through the use of subsidies.[42] For the US, international agreement on the use of subsidies was a precondition to effecting sustainable domestic reforms that would not prejudice the long term health of the US agriculture export industry. The Reagan Administration would table a 'double-zero' proposal for agriculture to eliminate completely both internal and export subsidies.[43]

The EU also was experiencing social disruption in its agriculture sector and increased financial burdens. Among the most important instruments of the Common Agricultural Policy was a price-support mechanism similar to that used in the US to prevent farmers' incomes from falling too low. The Commission would establish a 'threshold' price for individual commodities, and would intervene to purchase stocks from farmers at that price if the world market price fell below it. With falling world prices and a growing dependence on guaranteed prices, European farmers had increasing production such that by 1986 the EU produced 140% of world demand for butter and 118% of world demand for cereals. By the mid-1980s, internal prices were on average 30% higher than world prices, and, like the US government, the European Commission was burdened with excess supplies in storage. In 1985, it held a staggering 15,730,000 tonnes of cereals. As world prices continued to fall, the Commission was losing even more money as the real value of intervention stocks decreased. In 1985 alone, these fell from a value of Ecu 12 billion to Ecu 5.5 billion. The financial burden was so severe that the CAP had come to account for 60% of the entire EU budget from 1986-87. This had forced the EU to revise its budget to cover a shortfall of Ecu 2 billion in 1986, and of Ecu 5 billion in 1987.[44] The European Parliament reported that 'the CAP in 1986 and 1987 is facing... impending budgetary Armageddon.'[45]

The EU therefore had very pressing incentives to control spending on agriculture and to reform the CAP. There was no question that the CAP should be 'adjusted' and 'adapted' so that 'the share of public expenditure claimed by agriculture can be reduced.'[46] However, the EU resisted the suggestions of the US to alleviate the farming crisis by negotiating a more *liberal* agricultural trade regime in the Uruguay round. To liberalize to the extent that the US had suggested would have involved dismantling the mechanisms of the CAP.

The EU had always maintained that the CAP was primarily a social instrument. During the Second World War, Pétain had encouraged a 'retour à la terre' policy to increase the number of farmers. He emphasized the moral virtues of 'travail, famille, et patrie,' which reinforced the already deep association of farming with traditional moral values. The family farm was seen as a pillar of society and religion.[47] Michael Tracy had commented that, 'agriculture in France seemed hardly to be a subject for economic analysis: its importance was generally recognized almost without question and the rest of the community seemed to accept an obligation to preserve a large and reasonably prosperous agriculture.'[48] The protection of this social institution found expression in the

CAP. As outlined by the Treaty of Rome in 1958, the CAP was designed to meet both social and economic objectives.[49] As the first common policy of post-war Europe, it was imbued with an additional importance as a symbol of European unity. Though the issue of agriculture was discussed in various GATT negotiations, there had never been a serious commitment to liberalization. As late as the Tokyo round in 1973, a European Council declared that the CAP was 'basic to its unity and fundamental objectives,' and that 'its principal mechanisms ... do not constitute a matter for negotiation.'[50]

For the EU, the international management of world agriculture through the Uruguay round would both alleviate the financial burden caused by low world prices and at the same time safeguard the social objectives of the CAP. It preferred to manage markets, to stabilize international prices and to regulate 'supply, demand and stocks, and, failing that, a division of the market.'[51] The EU therefore agreed to a negotiating agenda for agriculture that mandated a 'phased reduction of the negative effects' of agricultural protection, but not the actual instruments of protection.[52]

The US exerted pressure on the EU in a number of ways to conform with its preference for liberalization. At every opportunity, the US condemned various policies of the CAP, and either initiated GATT dispute settlement procedures to investigate the legality of the subsidies, or, acting on its own determination, threatened to retaliate unilaterally against the EU with trade sanctions. Through such instruments as the Export Enhancement Programme (EEP) the US targeted traditional European agricultural markets with subsidized sales.[53] The 1985 Farm Act lowered the price of main agricultural commodities, such as by 25% for grains, which exerted downward pressure on world market prices. At the same time, the US devalued its dollar, which affected the world market price for many agricultural commodities. In fact, the structural influence of the devaluation of the US dollar alone in the late 1980s caused the costs of the CAP to increase by approximately Ecu 7 billion.[54] It is interesting to note in this context that the French government insisted on the devaluation of the dollar in the interests of its *overall* economic policy, which goes some way to illustrate just where its priorities lay.

Notwithstanding such pressure, the EU attempted to 'adjust' the CAP through further management measures. In 1987, the EU instituted a programme of 'budget stabilizers' which suspended guaranteed purchases if production reached a set threshold. The intent was that this production threshold could be lowered to give farmers an incentive to reduce production, and to compensate them with direct payments for land 'set-aside,' or taken out of production. While this approach seemed consistent with the EU's preferences, it caused two fundamental problems.

The first was its effect on the EU's position in the GATT negotiations. In return for agreeing to a reduction in cereals production, France secured a commitment from the Commission to seek a 'rebalancing' of international commitments on the import of cereals substitutes. The EU had accorded the US a 0% tariff for corn gluten and soya in the Kennedy round of the GATT as part of a package to compensate the US for the trade diversion effects of the then newly implemented CAP. France now argued that it would be unfair to limit European cereal production if the market could be taken by cheap imports of US cereal substitutes. The EU therefore argued that it should be permitted to raise the tariff on oilseeds in exchange for lowering subsidies on cereals. The US, under pressure from the American Soyabean Association, could agree to rebalancing only under pain of igniting factional conflict in Congress within the farm lobby. This contributed to the deadlock.

However, the second difficulty with the budget stabilizers regime provided an impetus to the GATT negotiations. This was that they neither corrected structural surpluses, nor did they improve the condition of European farmers. By 1990, only 500,000 acres of the most marginal quality farmland had been taken out of production, and the cereal harvest regularly exceeded production thresholds. Furthermore, many farmers had shifted production to oilseeds, causing oversupply in that sector as well. Average farm incomes declined by 3.1% from 1988 to 1990. Moreover, approximately 20% of the largest farms, which were essentially agri-businesses, were receiving 80% of subsidies. Thus this average decline in farm incomes masked a sharp accentuation of despair at the lower end of the spectrum, which was composed of small-holders. [55]

This situation illustrated to the Commission the ineffectiveness of politically-manufactured stability, and in particular, of price-support mechanisms. These encouraged overproduction, placed a large financial burden on public treasuries, benefitted the larger farmers over the smaller ones in need of social support, and diverted funds away from alternative means of support. Then EC President Jacques Delors admitted in December 1990, 'we know we have to reform [the CAP].'[56] From 1991, the issue was pursued on two parallel tracks. The Commission attempted to reform the CAP which involved much heated internal debate, and at the same time it attempted to crystallize the CAP reforms in a GATT treaty, which involved as much debate with the US. The 'MacSharry Plan' for the CAP involved price reductions, compulsory land set-asides and compensatory payments that were 'decoupled' from production. This would enable the CAP to be reconfigured in such a way that real reductions in both internal supports and export subsidies could be effected. This would both satisfy the Americans, and, more importantly, give effect to the social mandate of the CAP.

Technically, there was a linkage between CAP reform and the Uruguay round negotiations, though this was denied by the EU. The former was a precondition for the EU to be able to agree to a deal that would be acceptable to the US. The EU maintained that the reform of the CAP was for the benefit of the EU, not the US, but there was sufficient scope for European farmers to believe otherwise. Because the CAP had always been portrayed in the language of 'social responsibility,' to them the CAP had symbolic power. It signified protection from unstable world markets, and safety for their incomes. Without the social policies of the CAP, many farmers believed their livelihoods would be destroyed. The very words 'reform of the CAP' were received by some as a threat to social stability. Anger was vented both against the US, for being a predatory power, as well as against the European Commission, for being a traitor. The 20,000 farmers protesting on the streets of Brussels outside the GATT ministerial meeting in December 1990 illustrated their anger by burning effigies of Raymond MacSharry, the EU Agriculture Commissioner, alongside effigies of Clayton Yeutter, the US Trade Representative. The European Confederation of Maize Producers announced its 'indignation that the trading blackmail used by the United States has been effective in making the EEC give way.'[57] French MEPs accused MacSharry of 'aligning ... totally with American demands [and] abandoning farmers in Europe so that farmers in America can survive.'[58]

Therefore, both the United States and the European Commission had similar interests in a GATT agreement on agriculture in the interest of restoring stability. This is by no means to suggest that the debate over the details of the final agriculture package agreed at Blair House in Washington in November 1992 was not exceptionally difficult. It involved arduous negotiation both between the US and EU, and within the EU to the extent that Agriculture Commissioner MacSharry had accused Delors of sabotage and tendered his resignation in anger. It is ironic that, as time passed, the hostilities between the US and the EU increased at the same time that the EU came to the view, similar to that of the US, that price-support mechanisms had aggravated the problem. During the time that the US refused to negotiate constructively with the EU for the first four years of the Uruguay round by not compromising its 'double-zero' proposal, relations over the agriculture issue between the transatlantic partners was tense, but was essentially in a stalemate. As the trade partners engaged in constructive negotiations, tensions certainly escalated, but it is important – indeed crucial – to recognize the underlying similarity in interests that had moved them to that stage.

It was the combination of arduous negotiation over detail between the US and the EU, and, importantly, the failure of the EU to exercise effective leadership at home that had caused this issue to assume such a central importance in the Uruguay round. Though the US and the EU were coming closer to agreement, the pressure that the US had exerted upon the Commission for the first four years had contributed to the perception that the US was the enemy of European farmers. Following the signature of the Blair House Accord, the US Embassy and MacDonald's restaurants alike were targets for farmers' protests. Moreover, it was very difficult, once the European Commission was ready to compromise, for it to do so without appearing as though it was 'giving in' to the Americans.

CINEMATOGRAPHIC FILMS: CULTURE OR COMMERCE?

The widening of the agenda to encompass agriculture raised concerns for 'economic security.' Similarly, the inclusion of audio-visual services on the negotiating agenda of the Uruguay round raised concerns about 'cultural security.' The issue became couched in the language of maintaining a distinct 'identity,' and in the language of resistance against American 'cultural imperialism.'

The audio-visual services issue concerned two European Directives, the 'Television Without Frontiers' Directive of 3 October 1989 (which came into force on 3 October 1991) and various 'MEDIA' Programmes.[59] The former established a quota for 51% European content for television programmes aired in the EU. The latter is a subsidy programme to assist in the funding, production, and distribution of cinema films, mainly by assisting cooperative productions among member states. The television directive is perhaps more commercially distorting, since the quota is emphatic: it restricts the broadcast of US television programmes.

The US therefore challenged the Television Without Frontiers Directive in the GATT on 23 October 1989 on the basis that its local content quota violated the GATT.[60] The European Union retorted that television programming is exempted from the GATT because it is a powerful medium to define and shape national values.[61] The debate continued in 1990 in the services negotiations of the Uruguay round as the Group of Negotiators on Services (GNS) created a special audio-visual working group to study the issue. The draft services agreement agreed to the 'special cultural status' of audio-visual services, which the European Union endorsed.[62] The EU, with the support of the European Parliament, sought the inclusion of a 'special cultural clause' in the final services agreement.[63] France, however, was not satisfied with the mere recognition of the specificity of the culture industry. French directors, actors, writers, and technicians quickly formed an alliance with their European counterparts. Under pressure from this alliance, French Communications Minister, Alain Carignon argued for a 'cultural exemption.' France desired audio-visual services to be excluded completely from the GATT.[64] At the eleventh hour, on 13 December 1993, President Clinton agreed to disagree with the EU on this issue, and withdrew the United States' insistence on a code for audio-visual services.

The language in which the debate was framed is perhaps more interesting than its outcome. The US argued that the product of its audio-visual 'entertainment industry' is a commodity like any other, and should therefore be subject to the liberal principles of the GATT.[65] Many in the EU, however, and particularly the French, insisted on referring not to an audio-visual industry, but to a 'cultural industry.' For instance, French Culture Minister Jacques Toubon denounced a 'US cultural invasion,' and warned that France would veto a services agreement that did not protect it from 'the Coca-Cola-McDonald's-Disney World lifestyle.'[66] The film producer Claude Berri stated that, 'if culture cannot be treated as an exception in GATT negotiations, Europe's cultural identity will die.'[67]

The latter arguments are persuasive. In 1992, *The Economist* suggested that 'information technology... is beginning to cause a deeper social transformation, by affecting the flow of information and ideas by which people define their culture.'[68] In an era where the information that reaches individuals on a daily basis can come from any part of the globe, this social transformation may engender a primordial, defensive reaction to identify with a primary community which embodies the values and symbols of an individual's identity. As the world becomes larger, individual security within a particular community may become more important, particularly if there is a perceived threat of a loss of identity from an 'invasion' of a predatory culture, as the statements above would seem to indicate.

Indeed, the propensity for communication, and particularly symbols and images to be used as a form of political control has long been recognized. Bourdieu has argued that the 'symbolic power to impose the principle of the construction of reality – in particular social reality – is a major dimension of political power.'[69] It is for this reason that the 'Voice of America' was an important component of the US ideological campaign against communism, and several states have banned satellite dishes.[70] With the seeming globalization of liberal, capitalist values, and with prosperity in many countries being identified with the possession of brand-name consumer items[71], one may even speak of a Gramscian hegemony of values – one that the US was attempting to propagate through the GATT, an institution which is the very embodiment of such a liberal ideology. The consequence of a globalizing culture has been lamented by Daniel Singer as, 'a sinister uniformity of heroes and models, metaphors and dreams.' He continued: 'Mastery of the image may well become both the instrument and the symbol of leadership in the New World Order.'[72]

Neither is it novel to suggest that increased communication between different cultures can result in insecurities. Some studies of nationalism have argued that modernization and increased communications can cause people to become self-aware, and to reinforce and amplify their group solidarity.[73] The attempt to liberalize 'cultural industries' in the Uruguay round may have caused the two concepts of economic security and the communications-engendered nationalism to meet. In this context, the European Commissioner for Audiovisual and Cultural Affairs, Joao de Deus Pinheiro, stated that, 'historically, [Europe] is a place where attempts at cultural hegemony have always produced a return to nationalism.'[74]

It is not only the EU that has resisted the liberalization of the trade in 'cultural' services. NAFTA limits ownership by NAFTA signatories of Mexican cable television systems to 49%[75], and cultural industries were excluded from the US-Canada Free Trade Agreement due to the fact that Canada also promotes local content in its television broadcasts. At a 1994 hearing of the Canadian Radio-television and Telecommunications Commission (CRTC) concerning the corporate take-over of Maclean Hunter to create a giant multimedia service provider, advocates of the deal installed an 18 inch satellite dish on the roof and flooded the hearing room with 300 channels of American programmes to reinforce their point that the protection of Canadian culture depends on developing its own national industry.[76] The Uruguay round could represent a moment of intersection between economic security, where culture is commodified, and communication, where culture is predicated upon the technological construction, or representation, of social reality.[77]

Having considered this position, however, another argument is perhaps more persuasive. The motivation of the US to ensure an export market for its entertainment industry, and the motivation for the EU to protect its less competitive film-makers can be explained in a word, 'money.' Films are the second largest export earner for the US, after defence industries.[78] In 1992, the US earned $3.15 billion on the sale and royalties of television, cinema and video in the EU[79], and the US industry has become heavily dependent on export markets (see the table below). In 1990, only 30% of its revenues were accrued from the domestic US market, as opposed to 80% in 1980.[80] The world television programming market was worth $80 billion in 1993, and is estimated to be rising at a rate of 10% annually, with pay-TV adding to the potential for generating revenues.[81] Moreover, the capability to regenerate profits in this sector is unlike almost any other. A manufactured good depreciates with consumption; the same film (or television programme, sound recording), produced once, can be sold in many different markets simultaneously, released on video, and sold for television royalties. It was therefore important for the US to secure a GATT agreement, even in principle, in this sector.

	US Receipts in the EU (MECU)		EU Receipts in the US (MECU)	
	1990	1992	1990	1992
Cinema	975.2	733.6	43	63.6
Television	1,099.1	1,417.3	80.8	81.7
Video	1,124.0	999.3	88.6	102.3
Total	3,198.3	3,150.2	212.4	247.6

Source: IDATE, IMO Report 1993-1994.

The European position can also be explained as outright commercial protectionism. The resistance was not a broad-based, popular nationalist or social movement against American culture, but was propagated by a small industry lobby and governments. A handful of directors and actors resisted the American 'cultural onslaught' because they feared that a level playing field which would attack their quotas and subsidies ($416 million annually in France) and expose their deficiencies as film-makers. Europeans regularly vote with their money, and spent $923 million at the box-office on US films in 1992.[82] On the other hand, the share of the European market enjoyed by European film-makers has declined to 20%.[83] It could be that Hollywood has an intangible competitive advantage in the production of visual entertainment.

Whether the audio-visual debate really did concern culture or commerce – or the shade of grey in between – is difficult to ascertain. It is for this reason that it was difficult for American negotiators to argue their case in the GNS: the debate hinged on whether audio-visual services are a commodity, or an expression of culture. But whatever one's opinion of the reasons for such voices of dissent, cultural or commercial, the fact remains that as technology shrinks the global marketplace, such debates between the US and the EU in the audio-visual services negotiations are likely to grow. With the growth of satellite television broadcasts and particularly with the extension of fibre-optic cables, the modes for the delivery of films are likely to increase. Similar arguments could be raised in future in the context of pay-TV, or over video-on-demand over Internet-like networks.

'NEW' ECONOMIC SECURITY

What is interesting about the trade in agriculture and audio-visual services is that both issues raised concerns about 'economic security,' loosely defined in a context of other forms of security. There is nothing new about international trade, *per se*, engendering fear about competition and social dislocation through unemployment. Fundamentally, all discussions of economic security, whether they are manifest in the context of trade liberalization or otherwise, are political discussions about the preservation of a way of life.[84] The concept of economic security has a long and varied intellectual heritage. The literature on the economic instruments of warfare has long recognized the strategic value of manipulating devices and of economic coercion.[85] Nearly all theories of International Political Economy can be interpreted as divergent views about the proper way in which to assure social and economic security, and as differing perceptions of asymmetrical market power and the ideological justifications of successive international economic systems.[86]

The current liberal trade system has always recognized that liberalization could cause concerns for societal security. As shown above, the consensus that underlined the very formation of the GATT was forged between Britain's emphasis on safeguarding employment and the United States' insistence on a general agreement on liberalization in principle. To be politically acceptable, general principles were peppered with exceptions, such as in the case of balance of payments difficulties, and to protect against import surges by such means as safeguards and escape clauses.[87] The character of the post-war international economic system was a 'compromise of embedded liberalism' between the more laisser-faire values of the US and the prerogatives for social stability valued among European states.[88]

The concerns raised in the agriculture and films negotiations centred on the character of power exercised in an asymmetrical relationship. The US enjoys a naturally-endowed comparative advantage in the production of main agricultural staples, including grain and soyabeans, which were at the heart of the dispute in the Uruguay round. The US also has a considerably more commercially viable production centre for films in Hollywood and the film industry based in the US enjoys a vertically-integrated global distribution network for them. Thus, the concerns that have been raised in these issues share the traditional features of economic security. There is a basic situation of market dominance on one side and fears of industrial decimation on the other. The debates have centred on the vulnerabilities and sensitivities of the weaker actor in the face of predatory trade policy.

However, one could argue that there is a fundamental difference between the concept of economic security as traditionally conceived and the character of economic insecurities that were raised by the issues of agriculture and audio-visual services in the Uruguay round. Traditional theories of International Political Economy have assumed that production is a means to achieving prosperity. They agree that a sound national economy is a necessary prerequisite for economic security, though they differ on the means of achieving it. By contrast, the objections raised over agriculture and audio-visual services in the Uruguay round show that the association between liberalization and insecurity was perceived to be more direct. The impact on the 'good life' would result not from unemployment and a lack of revenues, but from a direct attack upon national values, culture, and identity.

Such essentially non-economic, normative arguments sit uncomfortably within the liberal trade institution because they are alien (but not irrelevant) to its language. The consensus on embedded liberalism that undergirded the GATT relied principally on the traditional issues of social disruption due to unemployment and readjustment as a result of liberalization, not about the protection of 'identity.' For the same reason that NTBs have been difficult to bring within GATT disciplines – namely, the difficulty in defining a *bona fide* NTB as opposed to a *bona fide* safety standard – so will claims of preserving cultural integrity.

The agriculture and audio-visual disputes have shown that even though there was a relatively small constituency against liberalization in each case, the social construction of the issues in both cases made it difficult to compromise in international fora. The case of agriculture shows that even where the interests of the European Commission were more or less similar to those of the US, the Commission was forced to undertake a campaign of intellectual leadership to convince its own domestic interests that it had not 'sold out' to the US and that it was acting in their interests.

It is likely that the agriculture dispute will subside in the long run. The crisis was due to a structural surplus caused by price-support policies. The immediate crisis was resolved by virtue of an obsolescing bargain between states and their farmers whose political influence was no longer commensurate with their economic importance. The farm population as a proportion of the active workforce in the EU has declined from 30% in 1950 to 7.7% in 1990, and it is, on the whole, an ageing population that is continuing to decline in numbers.[89] Similarly, US farmers constituted only 3% of the total civilian employment by 1988, and the crisis of the 1980s had caused the most inefficient farmers to become bankrupt.[90]

However, the dispute over audio-visual services – while not new, it first surfaced in the 1930s – is symptomatic of a continuing process of globalization that is accelerating with the advent of high-technology delivery systems, and in the globalization of the marketing structures of the service industries. There is every reason to believe that the arguments raised in the audio-visual negotiations of the Uruguay round are a prelude to a larger debate.

GLOBALIZATION AND THE POLITICS OF TECHNOLOGY

Several factors could contribute to both an intensification of the disputes concerning the 'cultural industry,' and to its widening to other international fora. Among these are advances in technology, the realization of the commercial potential of new audio-visual services, the fact that international discussions of market access for these new entertainment services will take place within the larger context of discussions of the global information infrastructure, and that the issues involved will not be confined only to trade, but will involve investment and competition policies as well.[91]

Technological developments, particularly the digitization of transmissions, is blurring the traditional distinction between telephone and television signals. Both signals now can be carried together, enabling the fusion of telephone carriers and cable television networks in the commercialization of video-on-demand services. Digitization also compresses signals, which increases the amount of information that can be carried over a particular band, thus also increasing the number of channels available. Legislative frameworks in both the US and many European states have responded to this technological development through the deregulation of previously autonomous television and telecommunication services. From 1991 to 1993, the US amended its telecommunications legislation, which dated from the 1930s, to permit common (telephone) carriers to provide video services over telephone cables.[92] Alliances between the two industries in the US quickly followed. Among the results of this is the 'Full Service Network' interactive television system unveiled by Time-Warner in cooperation with Silicon Graphics, AT&T, and Scientific Atlanta among others.[93] Deregulation in Europe has been slower, due to the persistence of national monopolies in many member states.[94] However, European communications companies are investing in fibre-optic networks in anticipation of legislation similar to that of the US by 1998.[95]

Underlying this is the realization of the commercial potential of the home entertainment market through these new technologies. Former EU Commission President Delors, in particular, was an advocate of its expansion. He stated that, 'the culture industry will tomorrow be one of the biggest industries, a creator of wealth and jobs.... We have to build a powerful European culture industry that will enable us to be in control of both the medium and its content.'[96] Commissioner Pinheiro projected that the current employment of 1.8 million in the audio-visual industry in Europe could double as early as the year 2000.[97] In parallel with the plans of the Clinton Administration for a National Information Infrastructure (NII), the European Commission has outlined an Information Services Market.[98] However, without a European film and television industry to service the content of such information systems, video-on-demand could represent new avenues through which the American film industry can gain access to the European market. As *Time* magazine observed, 'the giant trucks of Hollywood are hurtling down the information highway and pushing horse and buggy European producers onto country lanes.'[99]

If the real commercial considerations that are at stake in these new modes of delivery for audio-visual services become couched in terms of 'cultural protection,' these issues will be very difficult to resolve. There are indications that such arguments will surface in other international fora. This was foreshadowed during the audio-visual debate in the Uruguay round. There, the European Commission outlined several 'minimum guarantees' that it would require as prerequisites for agreeing to the audio-visual section of the services agreement. Among these was the 'preservation of the ability to regulate existing *and new technology and transmission methods*.'[100] Such exceptions were also raised at the G7 'Information Society' Summit in Halifax in February 1995. Although the G7 communiqué affirmed the principles of liberalization, privatization and open access, it has been suggested that the wording of maintaining 'free and open' information channels was insisted upon by the US, while the word 'fair' was included due to 'European fears that the superhighway will accelerate the globalization of American mass culture.'[101]

The issue of protecting 'culture industries' also surfaced in the context of a proposed OECD Investment Code. While information, as a service, can be transmitted, or traded, across borders, this can require investment in the infrastructure, which is the means for its supply. In the context of a global investment agreement, the EU has insisted upon an exemption for 'culture industries.'[102] This could be a bargaining manoeuvre to put pressure on the US to amend its competition policy, particularly the restrictions that it places on broadcasting.[103] Notwithstanding, it is the nature of the new forms of audio-visual services to implicate not only trade, but investment and competition policy. Given the objections for reasons of 'culture' that have been raised even at this early stage, it seems reasonable to conclude that this issue will gain prominence in future.

CONCLUSION

The issue of agriculture raised concerns for 'economic security,' which centred on the social value attached to programmes for the protection of farmers. Economic security, as expressed in this issue, was due to a subjective belief on the part of farmers in the value of the social institution of the CAP. That such non-economic arguments about maintaining socially valued institutions intruded into international trade negotiations is symptomatic of the widening of the agenda of the GATT to engage in discussions on agriculture in a serious way. On the other hand, whilst the widening of the agenda to encompass audio-visual services also raised concerns for economic security, it was argued that maintaining a distinct culture was put forth as an excuse to shelter a relatively inefficient industry in Europe. Moreover, there are purely commercial reasons for wishing to engender growth in what promises to be a dynamic industry in future. There could be elements of wishing to safeguard a developing industrial policy for the electronic information and entertainment sector. Importantly, unlike the farm community, which is declining as a political constituency, the businesses engaged in the new technologies of the global information age promise to generate substantial revenues, and to employ more people.

These interpretations of the new economic security inform this analysis, the principal burden of which has been to contextualize the US-EU trade relationship within a broad, structural, conception of the international trade system. The following conclusions can be drawn. The first is that despite the sound and fury during the tense negotiations between these actors in the Uruguay round, had there not been a sufficient congruence of interests between the US and the EU, it is unlikely that the trade partners would have found themselves engaged in the negotiations at all. While the US and the EU were divided over the issue of agricultural liberalization, in other issues in the Uruguay round, such as trade in services, TRIMS, and TRIPS, the US and the EU had more or less similar positions, and found themselves on the same side of a northern-developed country consensus, against a southern-developing country resistance. Those who hailed the end of the GATT were wrong.

Although the issue of agriculture caused the most tension between the transatlantic partners, their interests were fundamentally not that dissimilar. Ultimately, the US and the EU, having employed similar support programmes and finding themselves both affected by international surplus-capacity in agriculture, had similar interests in controlling spiralling budgets for domestic agricultural price supports, storage of surpluses, and export subsidies. That the dispute over agriculture did not escalate to the point of imperiling the Uruguay round is testament to the fact that despite the political sensitivities, and the media limelight, endogenous pressures for protection did not in the end take precedence over fundamental state interests which the US and the EU shared. Agriculture nevertheless did cause the most anxiety about the success of the Uruguay round.

Agriculture seems to illustrate *par excellence* the model of 'pyramidal negotiations' in the GATT. The US and the EU both dominated the pace and progress of the negotiations by controlling the progress of this one issue. The EU caused delay because it was engaged in a process of redefining a domestic bargain with its farming constituencies. The US refused to compromise its position until that bargain was struck, both for the sake of obtaining a satisfactory agreement and because it did not wish to factionalize its own farm lobbies. To be sure, both the US and the EU attempted to externalize the difficulties that they experienced in this sector. The escalating subsidy war was only the most visible attempt to thrust the burden of adjustment on to the other. Yet, neither actor could ameliorate the crisis by acting unilaterally. Power politics must therefore be contextualized as the surface manifestation of attempting to gain a *better* deal at the negotiating table, rather than at the root of the relations between the transatlantic partners. At a more fundamental level, the GATT negotiations must be viewed as the international manifestation of each partner attempting to manage domestic pressures. While the international rivalry captured the attention of the media, it was the unfolding of the domestic game that caused the US and EU to shape and to control the Uruguay round within a pyramidal structure.

The most important conclusion that can be drawn, however, concerns the interplay between the macro-political forces which, at a structural level, drove the transatlantic partners to cooperate in convening the Uruguay round and to negotiate the new issue of services, and the micro-social tensions that this caused. It was argued that the transatlantic partners shared a desire to promote the stability of the trade system for political reasons and to gain market access for vibrant new sectors of their economies for commercial reasons. Thus, they cooperated in launching the Uruguay round of the GATT. It was also shown that the issue of services raised some differences of opinion between the US and the EU, most notably in audio-visual services. Whereas the structural imperatives, namely global oversupply, forced the US and the EU into an, albeit difficult, accommodation on the issue of agriculture, the structural imperatives influencing the growth of the international trade regime to include trade in services forced a divisive issue of commerce to the fore between the US and the EU.

It was suggested that the audio-visual dispute may foreshadow a larger debate. The Uruguay round was concerned with the fairly straightforward issue of quotas for television programming, and subsidies for films. In future, the modes of delivery for the entertainment industry could encompass a greater use of satellites, cable systems, and tailored consumer services such as video-on-demand. One might suggest that this will resolve (or exacerbate) the issue by enhancing consumer choice. While the European Commission may mandate that a certain quota of

European programmes be available, there would be very little that it could do to force consumers to 'demand' a certain proportion of European content in their viewing, if consumers were to control the programmes that enter their homes. However, the issues involved are complex. Future negotiations are likely to concern investment rules as these relate to ownership and access to the modes of delivery, to competition policy, and to intellectual property protection. That capitalizing on these new services is a fundamental interests of both the US and the EU is likely to make the debates perhaps even more lively than those over agriculture. To be sure, arguments of cultural imperialism and of ensuring the 'security' of distinct cultural identities will be raised. However, one should not lose sight of the fact that such issues will relate to the larger question of the rules to govern the global information infrastructure. And this is a technological development that, by its very nature, *requires* international cooperation.

Thus, in conclusion, the trade relationship between the US and the EU is likely to become complex as new issues blur the distinction between investment, competition and 'trade,' strictly defined. It is also likely that there will be intense competition in these new areas. But however bitter the disputes over 'identity' and 'security' may become, the US-EU trade relationship will remain within a structure of growing interdependence.

NOTES

1. I would like to thank John Groom, Dan Hiester, Phil Deans, Dominic Powell, and Robert O'Brien for their helpful comments on this chapter. Any errors, of course, remain my sole responsibility.
2. In the interest of clarity, the present name of the EU is used here in the context of events that took place both before and after 1 January 1995.
3. He announced this after the Uruguay round had failed to produce a document by on of its many deadlines. For his reasons why he believed that the 'GATT bled to death' (p.76), see Thurow, *Head to Head: The Coming Economic Battle Among Japan, Europe, and America*, Morrow, New York, 1992, esp. pp.76-85.
4. A qualification needs to be made here. This is perhaps the greatest lesson in the context of the US-EU relationship, and the structural forces that seem to drive the GATT process and to support institutionalized liberalization. This author would not suggest that this focus is more 'important' than normative considerations raised by the Uruguay round, for instance the discussions on extending patents for pharmaceutical companies, where developing countries argued that at issue was literally the difference between life and death.

5. This is the most recent figure given by the European Commission. See 'Commission Sets Out to Revamp US Relations,' *The Reuter European Community Report*, 26 July 1995. All subsequent dollar figures are also given in US dollars.

6. There is some debate as to whether Canada or the EU is the US largest trade partner. This is exemplified by the contributions to this volume by Robert O'Brien and Stephen Woolcock.

7. John Condliffe, *The Commerce of Nations*, W.W. Norton, New York, 1950, p.219.

8. See Gilbert Winham, 'International Negotiation in an Age of Transition,' *International Journal*, Vol.XXXV, No.1, Winter 1979-1980.

9. 'Surprise, Surprise: GATT Comes Right,' *The Economist*, 18 December 1993, p.13.

10. Although the negotiations on trade in services were legally separate but parallel, in practice linkages spread to this area during the MTN. Once the Uruguay round was concluded, however, the discussions on services, particularly financial services, continued.

11. Stephen Lukes, *Power: A Radical Interpretation*, New York University Press, New York, 1986.

12. For an elaboration of the agriculture negotiations of the Uruguay round, see Jarrod Wiener, *Making Rules in the Uruguay Round of the GATT: A Study of International Leadership*, Dartmouth, Aldershot, 1995.

13. The prenegotiations for the round are discussed by Alan Oxley, *The Challenge of Free Trade*, Harvester Wheatsheaf, London, 1990; and Ricardo Caldas, *Brazil and the GATT*, Ph.D Dissertation, International Relations, University of Kent, 1995 (unpublished).

14. There are clauses relating to primary commodities, minerals and agriculture in the original GATT (1947), and other issues had been introduced, such as civilian aircraft in the Tokyo round.

15. That is, until attention shifted to their dispute over public procurement, the trade in television and films, etc.

16. Former EU Commission President Jacques Delors has been quoted as remarking on the 'deep relationship between the world's premier powers.. descending to the level of disputes about pasta and hormones.' In M.M Nelson and G.J. Ikenberry, *Atlantic Frontiers: A New Agenda for US-EC Relations*, Institute for International Economics, Washington D.C., 1993, p.9.

17. See GATT, *Basic Instruments and Selected Documents*, Geneva, various years. In comparison to actual disputes, there has been a relatively small number of GATT dispute panels actually convened. Of the thirty-six panels between the US and the EU, the US brought twenty-one complaints and the EU brought fifteen. The US became disillusioned with the GATT dispute settlement procedure, which the respondent was able to block by refusing to accept its decision. Following the EU's blockage of the 1981 dispute panels on tinned fruit and pasta, the US increasingly resorted to unilateral measures. However, the normative power of the GATT panel on oilseeds proved useful in the propaganda war in the final stages of the Uruguay round.

18. This is the revised figure since the conclusion of the Uruguay round estimated by the IMF. See, Richard Harmsen and Arvind Subramanian, 'Economic Implications of the Uruguay Round,' *International Trade Policies: The Uruguay Round and Beyond*, IMF, Washington, 1994, p.1.

19. William J. Drake and Kalypso Nicolaïdis reported that 'there was no way [that a services agreement] could have been concluded even without the agricultural debacle,' at the 1990 Brussels Ministerial meeting. This was due as much to the US refusal to agree to unconditional MFN as part of the Draft of the General Agreement on Trade in Services (GATS) to maintain sectoral reciprocity in such areas as telecommunications as it was to any intransigence of its trade partners. However, the 20,000 farmers protesting outside of the venue provided a convenient scapegoat. See 'Ideas, Interests, and Institutionalization: Trade in Services and the Uruguay Round,' *International Organization*, Vol.46, No.1, 1992, p.88.
20. Jagdish Bhagwati, *Protectionism*, MIT Press, London, 1988.
21. *Ibid.*
22. See, for instance, Robert Gilpin, *The Political Economy of International Relations*, Princeton University Press, Princeton, NJ., 1987; and Robert Baldwin, 'The New Protectionism: A Response to Shifts in National Economic Power,' in Jeffrey A. Frieden and David A. Lake (eds.), *International Political Economy: Perspectives on Global Power and Wealth*, Unwin Hyman, London, esp. p.368.
23. See Gilpin, *op. cit.*
24. See Susan Strange, 'The Future of the American Empire,' *Journal of International Affairs*, Vol.42, No.1, 1988; and de Anne Julius, *Global Companies and Public Policy: The Growing Challenge of Foreign Direct Investment*, Pinter and the Royal Institute of International Affairs, London, 1990.
25. See Susan Strange, 'Protectionism in World Politics,' *International Organization*, Vol.39, No.2, 1985; and Strange, *States and Markets: An Introduction to International Political Economy*, Pinter Publishers, London, 1988.
26. This point is made by I.M. Destler, *American Trade Politics: System Under Stress*, Institute for International Economics, Washington, 1986.
27. IMF, *op. cit.*, Vol.I: Principal Issues, p.15 fn.35.
28. United States Congress, Office of Technology Assessment, *International Competition in Services*, Government Printing Office, Washington D.C., July 1987; and United States Congress, Office of Technology Assessment, *Trade in Services: Exports and Foreign Revenues*, Government Printing Office, Washington D.C., 1987.
29. Drake and Nicolaïdis, *op. cit.*, pp.37-100. See also: 'Getting Services on the Agenda By Working the Washington Crowd,' *National Journal*, 30 August 1986, pp.2060-2061; 'Lobbying for Free Trade,' *National Journal*, 20 April 1991, pp.942-943; and Bernard Hoekman, 'Market Access Through Multilateral Agreement: From Goods to Services,' *World Economy*, October 1992, esp. p.714.
30. 'Caveat Vendor,' *The Economist*, 1 May 1993, p.77.
31. France, with high unemployment and a volatile currency in the early 1980s, argued that the problems in international trade stemmed not from a return to protectionism, but the fact that the Reagan Administration had caused the dollar to be overvalued. This increased the price of US exports and caused imports to be cheaper, and this led to the demands for protection. France agreed to participate in a GATT round only after the US had devalued the dollar.
32. GATT, *International Trade, 1988-89*, Geneva, 1989. Vol.1, Table 25.
33. OECD, *Services: Statistics on International Transactions*, Paris, 1993.
34. 'Brussels Firm on Farm Trade,' *Financial Times*, 12 September 1986, p.6.
35. 'Falling Exports, Rising Support Payments Throwing Farm Economy Out of Sync.' *National Journal*, 24 November 1984, p.2251.

36. 'Large Surplus, Falling Trade Prompts Review of Methods to Reassure Foreign Clients,' *Congressional Quarterly*, 27 November 1982, p.2911.

37. 'Farming: Invisible Support,' *The Economist*, 11 December 1982, p.39.

38. 'President's Proposal Expects Record Food, Farm Costs to Fall as Economy Mends,' *Congressional Quarterly*, 5 February 1983, p.273; 'Writing a Blank Cheque,' *National Journal*, 23 March 1985, p.625.

39. This is spirit of the Agriculture Adjustment Act of 1933. There were several permutations of government programmes since that time, from Eisenhower's 'soil banks' to 'set asides,' loans to farmers on which they were permitted to default if the value of the crops depreciated below a certain level, and 'blended credit' wherein the government would give farmers a ratio of government reserves to export to make-up a shortfall in profits. See Murray R. Benedict, *Farm Policies of the United States, 1790-1950: A Study of Their Origins and Development*, Octagon Books, New York, 1966.

40. 'Writing a Blank Cheque,' *op. cit.*, p.625.

41. 'Regional and Ideological Rifts Divide the Agriculture Lobby,' *Congressional Quarterly*, 27 August 1983, p.1711; 'Writing a Blank Cheque,' *op. cit.*, p.625.

42. Green Europe, *The Agricultural Situation in the European Community*, 1987 Report, T/166-167.

43. United States, 'Proposal to the Uruguay Round Negotiating Group on Agriculture,' UR-0186, GATT, 7 July 1987.

44. 'Debatisse Report,' *Session Documents*, European Parliament, A-155/87, 2 October 1987, pp.48-61.

45. 'Report Drawn up on Behalf of the Committee on Agriculture, Fisheries and Food,' Rapporteur: Mr. Provan, *Working Documents*, European Parliament, Doc.A-2-8/86/Part B, 26 March 1986.

46. 'The Hague European Council,' *Bulletin of the EC*, 6-1986, p.10, pt. 1.1.11, 1.1.12.

47. Quoted in M.C. Cleary, *Peasants, Politicians and Producers: The Organization of Agriculture in France Since 1918*, Cambridge University Press, Cambridge, 1989, p.92.

48. Michael Tracy, *Government and Agriculture in Western Europe, 1880-1988*, 3rd.ed., Harvester-Wheatsheaf, London, 1989, p.231.

49. Article 39(1)b states as one of its objectives: 'to ensure... a fair standard of living for the agricultural population, particularly by increasing the individual earnings of persons engaged in agriculture.' *Treaty Establishing the European Economic Community*, 1958, Title II 'Agriculture.'

50. Council of the European Communities, *The Development of an Overall Approach to the Forthcoming Multilateral Trade Negotiations in GATT*, I/135/73 (COMER 42), Luxembourg, 29 June 1973.

51. European Communities Economic and Social Committee, *GATT: Towards a New Round*, Office for Publications of the European Communities, Luxembourg, 1986, p.40.

52. GATT Ministerial Declaration on the Uruguay Round (Punta del Este Declaration), GATT, *Basic Instruments and Selected Documents*, 33rd Supplement, 1987, p.19.

53. The EEP was later renamed the Bonus Incentive Commodity Export Programme (BICEP). As its acronym suggests, the US was flexing its muscles.

54. 'Currency Confusion in Grain Trade,' *Financial Times*, 6 August 1985, p.22.

55. Commission of the European Communities, *The Situation on the Agriculture Markets – 1988 Report*, (COM(88) 795 final).
56. 'Mr. Delors on the Future of Agriculture,' *Agence Europe*, 3 January 1991.
57. 'Agriculture,' *Agence Europe*, 9 January 1991.
58. French MEP Martinez, quoted in 'Situation in Agriculture,' Debates of the European Parliament, *Official Journal of the European Community*, No.3-409, 10 October 1991, pp.262-271.
59. Council Directive 98/552 of 3 October 1989 on the Coordination of Certain Provisions Laid Down by Law, Regulation or Administrative Action in Member States Concerning the Pursuit of Television Broadcasting Activities. *Official Journal of the European Communities*, L/298, 1989, p.23; and Measures to Encourage the Development of Industry of Audiovisual Production, implemented annually since 1992.
60. GATT, *GATT Focus*, Vol.66, No.3, 1989.
61. Art. XX of the General Agreement permits states to restrict the import of goods that wold affect 'public morals'; Art. IV relating to cinematographic films permits screen quotas. For the finer points of the interpretation of the GATT in this context, see: Jon Filipek, '"Culture Quotas"0: The Trade Controversy Over the European Community's Broadcasting Directive,' *Stanford Journal of International Law*, Vol.28, 1992; and Lisa L. Garrett, 'Commerce Versus Culture: The Battle Between the United States and the European Union Over Audiovisual Trade Policies,' *North Carolina Journal of International Law and Commercial Regulation*, Vol.19, 1994.
62. 'Services: Audio-Visual Working Group,' *GATT Focus*, Vol.10, 1990, p.75.
63. 'GATT/Broadcasting: Towards a Cultural Code in the GATT,' *Europe Information Service: Tech Europe*, 9 September 1993.
64. 'GATT/Film Industry: France Argues Case for Excluding Audio-Visual Sector,' *European Information Service: European Report*, 18 September 1993.
65. It is interesting to note that Universal is owned by Matsushita, Columbia by Sony, Fox by Rupert Murdoch, and MGM by Crédit Lyonnais!
66. 'Europeans Battle American Cultural Juggernaut in Trade Talks,' *The Gazette* (Montreal), 6 October 1993, p.B3; and 'France, Defiant, Holds Out for GATT Exemptions,' *The Reuter European Community Report*, 11 October 1993.
67. '*Germinal* Film Joins France's GATT Battle,' *The Independent*, 1 October 1993, p.10.
68. 'Brother Robot,' Survey of Artificial Intelligence, *The Economist*, 14 March 1992, p.24.
69. Bourdieu, *Outline of a Theory of Practice*, Cambridge University Press, Cambridge, 1977, p.165.
70. The omission of specific examples is deliberate here. One could cite South Africa controlling television under its apartheid regime, or some Muslim countries and China banning satellite dishes. Each case illustrates an attempt to filter outside ideas. But as some countries, including China, also counterfeit US home videos, general statements can become difficult.
71. It is true that in the high growth areas in Southeast Asia most people demand Japanese goods, except for a few luxury goods from Europe. However, the second-best known word worldwide is reputed to be 'Coke,' second only to 'ok.'
72. Daniel Singer, 'GATT and the Shape of our Dreams,' *The Nation*, 17 January 1994, p.54.

73. See for instance, Karl Deutsch, *Nationalism and Social Communication: An Inquiry into the Foundations of Nationality*, Harvard University Press, Cambridge, Massachussets, 1966.

74. 'More Transatlantic Film Cooperation Good for Industry Profits,' *PR Newswire*, 1 March 1994.

75. North American Free Trade Agreement, Annex, Mexico, p.I-M-15. Available through the world wide web home page of the Graduate School of International Relations, University of Kent at URL: http://snipe.ukc.ac.uk/international.

76. 'Showdown: Ted Rogers and Regulators Clash over his Plans to Create a New Multimedia Giant,' *Maclean's*, 3 October 1994.

77. This can be a product of 'globalization,' if this is understood to be a natural extension of capitalism. As one colleague has pointed out to me, this could reinforce Karl Polanyi's argument of the impact of commodification of societies. Technological changes may have altered the pace of change, but not the change itself.

78. 'What's Hot, What's Not,' *The Economist*, 4 May 1991, pp.118-119.

79. IDATE, *IMO Report*, 1993-1994. Available on the world wide web at URL: http://www.earn.net/EC.

80. 'Gone With the Cash,' *The Economist*, 3 November 1990, pp.93-94.

81. IDATE, *IMO Report*, 1993-1994. Available on the world wide web at URL:http://www.earn.net/EC.

82. IDATE, *IMO Report* 1993-1994. (Reported figure of Ecu 733.6 million. Calculated at current rate of exchange of 1.26 ECU/US$). The author recognises that this statement ignores Gresham's law: if there were a greater supply of European films, the attendance figures could be higher.

83. It is not that the French do not have good ideas. 'Trois Hommes et un Couffin' made only $3.5 million at the box office in the US, but the Americanized version of 'Three Men and a Baby' generated $170 million. 'French Films, American Accents,' *The Economist*, 27 February 1993, p.105.

84. See Barry Buzan, 'The Interdependence of Security and Economic Issues in the "New World Order",' in Richard Stubbs and Geoffrey R.D. Underhill, *Political Economy and the Changing Global Order*, Macmillan, London, 1994, esp. p.89.

85. See, for instance, David A. Baldwin, *Economic Statecraft*, Princeton University Press, Princeton, NJ., 1985.

86. See, in particular, an excellent collection by Klaus Knorr and Frank N. Trager, *Economic Issues and National Security*, University of Kansas Press, 1977.

87. Articles XII and XIV, respectively.

88. This is John Gerrard Ruggie's term. See: 'International Regimes, Transactions, and Change: Embedded Liberalism in the Postwar Economic Order,' in Stephen Krasner (ed.), *International Regimes*, Cornell University Press, Ithaca, 1983, esp. pp.195-232.

89. See Rosemary Fennell, *The Common Agricultural Policy of the European Community: Its Institutional and Administrative Organisation*, Granada, London, 1971; and Ian Barnes and Jill Preston, *The European Community: Key Issues in Economics and Business*, Longman, London, 1990.

90. 'The Numbers Game: How You Gonna Keep 'Em on the Farm?,' *National Journal*, 24 November 1990, p.2885.

91. This list is kept brief so as not to prejudice a wider argument made elsewhere. See Keith Webb and Jarrod Wiener, *The Internet and International Relations: The Politics of Global Communications*, forthcoming.

92. US Congress, HR 1504: 'Communications Competitiveness and Infrastructure Modernisation Act of 1993'; US Congress, S.1086: 'Telecommunications Infrastructure Act of 1993.

93. 'Ready for Prime Time?,' *Time International*, 26 December 1994-2 January 1995, pp.86-87.

94. The European Commission deregulated information services delivered by telephone in 1990, but this was challenged by Belgium, Italy, Spain and Greece. 'Telecoms Regulation: the Last Stand,' *The Economist*, 22 February 1992, pp.85-86.

95. Eighty-three cable companies have already laid 29,000 kilometres of fibre optics in Britain alone. 'Wiring the World,' *Time International*, 17 July 1995, p.61.

96. Quoted in Garrett, *op. cit.*, fn.116.

97. 'Hollywood to the Rescue as Culture War Abates,' *International Herald Tribune*, 8 April 1994.

98. For US legislation, see P.L 102-94: 'The High Performance Computing Act of 1991,' and the proposed amendment in US Cong. H.R. 1757, 'High Performance Computing and High Speed Networking Applications Act of 1993' of 21 April 1993. For the Clinton Administration's plans, see: Executive Office of the President, 'The National Information Infrastructure: Agenda for Action.' For the EU programmes relevant to its information technology programm, see in particular: Commission of the European Communities, 'Proposal for a Council Decision Setting Up a Programme for an Information Services Market,' COM(570) final, 23 January 1991. Available on the world wide web at URL: http://www/echo.lu/programmes/en/DELTA_2.html. Martin Bangermann's report can also be accessed at: http://www.earn.net/EC.

99. 'Invasion of the Profit Snatchers!,' *Time International*, 27 February 1995, p.49.

100.'EC Ministers Outline Trade Goals for Cinema and TV,' *Reuters European Community Report*, 5 October 1993. Emphasis added.

101.'Rivals and Allies Circle the Info-Highway,' *International Herald Tribune*, February 26 1995, p.15. See also 'World Jousts Over the Superhighway,' *Computer Weekly*, 2 March 1995, p.14. The G7 communique can be found on the world wide web at URL:http://ttg.sba.dal.ca.g7/textserver.html

102.'US to Oppose EU Bid to Exempt "Culture" from OECD Investment Accord,' *International Trade Reporter*, Vol.12, No.21, 24 May 1995, p.882.

103.'Bonn Wants EU Initiative for Access to US Market,' *Reuter European Community Report*, 17 February 1995; 'US, EU Officials Discuss Common Rules on Telecom-munications,' *BNA Management Briefing*, 19 July 1995.

7 EU-US Commercial Relations and the Debate on a Transatlantic Free Trade Area

Stephen Woolcock[1]

This chapter focuses on the future of transatlantic commercial relations. There is already an extensive literature on the extent of transatlantic economic ties, issues in macro-economic relations, the problems of market access in each market and regular detailed reports on current difficulties.[2] This chapter discusses possible trends in US-EU commercial relations (trade, investment and market access issues), summarizes the various ideas for deepening transatlantic commercial links and considers the advantages and drawbacks of each of the broad policy options.

By way of introduction the chapter considers three possible scenarios for transatlantic economic relations: a continuation of the status quo, drift and deepening. The chapter then stresses how transatlantic commercial relations must always be seen in the context of transatlantic security relations, macro-economic cooperation, or as is more often the case non-cooperation, as well as the impact of relations with third countries and the multilateral system. There has always been a tenuous link between trade and security in US-European relations. In 1995 the link was unusual in that the most persistent calls for a Transatlantic Free Trade Area (TAFTA) came from politicians and security experts seeking to strengthen and consolidate transatlantic relations at a time of weakening of security ties in the post-Cold War era. The links with macro-policy and third countries cannot be over emphasized. With regard to the later the central roles of both the US and EU in the international economy mean that bilateral relations cannot be considered without reference to their impact on third countries or on the multilateral system, such as in the World Trade Organization (WTO), and the Organization for Economic Cooperation and Development (OECD).

COMMERCIAL POLICY IN CONTEXT

Transatlantic commercial policy cannot be considered in isolation, but must be seen in the context of a complex set of factors. These factors have shaped past policy and are certain to continue to shape, if not determine, transatlantic commercial relations in the future. In a short chapter it is not possible to do more than summarize these factors and point to the potential influence they may have on commercial relations in the future.

The Linkage with Security

The security imperative in transatlantic relations during the Cold War was seen by many as helping to moderate commercial disputes. Faced with the need to maintain a common front vis-à-vis the USSR, disputes over trade in specific sectors or differences over how to conclude trade negotiations were played down so as not to rock the boat of transatlantic political and security relations. Security took precedence, so that in 1978, for example, differences over how to conclude the Tokyo Round of trade negotiations were overcome so as not to jeopardize the negotiations on the twin track strategy of NATO. It has therefore been argued that the end of the Cold War and the end of the security imperative could result in greater trade tensions. In reality, the growing intensity of transatlantic commercial links has provided a disincentive against trade wars in its own right for a number of years. But there are still knock-on effects of changes in the security relationship. When security concerns dominated, the transatlantic dialogue was conducted mainly by a fairly select group of people in the security community. This group therefore had a shaping impact on US-European relations. As commercial relations have assumed a larger role in the relationship, more numerous and diverse constituencies have become important. This adds many new dimensions to transatlantic relations and deepening economic relations bring the interests of this wider group of constituencies into play. Transatlantic relations must not only cope with the passing of the generation that experienced the Second World War and the post-war cooperation, it must also cope with a broadening in the number of constituencies whose support is needed for solid transatlantic links. Recognition of this fact has found expression in a series of initiatives to rejuvenate and broaden the scope of the transatlantic dialogue.

The linkage between security and commercial links can run both ways. As noted above the current proposals for a TAFTA have come from – predominantly European – politicians concerned with increased tensions in US-European security relations as a result of differences over the pace of potential NATO enlargement and how to respond to the war in Bosnia. The linkage between commercial and security relations is complicated by the lack of symmetry. In international security the US retains a clear leadership role, at least as long as Europe has only a weak Common Foreign and Security Policy (CFSP) and no defence identity (ESDI). In the field of commercial and monetary relations the US has ceded its leadership role over the years. This has occurred because the US is no longer able or willing to pay the domestic price, such as offering non-reciprocal benefits to countries to ensure that they support a liberal multilateral trading system. In monetary affairs the US ceded a large measure of leadership when it floated the dollar in the early 1970s. In both trade and monetary affairs the EU has become more and more important and, together with other countries, such as Japan, now shares in shaping the 'rules of the game.' This asymmetry between US dominance in security and relative weakness in commercial and economic relations will continue to create difficulties in managing transatlantic relations.

Commercial relations must also be seen in the context of macro-economic coordination, or non-coordination, and international monetary policy. As a larger, less trade-dependent economy, the United States was, in the past, able to conduct domestic policy without significant external constraints. It was also able largely to neglect the impact that national policy decisions had on the rest of the world. The smaller, more trade dependent, European economies tended to suffer from the effects of exchange rate instability. When fiscal adjustment was needed to redress imbalances in the world economy, the US was therefore able to limit or contain the costs of adjustment more than the individual European countries.[3] This has had important implications for transatlantic economic relations. As a result, all new initiatives, such as the 1990 Transatlantic Declaration (TAD) and the debate on TAFTA in 1995, have been accompanied by European calls, usually led by France, for more systematic efforts to ensure stable exchange rates, rather than rely on ad hoc intervention when it suits the US Treasury. European efforts to limit exchange rate fluctuations, whether in the shape of the currency snake, the EMS or EMU were also, in part, in response to this imbalance in the relationship with the US dollar.

Today the relative decline in the importance of the US economy, increased US trade dependence and the moves towards a single European currency have brought about real change. If the EU does create a single currency, transatlantic monetary relations in the 2000s will be radically different. By then the EU, or a core group of EU currencies, could be as indifferent to external constraints as the United States was in the 1970s and early 1980s. Countries participating in such a core currency might, as the US did in the past, choose to focus on domestic policy objectives and neglect calls for policy adjustment to facilitate transatlantic or international economic coordination. The US, on the other hand, will face growing external constraints. US trade dependence is already on a par with that of the EU as a whole, and domestic constituencies may become as sensitive to monetary policy decisions taken elsewhere as they are now to trade policy. It is unclear how these US constituencies will respond to such increased dependence on other countries' macro-economic policy. Will they seek to insulate the US economy, or call for greater cooperation with Europe and, if the latter, will the EU listen?

EU-US commercial relations are also shaped by relations with third countries. Perhaps the most consistent European criticism of US commercial policy during the last ten years has been its readiness to deploy unilateral trade measures when the US's trading partners are seen, by the US, as indulging in 'unfair' trading practices. This will continue to be a problem as long as aspects of commercial policy are not covered by multilateral rules.[4] These unilateral actions have not always been taken against the EU, but also against third countries and have often resulted in bilateral agreements, such as those between the US and Japan on semi conductors, auto parts, and computers. Although these nominally include the principle of most-favoured-nation treatment (MFN) – in other words that the resultant market opening should be extended to all countries – these agreements are seen by the EU as the source of trade diversion. The EU also concludes bilateral agreements with third countries, including Japan, such as the EU limitation of car imports until 1999.

Another area in which relations with third countries has implications for transatlantic commercial relations is the use of aggressive export strategies. The recent push by the US to enhance exports in major emerging markets, such as China and other Asian countries, has provoked criticism in Europe, although the US Administration claims that it is merely beginning what European governments have done for years. In short, how the US and EU deal with third countries can have a profound effect on transatlantic relations. Efforts to deepen US-EU economic ties can be undermined by conflict in third country markets or trade distortions resulting from bilateral deals.

This brings us to the question of the US and EU roles in the world trading system. Here the issue is not so much a question of multilateralism or regionalism, but how far each is prepared to go in supporting the multilateral trading system even when this is not always in narrowly defined 'national' interests.

In the first 25 years or so of the post-1945 trading system, the US provided the leadership required to sustain a reasonably strong multilateral order. But the US is no longer able or willing to provide this kind of leadership into the 2000s. It is questionable whether the EU can fill, or partially fill the vacuum, given the lack of agreement on EC competence on some of the 'new commercial' issues, such as trade and investment, trade and the environment and even some aspects of services. The growth in regional agreements in the 1990s suggests that the vacuum may be filled by regional agreements. If the US and EU cannot shape multilateral rules, they can shape the rules in regional structures (NAFTA, FTAA and the wider Europe) in which they each still retain, or are establishing, hegemonic roles. If the US and EU continue down a regional route to addressing some of the 'new' issues, the multilateral system may suffer and the potential of competing regional approaches may increase.

Even if both the EU and the US pursue multilateral 'solutions,' they may, as in the past, adopt strategies of coalition-building within the framework of multilateral negotiations in order to outflank or counter the position of the other. The US used such a strategy in the case of agriculture and the EU in financial services in the Uruguay Round of the GATT. Would a TAFTA help to limit the risk of competing regional approaches to trade rules emerging or would it undermine the letter and spirit of multilateralism? Should the EU and US push for a TAFTA as part of a means to provide a form of shared leadership of the multilateral system? In such a case, would this amount to shared hegemony, and would it be benign?

Last, but by no means least, transatlantic commercial relations are hostage to domestic pressures. This applies to the competence of the negotiators as well as the whole range of domestic economic and political structures that shape policy. On this issue, the EU has the more obvious problem of getting national governments to recognize EU competence in areas such as investment, trade and the environment, or air transport. The issue of competence was not resolved by the 1994 European Court ruling on European Community competence in ratifying the conclusions of the Uruguay Round. In the US, the competence issue may be less obvious but will be no less important in future. Individual states retain competence on policies which affect the future commercial policy agenda. This is partially the case for investment, competition policy, environmental and other standards, and public purchasing. With the Republican-led Congress keen to push further competencies down to the state level, limitations on the federal government's competence on commercial policy issues are likely to increase. Even at the Federal level, Congress has shown a greater desire to shape commercial policy and thus tie the hands of the Administration, regardless of the political hue of the Congress or Administration.

THREE SCENARIOS FOR TRANSATLANTIC COMMERCIAL RELATIONS

It is possible to envisage three broad scenarios for transatlantic commercial relations over a five to ten year period: i) a continuation of the status quo; ii) drift at a greater or lesser pace; and iii) a deepening of economic ties. Scenarios of trade war and economic tension spilling over into political relations, on the one hand, and a transatlantic economic community with far reaching policy approximation and integration, on the other, are highly unlikely and therefore not considered in depth. The importance of trade and investment links rules out the former and deep-seated structural and regulatory policy differences rule out the latter.[5]

Status Quo

The transatlantic commercial relationship – including trade and investment – is the single most important one in the international system. Two-way trade in 1993 was Ecu 170 billion. In 1994 the EU registered a trade surplus of some Ecu 8 billion, because US economic growth was higher than European growth, but in the early 1990s the US had a sizeable trade surplus when EU growth was higher than that of the US.[6] The US exports more to Asia than Western Europe, but has had a persistent, structural trade deficit since the mid-1970s, which is now in the order of $100 billion.

In 1993 the stock of EU investment in the US was some $240 billion. This represented 53% of total foreign direct investment in the US and was on a rising trend, compared to the 33% and falling for Japan. The EU (15) also receives over 40% of US FDI overseas, a total of about $220 billion. This significant mutual dependence finds expression in the figure of approximately 3 million jobs each in the US and EU

created by investment from the other side of the Atlantic. The
scenario is therefore that such a close economic relations
important to be damaged by short or medium term adver:
whether economic, political or security related. Mechanisms
established over the years to cope with disputes that might
potential of escalating into a trade war. Constant communicati
levels also limits the dangers of drift.

A Drift Scenario

The drift scenario also assumes that the commercial relationship is
important to be threatened by short term tensions in political or securit
relations, but that over the years, increased growth in US intra-regional
trade and investment, including commerce with the fast growing Asian
economies, combined with similar growth in intra-regional commerce in
Europe, will reduce the relative importance of the transatlantic economic
relationship. Developments in monetary policy, such as the creation of
a single currency by core EU members, could result in less macro-
economic policy cooperation unless attitudes change dramatically on both
sides of the Atlantic. A less trade-dependent EU could focus on internal
objectives and the US has, in any case, never shown any interest in
enduring cooperation on exchange rates when Europe wanted it.

In the post-Cold War era, both sides may reasonably feel that they
can afford to hold differing views of international security, to engage in
more open competition for markets, and to pursue their own agenda to
shape the international rules for trade and investment. Regional agreements, along the lines of NAFTA, FTAA or APEC could then become
the source of strategic commercial competition, rather than a means to
promote greater multilateral liberalization. If the WTO is not able to
integrate all the 'new commercial' policy agenda items, it is probable that
regional approaches to such issues as trade and the environment,
competition policy, and labour standards could emerge. Over time these
regional approaches could well develop divergent sets of rules, thus
creating the potential for competing regional approaches to the 'rules of
the game.' Against such a background trade frictions could increase and
would be likely to have more adverse effects.

To complete the picture, domestic political trends could result in
continued divergence rather than convergence in areas of regulatory
policy. In the early 1990s one could point to signs of convergence
between Europe and the US. In Europe, the creation of a genuine internal
European market had reduced national state intervention and in many

areas replaced discretionary policies with rules-based approaches based on European law. In the US the Clinton Administration appeared to want to introduce a more active industrial policy.[7] However, the election of a Republican controlled Congress in 1994 reversed this process. Thus while the EU may be moving slowly towards greater deregulation and liberalization, the US is moving rapidly towards an even smaller federal state option which will once again result in divergence.

A Deepening of Economic Links

The deepening scenario could result from an awareness, on the part of both the US and EU, that they need to cooperate closely, not only to ensure a sound economic foundation for a transatlantic political and security relationship, but also to provide stability in the management of the international economy and to shape the commercial 'rules of the game' in a manner that reflects their common interest in a liberal, rules-based multilateral system. Together, the US and EU could still shape the development of the multilateral system, which might otherwise stagnate if a more diverse WTO (including powerful countries at different levels of development and with different interests, for instance, China and Russia) fails to maintain the momentum behind international economic integration.

Such a deepening of transatlantic commercial relations, through a trade agreement, the development of a single transatlantic market, or possibly even a commitment to greater macro-economic cooperation, would provide a solid foundation for continued security and political cooperation. This might undermine the spirit of a genuine multilateral commercial order, in the sense that a transatlantic *excuse* would be difficult to distinguish from joint hegemony, at least when it came to shaping the 'rules of the game' in certain 'beyond the border' issues.

To agree on a transatlantic *excuse* it would be necessary to have continued approximation of domestic regulatory policy objectives in the US and EU. This could be brought about by intensified regulatory cooperation. As the objectives of domestic policy become accepted as being broadly equivalent in the EU and US, the case for border measures to defend national policies, on standards, competition, fair trade, or the environment would weaken. It would then be possible to agree to remove border measures and to reach some form of accommodation of the remaining differences in policy, perhaps through mutual recognition agreements. This process would be driven, as it has been in other regional agreements, by market-led developments.

THE PROPOSALS

The current basis of EU-US relations is the Transatlantic Declaration (TAD), which was signed in November 1990. Although this includes security and political dimensions, its core relates to cooperation between the then European Community and the United States government. The TAD essentially codified the already extensive cooperation between all institutions of the EU (Commission, Council and Parliament) and the US Administration and Congress. The TAD was a facilitating agreement rather than one which set specific objectives. (It is salutary to recall that attempts to introduce specific objectives, such as liberalization of agricultural trade or the competition of the Uruguay Round, were very nearly responsible for the failure of negotiations of the TAD in the summer of 1990.) In facilitating enhanced EU-US cooperation, the TAD has a mixed record. There have been specific agreements, such as the US-EU agreement on competition policy in 1993, the understanding on regulatory cooperation (agreed at sub cabinet level in 1995) and the more recent agreements on educational exchange and cooperation in humanitarian aid. The political cooperation procedures established in the TAD also resulted in common positions in foreign policy.[8] But there were also failures, such as in the case of the working groups set up in June 1993 in Berlin to seek greater cooperation in the areas of international crime, drug trafficking and support for Central and East European countries.

Over and above the facilitating agreements or declarations, there have also been more specific proposals concerning a deepening of transatlantic economic relations. For example, the former British Prime Minister Margaret Thatcher proposed a Transatlantic Free Trade Agreement in 1990, although her motivation was as much anti-European as Atlanticist. The timing of subsequent proposals by British ministers in the conservative government, such as the speech by Foreign Secretary Malcolm Rifkind at the 1995 Conservative Party Conference, might also be tainted with such suspicions. In 1990 Mrs Thatcher's proposal was not well received in the rest of the EC, because it was perceived as an effort to undermine the 1990/91 Intergovernmental Conference and efforts at deepening European integration. It also came in the midst of multilateral negotiations in the Uruguay Round.

The recent interest in proposals to deepen transatlantic economic relations began in 1994, with the suggestion by Canada's Prime Minister Jean Chrétien that NAFTA and the EU should negotiate a TAFTA. The Canadian motivation appeared to be a mixture of a desire to strengthen its own transatlantic ties with Europe, promote further liberalization internationally, as well as redress the imbalance in its commercial relationship with the US. In 1994 the Transatlantic Policy Network (TPN), a joint European and American group led by business and European parliamentarians, proposed putting EU–US relations on a treaty basis.[9] The TPN was interested in providing a sound basis for transatlantic relations by intensifying economic relations.[10]

In 1995, proposals were made for more dramatic, symbolic agreements. The German Minister of Foreign Affairs, Klaus Kinkel, made a speech in Canada in April 1995 calling for a TAFTA. His motivation was to consolidate and underpin EU-US relations and transatlantic relations at a time when there were real tensions in security and political relations as a result of tensions over the enlargement of NATO (which the US favoured but on which European countries were more cautious) and Bosnia (on which the US Congress was pressing for lifting the arms embargo, which the EU wished to retain). There was also a general concern about potential US isolationism emerging as new generations of politicians sought to define the US role in the post-Cold War era. What was called for, therefore, was a 'big idea,' something symbolic, that would catch the imagination of politicians and public opinion. Detailed negotiations on regulatory cooperation were unlikely to fit the bill. Other European politicians came forward with similar ideas, such as the incoming European Commission President, Jacques Santer, in his speech to the European Parliament and the British Minister of Defence and later Foreign Secretary, Malcolm Rifkind. These proposals were short on detail, but they were clearly aimed at finding a 'big idea' rather than detailed economic groundwork.

Although most of the suggestions for a new initiative came from the European side and reflected a general European concern about the potential volatility in US policy, there were also US speeches in favour of closer ties. For example, House majority leader Newt Gingrich proposed a transatlantic free trade zone. He argued that 'the United States and Europe will drift apart unless we have projects large enough to hold us together... We're not going to stay together out of nostalgia.... And my suggestion in part is that we want to start looking at a free trade zone that includes the US and Europe.'[11]

The US Administration reacted coolly to such ideas and new initiatives. The Administration was engaged in strengthening economic ties with other regions, such as Asia, where economic growth was more dynamic than in Europe, and with Latin America, where there was a desire to ensure that the trend towards economic liberalism was consolidated. After all, the Clinton Administration had promoted the idea of APEC and, at the Seattle APEC summit in late 1993, set the target of 2020 for free trade within APEC. In Miami in December 1994 President Clinton also gained an agreement from other countries to seek free trade in the western hemisphere (in the form of a Free Trade Agreement for the Americas) by 2005. It was not that the Clinton Administration considered these regions more important than Europe, but simply that commercial relations with Europe were generally not thought to be in need of strengthening. The objective was to bring US commercial relations with other regions up to the level that it had reached with Europe. But to some people in Europe it appeared that the US was concluding regional agreements with everyone but Europe.

The next step came at the biannual EU-US summit in May 1995. Presidents Clinton, Chirac (President of the European Council) and Santer (European Commission) agreed to establish a Group of High Level Representatives, consisting of representatives of the Council Presidency (Spain), the European Commission and the US Administration, to consider ways of strengthening EU-US relations and report to the next EU-US summit in December 1995. In response to this the EU, in the shape of a European Commission communication to the Council and the US, in the shape of a speech by Secretary of State Warren Christopher, produced broad policy outlines.

The Initial US Proposals

The July 1995 speech by Warren Christopher covered the spectrum of US-European relations from security (enlargement of NATO), to political cooperation (on international crime and the proliferation of weapons of mass destruction), to proposals on cooperation on technical barriers to trade.[12] Mr Christopher argued that efforts to strengthen US-EU economic relations should be no less ambitious than those in Asia Pacific or the western hemisphere. He also said that TAFTA deserved serious study. But the speech reflected the predominant view in the US Administration, and Washington in general, that this was not the time for a major new initiative. As its title (*Charting a Transatlantic Agenda for the 21st Century*) suggested, the speech was an early attempt to shape the agenda. It did not include any 'big ideas.' The speech listed the extensive cooperation already being undertaken. This list included, for example, joint work on a Multilateral Investment Agreement (MIA), cooperation on high technology, technical barriers to trade, an open skies policy for air transportation, completion of the unfinished business of the Uruguay round (basic telecommunications liberalization, audio-visual and financial services) and a joint code on commercial bribery.

The speech referred to the Transatlantic Business Forum (TBF), which had been initiated by the US Department of Commerce in talks with the European Commission in early 1995. The objectives of this initiative were unclear, but it certainly sought to involve business in setting the objectives for detailed commercial negotiations. In its preparatory meetings the TBF called for 'further liberalization,' work on the mutual recognition of regulation and test results to reduce barriers to trade resulting from technical policies, and regulatory cooperation. The TBF received somewhat less than full endorsement from European business circles, which argued that there were channels for transatlantic business contacts already in existence, via, for example, UNICE (the Union of European Industry and Employers Confederations), the European Round Table of Industrialists (ERT) and the TPN. As a result, efforts to sign up chief executives for the TBF by the European Commission and US Department of Commerce did not produce the expected support.[13] This is not surprising, as most international companies operating in Europe and the US had few major difficulties, as is evidenced by the fact that something in the order of 30% of US-EU trade was accounted for by intra-company trade of multinational companies.

The position of the US Administration, as reflected in the Christopher speech, broadly coincided with a continuation of the status quo. There was no urgency in efforts to deepen commercial links to counter a drift scenario. The speech clearly favoured continued work to strengthen links but there was no new initiative. The idea of a TAFTA was not ruled out, but in an important passage in the speech, Mr Christopher appeared to set tough conditions on the TAFTA. Any agreement would have to avoid discrimination vis-à-vis third countries and be consistent with the WTO. The only way to avoid discrimination in a free trade agreement is to extend all concessions negotiated bilaterally to all other countries and thus offer MFN treatment. In such circumstances, the incentive to conclude a bilateral agreement is reduced, and it might be argued that it would make more sense to negotiate further liberalization multilaterally right from the start. The condition of compatibility with the WTO (Article XXIV on free trade agreements and customs unions) is likely to mean that sensitive sectors, such as agriculture and shipping, would have to be included to satisfy the 'substantially all trade' requirement of Article XXIV. These issues proved highly contentious during the Uruguay round, and it is not clear how an agreement would be easier to achieve in bilateral negotiations than in multilateral talks, where a larger package deal is usually available.

In 1995, the attention of the US Congress was not focused on Europe, or on international affairs. From 1988 to 1989 Congress focused on developments in Europe, as a result of the EC-92 initiative and subsequently more negatively in the context of battles over agricultural trade in the Uruguay round. Thereafter, most members of Congress shifted their attention to whether the Republican 'Contract for America' of 1994 would be implemented and how this would affect the outcome of the 1996 Presidential election. The Republican-controlled Congress after 1994 sought substantial cuts in US international financial commitments, such as to the UN and to foreign aid. But this did not necessarily amount to an isolationist position. There remained a conservative internationalist view, as reflected in the speeches by House Leader Gingrich.

In summary, therefore, the US approach suggested support for the status quo. It did not appear to support the view that there were major problems in transatlantic commercial relations and that there was consequently no need to take new initiatives. If there were regional free trade initiatives with other regions, this was because of a need to develop commercial links with the Asia-Pacific region and Latin America. Commercial relations with Europe were not in need of development.

The European Proposals

The European Commission's proposals came in a Communication to the Council in July 1995[14], which was discussed in the General Affairs Council (composed of Foreign Ministers) in early October 1995. The Commission proposals followed initiatives taken by the EU in early 1993. At that time the concern was about drift as a result of the increased focus on domestic policy by the incoming Democratic Presidency.[15] Compared to the speeches made by national politicians calling for transatlantic free trade agreements or Atlantic communities, the Commission paper was more cautious. This was probably due to the desire to incorporate both the political objectives of the ministries of foreign affairs in countries such as Germany, Britain and Sweden, which were concerned about drift in the security and political relations, and the disinclination of ministries of trade and economics to get drawn into a commitment to negotiate on the 'non-negotiable' issues.

The Commission paper stressed the need for EU-US cooperation in virtually every field of foreign and commercial policy if progress was to be made in international negotiations. Indeed, the approach adopted by the Commission paper was that the US and EU should 'concentrate on maintaining the momentum of the multilateral process.' To this end, the paper included a reference to the possibility of an acceleration of the tariff reductions agreed in the Uruguay round, completion of the outstanding issues started in the Uruguay round, such as rules of origin and services, and joint efforts with the US to establish a WTO work programme for the twenty-first century to include the 'new commercial issues.' The Commission also called for multilateral discipline to oppose US unilateralism and to ensure that regional agreements were compatible with the WTO.

This did not mean that the Commission neglected bilateral cooperation. It recommended work to create a Transatlantic Economic Space. The use of the Economic Space idea appears to be an effort to give some new substance to the existing transatlantic cooperation, but not to commit the EU to specific treaties or free trade agreements. An Economic Space is a flexible concept with no definition in the WTO.[16]

The Commission's Economic Space proposal was essentially a building block approach. The Commission's proposals on specific areas of work was at least as challenging as the US calls for the inclusion of agriculture and audio-visual services. For example, there was a call for full mutual recognition agreements. In the discussions in 1994-95 the EU ran up against US resistance to mutual recognition because of the loss of regulatory sovereignty that they entailed. The US preferred recognition of test results only. This would mean that regulators in the US would be obliged to accept the results of tests carried out in EU member states, but not that products passed as suitable in the EU should automatically satisfy US requirements as well. The Commission paper also suggested that if work on cooperation in competition policies could continue this might, at some time in the future, result in an agreement that would preclude unfair competition and could thus obviate the need to use anti-dumping and countervailing duty actions in transatlantic commerce. This would be a major departure for the US, which has made significant use of such trade instruments in response to what it believed to be 'unfair' import competition from Europe, and other countries. Finally, the Commission paper proposed a dialogue on macro-economic policy, in which representatives of the Council of Finance Ministers would engage in a dialogue with the US Administration.

On balance, the European Commission proposals went further in seeking to deepen transatlantic commercial ties than those contained in the Christopher speech. Inevitably, these initial US and European

Commission proposals reflected their current interests and abiding preoccupations in transatlantic commercial relations. The US stressed that any agreement would have to include the liberalization of agriculture and audio-visual services and the European Commission wanted to engage the US on issues where it has been the demandeur. In the autumn of 1995 negotiations were under way to find a common wording in time for the December 1995 US-EU summit in Spain.

AN ASSESSMENT OF THE POLICY PROPOSALS

This section assesses the policy proposals that have been made, namely an Economic Space as suggested by the European Commission and TAFTA. It also discusses a third option of pursuing multilateral liberalization. Some of these options are not mutually exclusive and there are the further options of the status quo, or options which focus on political or security relations. After assessing the pros and cons of each option, the concluding section then considers which is most likely and how this might affect the future development of transatlantic commercial relations.

A Transatlantic Economic Space

This option is based on the Commission proposals. It is essentially a 'building block' approach to deepening commercial relations. In areas where agreement can be reached negotiations would proceed. It implies the adoption of either sectoral negotiations or negotiation by issue area. The possibility of a formal trade agreement some time in the future need not be excluded, but it is not set out as a clear policy goal.

The advantages of this approach are that it entails a low risk and that it is pragmatic. It is low risk because it avoids a commitment to complex negotiations on a trade agreement which may not succeed. The announcement of the intention to negotiate a TAFTA would raise political expectations which, if not fulfilled, could have an adverse impact on transatlantic political relations. By seeking to deepen commercial relations in an ad hoc manner it would also be possible to avoid politically sensitive issues. If there is sufficient progress in such negotiations, it would still be possible to negotiate a trade agreement at a later date.

A dialogue on some of the 'new commercial' policy issues, such as investment and trade and the environment, can help to ensure that the US and EU adopt a similar approach. This could in turn prevent competitive regional approaches emerging and smooth the way to agreements within the OECD or the WTO. As such, it may provide a form of joint influence of the agenda and shape of international agreements, but without the fanfare of a formal trade agreement. Even if a bilateral trade agreement were successful, it could undermine the multilateral system at a time when more and more countries are signing up to the WTO.

The main disadvantage of the building block approach is that it does not provide the 'big idea,' and thus the symbolism, that some believe is needed to ensure a continuation of sound transatlantic relations into the next century. The use of the name Economic Space is an attempt to make one big idea out of lots of smaller ideas or ongoing work. The EU used this approach to some effect with the EC-92 initiative. But in that case there were important political initiatives, such as greater majority voting, which provided an internal dynamic to the process. In the absence of a clear commitment to negotiate a free trade area, there is a danger that the building block approach will simply allow all difficult issues to be put aside. Selectivity means that there is no scope for trade-offs, such as greater liberalization of agriculture in return for binding discipline on 'unilateral' US trade remedies. Without such trade-offs it is difficult to see how any more progress could be made in bilateral talks than was possible in the multilateral talks in the Uruguay round. The building block option also does not, by itself, provide any guarantee against the US or EU reverting to unilateral remedies to difficult issues.

The TAFTA Option

Perhaps the strongest case for a TAFTA is not the commercial or economic benefit that would accrue from it, but the political symbolism of a joint commitment to deepen commercial relations. There are also economic benefits. Initial estimates suggest that an agreement eliminating all tariffs between the US and EU could result in a 10% increase in US exports to the EU and a 6% increase in EU exports to the US. More than half the US increase would be in agricultural products, and a sizeable share of the EU increase would be in sensitive sectors for the US, such as textiles and clothing.[17] With the elimination of NTBs, such as local government purchasing preferences, not to mention the effects of removing regulatory barriers to trade in the field of services, the benefits could be considerably greater. A trade agreement could therefore find support among business people as well as politicians. Even organized labour, at least in the US, might support a trade agreement with the EU because, unlike NAFTA, it would be with a trading partner with higher rather than lower labour standards. The same case might be made for environmental lobbies concerned about a race to the bottom resulting from trade agreements with Asian or Latin American countries.

A TAFTA would tie the US into a binding agreement and thus satisfy those in the EU concerned about US unilateralism, but this would only happen if the agreement went considerably further than tariff reductions. To remove the risks of disruption to trade as a result of trade remedies against perceived 'unfair' trade, it would be necessary to move closer to a kind of transatlantic common market (meaning the free movement of goods, capital and services). [18] If this were to happen there would be real benefits for business.

Assessments of a TAFTA must therefore take account of what type of agreement it might constitute. Considering first the option of a TAFTA as primarily an agreement to remove tariffs, the main disadvantage is that it would involve high risk with limited commercial benefits. The risk resides in the fact that negotiations may fail on sensitive sectors. If TAFTA excluded such sensitive sectors it would not be unique among free trade agreements, but such a move by the two major members of the WTO would undermine any prospect of developing effective multilateral discipline of regional trade and integration agreements. As such regional agreements have been multiplying, this would be very wounding to the credibility of the new WTO. An agreement which included the liberalization of agriculture and textiles would on the other hand be widely welcomed, even if it were a bilateral agreement.

Even if TAFTA were successful in removing all tariffs, including those in sensitive sectors, it would still discriminate against third countries. Although this would not be contrary to the letter of the WTO, which still allows free trade areas, the symbolic effect of the two largest trading entities concluding a free trade agreement would be damaging. There would be pressure to 'multilateralize' the liberalization at an early stage.

A TAFTA that went beyond tariffs and included significant non-tariff and regulatory barriers to trade would have different effects. Broadly speaking, the benefits for the US and EU would be greater, because a wide range of 'behind the border' barriers to trade would be addressed. The creation of an Atlantic common market would also establish a form of transatlantic *acquis*. This would preclude the risk of divergent competing regional approaches based on the North American and European models. Such an agreement would also lock the European and

American economies together and thus provide a firm economic basis for stable transatlantic relations into the next century.

The difficulty with this kind of an ambitious TAFTA is that it would be very difficult to negotiate. It would probably require the US to cede more sovereignty than the US Congress is likely to be willing to cede and more changes in the EU *acquis* than the EU is ready to accept. Although it could provide the basis for international agreements, it would also constitute a form of joint dominance of the multilateral system by the EU and US. Although this may be welcomed by those who believe that a pluralistic WTO will be unmanageable without joint leadership, it will undermine the spirit of the WTO.

The Multilateral Option

This brings us to the third option of joint leadership of the multilateral system. Rather than seek bilateral liberalization, the US and EU could jointly seek to strengthen the multilateral system. This would avoid all the dangers of undermining multilateralism. In the past the US provided leadership for the multilateral system, but it is now no longer able or willing to do so. The EU might aspire to leadership, but has in the past had difficulties being proactive enough to provide it. The case of the EU-led agreement on financial services in 1995 is so far one of the few in which the EU was able to make progress without US support. Joint leadership would therefore be more realistic, but there are dangers in this. As has been pointed out, future international negotiations will be shaped by a pattern of changing issue-based international coalitions.[19] There remains a danger that without sufficient power to influence the agenda alone, both the US and EU will be tempted to seek multilateral coalitions against each other.

CONCLUSIONS

It is possible to hold different views on the future of transatlantic commercial relations. The likely scenarios fall within the middle range that encompass a continuation of the status quo, drift or deepening. A dramatic deterioration in commercial relations is unlikely because of the importance of the existing links. The conclusion of some agreement establishing a form of transatlantic community or *acquis* is equally unlikely because of the continued differences in domestic policies and Congressional opposition to ceding sovereignty.

Of the middle range scenarios, a slow drift appears to be the most likely. This may be no more than a progressive erosion of the relative importance of transatlantic commercial links as trade and investment between the transatlantic 'partners' and third countries or regions increase. The drift may, however, be faster if regional approaches consolidate divergent approaches to international rules and no efforts are made to strengthen economic coordination between the US and the core countries of the EU within a single currency.

The impact of a slow drift in commercial relations will not be such as to precipitate any major initiatives. Indeed, one could argue that drift has been occurring for some time and that the only reason that proposals for deepening relations reached the agenda in 1995 was because they were put there by people concerned about tensions in the transatlantic security and political relationship.

There is little to offer in the option of a TAFTA limited to the removal of remaining tariffs. There are some trade benefits from this, but the risks of failure and the systemic risks of such an agreement for the multilateral system tend to argue against it. There is also little support for the idea in the US and the prospects of initiating any negotiation before the next Presidential election in 1996 seem slim. In Europe there is, in general, more support but France has come out against even a study of the impact of a TAFTA, on the grounds that it would 'undermine multilateralism' and also add to pressure for trade liberalization in agriculture.

A deeper form of economic integration in which there could be a transatlantic *acquis* on a broad range of commercial policy issues would be more worth the risk, but such an agreement would have to overcome major political hurdles related to sovereignty and the continued differences in approach to 'beyond the border' issues in Europe and the US.

If drift is the most likely scenario, this need not be seen as a negative development. If the EU and US jointly promote multilateral liberalization at the same time as their bilateral links decline in relative importance, this may indeed have a beneficial effect.

NOTES

1. The London School of Economics Centre for Research on the United States of America. The author wishes to acknowledge support from the Economic and Social Research Council as part of its Global Economic Institutions initiative.

2. Gary Clyde Hufbauer, *Europe 1992: An American Perspective,* The Brookings Institution, Washington, 1991; Stephen Woolcock, *Market Access Issues in EC-US Relations: Trading Partners or Trading Blows,* Royal Institute of International Affairs, London 1991; European Commission, *1995 Report on US Barriers to Trade and Investment,* Brussels, 1995; and United States Trade Representative, *1995 National Trade Estimate Report on Foreign Trade Barriers,* US Government Printing Office, 1995.

3. Randell Hanning, *Macroeconomic Diplomacy in the 1980s: Domestic Politics and International Conflict among the United States, Japan and Europe,* Atlantic Paper No. 65, London, 1987.

4. Stephen Woolcock, Jeffrey Hart and Hans van der Ven, *Interdependence in the Post Multilateral Era: Trends in US/EC Trade Relations,* MIT, Mass., 1985; Jagdish Bhagwati and Hugh Patrick, *Aggressive Unilateralism: America's 301 Trade Policy and the World Trading System,* University of Michigan Press, 1991.

5. See Stephen Woolcock, 'European and North American Approaches to Regulation: Continued Divergence?,' in William Wallace (ed.), *The End of the West,* (forthcoming), 1996.

6. European Commission, *1995 Report on US Barriers to Trade and Investment, op. cit.*

7. Woolcock, 'European and North American Approaches to Regulation,' *op. cit.*

8. Roy Ginsberg and Thomas Frellesen, *EU-US Foreign Policy Cooperation in the 1990s: Elements of Partnership,* Centre for European Policy Studies, Brussels, CEPS Paper No.58, 1994.

9. At the time of the Transatlantic Declaration there was also discussion of a treaty. Indeed, Secretary of State Baker had suggested that a treaty was one option in his November 1989 speech on transatlantic relations in Berlin. But at the time uncertainties about the future of Europe, and in particular about the future shape of the European Union, meant that a new treaty was not really given serious consideration.

10. The Transatlantic Policy Network, *Towards a Transatlantic Partnership: A European Strategy,* Brussels, 1994.

11. Newt Gingrich, 'An American Vision for the 21st Century,' 1 March 1995. Quoted in Glennon Harrison, *A New Transatlantic Initiative? US-EU Economic Relations in the Mid 1990s,* Congressional Research Service (95-983 E), 15 September 1995, Washington, DC.

12. US Department of State, *Charting a Transatlantic Agenda for the 21st Century,* Speech by Secretary of State Warren Christopher, Madrid, 2 June 1995.

13. Glennon Harrison, *The Transatlantic Business Dialogue,* Congressional Research Service (95-982 E).

14. European Commission, *Europe and the US: The Way Forward.* Communication from the Commission to the Council, COM (95) 411 final, 26 July 1995.

15. Michael Smith and Stephen Woolcock 'Learning to Cooperate: the Clinton Administration and the European Union,' *International Affairs,* Vol.70, No.3, July 1993.

16. Comparisons with the European Economic Space, which was the construction proposed by Commission President Delors to placate the members of EFTA seeking membership of the EC in 1988, are probably more confusing than useful.
17. Harrison, *op. cit.*
18. Mark Nelson and G. John Ikenberry, *Atlantic Frontier: A New Agenda for US-EC Relations*, Carnegie Endowment for International Peace, Washington DC, 1993.
19. Miles Kahler, *Regional Futures and Transatlantic Economic Relations*, European Community Studies Association/Council on Foreign Relations, 1995.

Index

Agriculture 3, 4, 9, 10, 14, 16, 112, 119, 128, 129, 131-135, 140, 141, 142-46, 150-152, 154-157, 168, 176-80, 182

APEC, *see* Asia-Pacific Economic Cooperation

ASEAN, *see* Association of South-East Asian Nations

Asia-Pacific Economic Cooperation 20, 104, 108-111, 120, 123, 170, 174

Association of South-East Asian Nations 85, 104, 106-108, 121

Balkans 12, 13, 30, 31, 33-36, 40, 48, 58

Bosnia 11-13, 29, 31-6, 45, 60, 69, 109, 166, 173

Brzezinski, Zbigniew 37

Bush, George 27, 28, 102

Canada ix, x, xvi, 9, 10, 29, 96, 98, 99, 102, 107, 108, 112-114, 121, 122, 130, 148, 173

Canada-United States Free Trade Agreement 96, 98

CAP, *see* Common Agricultural Policy

Caucasus 40

CFSP, *see* Common Foreign and Security Policy

Chechnya 38, 40, 51, 52

China 10, 96, 104-106, 108, 117-123, 148, 167, 171

Christopher, Warren 11, 32, 53-55, 104, 174, 175, 178

CIS, *see* Commonwealth of Independent States

CJTF, *see* Combined Joint Task Force

Clinton, Bill 5, 6, 8, 13, 19, 28, 32, 33, 36, 37, 45, 47, 48, 50, 51, 53, 54, 55-58, 61, 100, 109, 113, 117, 147, 153, 171, 174, 176

Cold War ix, xiii, xv, 3-5, 9-13, 17, 18, 20, 21, 26, 28, 31-35, 38, 42, 46, 51, 60, 61, 77, 82, 95, 96, 104, 119, 123, 124, 164, 165, 170, 173

Combined Joint Task Force 8, 35, 36

COMECON 82, 92

Common Agricultural Policy 131, 132, 134, 142-145, 152, 155

Common Foreign and Security Policy 2, 3, 7, 8, 67-69, 73-74, 76-78, 80-81, 85-93, 166

Commonwealth of Independent States 6, 46, 48, 54, 78

Crimea 40

Croatia 36

CUFTA, *see* Canada-United States Free Trade Agreement

Czech Republic 6, 36, 37, 39, 45, 49, 60

Delors, Jacques 3, 74, 75, 81, 82, 133, 144, 145, 153, 177

EAI, *see* Enterprise for the Americas Initiative

ECJ, *see* European Court of Justice

EEA, *see* European Economic Area

EFTA, *see* European Free Trade
    Area
England 27
Enterprise for the Americas Initi-
    ative 102
ERT, *see* European Round Table
    of Industrialists
EU, *see* European Union
Eurocorps 2, 3, 8, 30, 35, 81
EUROMARFOR 81
European Council 20, 70, 76, 88,
    142, 143, 174
European Court of Justice 69, 70,
    86
European Economic Area 82-84
European Free Trade Area   72,
    82-85, 177
European Round Table of Indus-
    trialists 175
European Union   viii, ix, x, xi,
    xv, 2-4, 7-8, 10, 14-17, 28-30,
    32, 38, 40-42, 45, 48, 53-54,
    67-70, 72-74, 78, 80-81, 83,
    85-86, 91-93, 109, 111-112,
    122-123,   128-136,   139-150,
    152-182

France 2, 4, 8, 26, 27, 29-31, 33,
    36, 39, 41, 53, 58, 59, 73, 77,
    109, 121, 135, 139, 140, 142,
    144, 147, 150, 166, 182
Free Trade Area of the Americas
    10, 103, 168, 170
FTAA, *see* Free Trade Area of
    the Americas

GATT, *see* General Agreement on
    Tariffs and Trade
General Agreement on Tariffs and
    Trade x, xvi, 1-4, 9, 14, 15,
    20, 72, 99, 108, 109, 113-115,
    128, 129, 130-140, 142-149,
    151, 152, 155, 156, 168
Germany 2, 3, 27, 31, 33, 36,
    41, 47, 53, 59, 73, 76, 82,
    85, 109, 139, 176
Gore, Al 47, 53, 102
Greece 32, 34, 41, 44, 49, 153
Gulf war 28, 31, 80, 90, 121

Hong Kong 104-106, 108, 120
Hungary 6, 36, 37, 39, 45, 47,
    49, 60, 85

IMF, *see* International Monetary
    Fund
Indonesia 105, 107-109
International Monetary Fund 1,
    15, 101, 123, 134, 139
Italy 27, 41, 49, 105, 109, 139,
    153

Japan   10, 20, 96, 100, 104-
    109, 115-121, 123, 128, 137,
    166, 167, 169

Kissinger, Henry 37

Kozyrev, Andrei 7, 39, 46, 49,
    53, 55, 57, 58

Maastricht Treaty on European
    Union xi, 7, 28, 29, 67, 68,
    73, 78, 79, 83-84, 86, 88,
    90-92
Malaysia 105-108, 110
Mexico 9, 10, 97, 98, 100-102,
    112, 114, 115, 122, 148
MIA, *see* Multilateral Invest-
    ment Agreement
Mitterrand, François 82

Multilateral Investment Agreement 175

NAC, *see* North Atlantic Council
NACC, *see* North Atlantic Cooperation Council
NAFTA, *see* North American Free Trade Agreement
NATO, *see* North Atlantic Treaty Organization
New Zealand 107, 108, 121
North American Free Trade Agreement 9, 10, 14, 15, 96, 100-103, 105, 107, 109, 111-115, 118, 122, 148, 168, 170, 173, 180
North Atlantic Cooperation Council 1, 6, 21, 46, 78
North Atlantic Council xi, 6, 30, 31, 34-37, 50, 56, 58, 68
North Atlantic Treaty Organization vii, viii, x, xi, xii, xiii, xiv, xv, 1, 2, 4-9, 11, 13, 14, 20-22, 26-42, 44-61, 69, 73, 74, 77-82, 84, 93, 121, 165, 166, 173, 174

OAS, *see* Organization of American States
OECD, *see* Organization for Economic Cooperation and Development
Organization for Economic Cooperation and Development 1, 15, 21, 109, 140, 154, 164, 179
Organization for Security and Cooperation in Europe 7, 29, 35, 39, 44-49, 51, 52, 54, 58, 59

Organization of American States 103
OSCE, *see* Organization for Security and Cooperation in Europe

Pacific Basin Economic Council 107
Pacific Century 10, 95, 96, 104, 105
Pacific Trade and Development Conference 107
PAFTAD, *see* Pacific Trade and Development Conference
Partnership for Peace 1, 6, 7, 21, 30, 36, 37, 44-47, 49, 51-53, 56-60
PBEC, *see* Pacific Basin Economic Council
PfP, *see* Partnership for Peace
Poland 6, 29, 36, 37, 39, 45, 49, 54, 60, 61, 82, 85
Portugal 3, 133

Russia xiii, 6, 7, 13, 27, 31, 33, 37-41, 44-61, 69, 120, 121, 171

Santer, Jacques 69, 79, 173, 174
SEA, *see* Single European Act
Singapore 104-107, 109
Single European Act 2, 7, 73, 83, 86-88, 91, 92, 120, 121
Single Market project 108
Slovenia 36
South Korea 29, 104-108, 121
Spain 3, 39, 133, 139, 153, 174, 178

TAD, *see* Transatlantic Declaration

TAFTA, *see* Transatlantic Free Trade Area

Taiwan 104-106, 108, 120

TBF, *see* Transatlantic Business Forum

TEU, *see* Maastricht Treaty on European Union

TPN, *see* Transatlantic Policy Network

Transatlantic Business Forum 184

Transatlantic Declaration 166, 172

Transatlantic Economic Space 177, 178

Transatlantic Free Trade Area x, 1, 16, 124, 164, 166, 168, 173-175, 178-182

Transatlantic Policy Network 173, 175

Turkey 29, 32, 34, 41, 44, 46, 85

Ukraine 40, 59

UN, *see* United Nations

United Nations 1, 3, 5, 11-14, 19, 28, 30-35, 47, 73, 77, 81, 87, 90, 93, 117, 123, 132, 150, 176

Western European Union xi, 2, 8, 29, 30, 35, 68, 69, 73, 74, 77-81, 84, 87, 93

WEU, *see* Western European Union

World Bank 1, 101

World Trade Organization 1, 14, 15, 21, 128, 164, 170, 171, 175-177, 179-181

WTO, *see* World Trade Organization

Yeltsin, Boris 7, 36, 37, 39, 50, 53-58